At Ease in the
WHITE HOUSE

AT EASE IN THE
WHITE HOUSE

The Uninhibited Memoirs
of a Presidential Social Aide

Stephen M. Bauer

with

Frances Spatz Leighton

A Birch Lane Press Book

PUBLISHED BY CAROL PUBLISHING GROUP

A Birch Lane Press Book
Published by Carol Publishing Group
Birch Lane Press is a registered trademark of Carol Communications, Inc.
Editorial Offices: 600 Madison Avenue, New York, N.Y. 10022
Sales & Distribution Offices: 120 Enterprise Avenue, Secaucus, N.J. 07094
In Canada: Musson Book Company, a division of General Publishing Co., Ltd., Don Mills, Ontario

Queries regarding rights and permissions should be addressed to Carol Publishing Group, 120 Enterprise Avenue, Secaucus, N.J. 07094

Carol Publishing Group books are available at special discounts for bulk purchases, for sales promotions, fund raising, or educational purposes. Special editions can be created to specifications. For details contact: Special Sales Department, Carol Publishing Group, 120 Enterprise Avenue, Secaucus, N.J. 07094.

Manufactured in the United States of America
10 9 8 7 6 5 4 3 2 1

Library of Congress Cataloging-in-Publication Data

Bauer, Stephen.
    At ease in the White House : the uninhibited memoirs of a
presidential social aide / by Stephen Bauer : with Frances Spatz
Leighton.
        p.   cm.
    "A Birch Lane press book."
    Includes index.
    ISBN 1-55972-061-1
    1. Presidents—United States—Anecdotes. 2. Presidents—United
States—Wives—Anecdotes. 3. White House (Washington, D.C.)–
–Anecdotes. 4. Bauer, Stephen. I. Leighton, Frances Spatz.
II. Title.
E840.6.B38   1991
973.92'092'2—dc20
                                                    90-32441
                                                    CIP

To Michael and Christopher

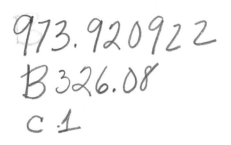

ACKNOWLEDGMENTS

A book is a gigantic jigsaw puzzle. This is to express sincere appreciation for those dedicated persons who helped put the gigantic puzzle together.

Allan J. Wilson, Oscar Collier, Susanne Paper, Lillian Rogers Parks, Shirley Gould, Kendall K. Hoyt, Sarah McClendon, Nineta Rozen and the History and Biography Divisions of the Martin Luther King Library of Washington, D.C.

And finally, Diane Sawyer and Sam Donaldson for their delightful and memory-refreshing views of the First Family Living Quarters, "PrimeTime Live," an ABC News Broadcast.

Contents

Foreword

*W*hen I arrived at the White House, I did not have the foggiest notion that I might someday write a book about my experiences. Over the following years, countless people asked me to talk about these events to the point that my best friend (and wife), Linda, finally suggested that I write a book. Her mentor, Laurel Lee, having recently completed making her diary notes into *Walking Through the Fire*, also provided enormous encouragement. Without their initial urging, there probably never would have been a book.

Later, Linda gave me the idea to work with my manuscript outline on the lecture circuit. Numerous appearances at dinner clubs across the nation gave me an opportunity to gauge the mood of the public and their level of interest in various aspects of the White House social life and lore. My intention was to write about what they thought was interesting and I hope the reader concludes that this book hits the target.

There was someone else who indirectly convinced me that a simple story of the everyday life of one man many be, for another, an interesting chronicle worthy of being recorded.

During my three years with the President's Army honor guard at Fort Myer, we periodically had formal dinners and invited special guest speakers. On one occasion, Walter Cronkite told us some captivating stories about his early days as a reporter during World War II. The morning of the Normady invasion, he was assigned to cover the airborne troops as they parachuted into France. When he arrived at the airfield, the Army commander refused him a parachute because he had not completed any of the necessary training.

No amount of arguing would change the officer's mind and the young reporter feared he might miss out altogether on the largest military attack in modern history. Finally sent down to the staging area for the glider troops, he boarded one of these flimsy crafts with an infantry platoon for the tow to the battle. Outfitted in a steel helmet and fatigues, he blended in with the troops.

Between the release from the tow plane and their landing, the troops knew they were in trouble because they could hear all the antiaircraft shells exploding in the air around them. The landing was quick and so abrupt that the glider literally split partly in two pieces, with the men, their helmets and equipment flying in all directions. Young Cronkite picked up a steel pot as they scrambled out the side of the ship under enemy fire, and he headed for the limited shelter available behind a hedgerow. Many of the men from the plane followed.

After a few moments of silence, one of the sergeants asked Cronkite where he thought they might be safest. He suggested another hedgerow and they all quickly headed to it. The sergeant once again asked for advice, since they were still taking enemy fire. Cronkite suggested another spot, to which the men responded as though it was an order. When the man asked for more instructions moments later, Cronkite became somewhat irritated. Walter pointed out that he knew nothing of combat tactics and asked why the man didn't decide for himself. Looking directly at his forehead the sergeant replied incredulously, "But you're the lieutenant!"

Walter took off his steel helmet to discover that he had somehow picked up the platoon leader's headgear after the hard landing, and all these men placed their lives in his hands because they thought everything he suggested had been an order from an officer.

The life of a White House Social Aide is much like correspondent Cronkite's early combat experience. People often mistake the uniforms for authority because of their interpretations of the surroundings. In fact, an aide must negotiate every event with the utmost of tact and diplomacy because he really has no significant power to direct the actions of visitors. Like the soldiers from the glider, guests respond to suggestions simply because they want to do the right thing. Without that edge a Social Aide would be lost.

From the first recorded Social Aide, Douglas MacArthur, who attended to Teddy Roosevelt's needs, to all the dozens of Social Aides who have served many First Families since, I applaud your sacrifices and dedication to duty. Your mastery of the art of making presidential social functions successful is well known among the select group of international celebrities who regularly attend them. Now, perhaps, your accomplishments will be more widely recognized by the general public.

I am grateful to many people for their help with this book. Writing about one's self is not an easy task. Frances Spatz Leighton helped immensely in focusing my part in these events as a character rather than as an observer. Her careful questioning and artful writing as well as her own experiences in Washington's power circles added much to my early efforts. Oscar Collier, as a trusted agent, led me each step of the way in the proper direction, despite my inclinations to wander. The staff at Carol Publishing Group was extraordinarily professional in their approach to every aspect of the project. As an editor, Allan J. Wilson was like a rock wall—dividing good from the otherwise with gracious ease.

To my many dozens of friends not named who have offered me solid encouragement over the past eight years, you can only begin to understand how much your support has meant. I thank you one and all.

And to my family. Linda was my cheerleader and conscience. Michael and Christopher are so inquisitive about everything that I simply had to record these events for them. Without their interest and support, nothing would have been possible, necessary or worthwhile.

The views expressed in this book are those of
the author and do not reflect the official
policy or position of the Department of
Defense or the U.S. Government.

Part One

Getting There
Is Half the Fun

1

First Encounters

*M*uhammed Ali, of all people—the most recognizable face in the world—was about to cause a social crisis at the White House.

The scene was the East Room. I was, at the moment, the White House Social Aide in charge of seeing to it that all the guests were in the State Dining Room before President Carter and the First Lady entered. Everyone was there except one impressive couple— Muhammed Ali and his new bride, Veronica.

She was a raving beauty with a face like an angel, a cloud of long black hair, and a streamlined body making her slim enough to be a model—which she was, or at least had been until the heavyweight champion billed as "the Greatest" became the focus of her life. That had been when he was married to someone else, and she had become almost a member of the family whom everyone called Cousin Veronica.

Now they were dawdling along, enjoying themselves, examining various art objects on display, talking and laughing. It was nearing the point where they might have to walk in to dinner *after* the President—a violation of protocol that could get a Social Aide into a lot of trouble—so somebody had to move them on.

Remembering my little run-in with Mrs. Ali some months back, I didn't want to be the one who annoyed her a second time. Then I had been the Introducing Aide as she approached the new President, Jimmy Carter, in the receiving line. She had indicated she wanted to be introduced to the President as Mrs. Ali.

I knew a lot about Veronica—she was always in the news—and Mrs. Ali she was not, at least not yet. Muhammed Ali had gone through a messy divorce, but they weren't married, even though Veronica had borne him a child in 1976 named Hana Yasmeen Ali.

I had ignored her wishes and introduced her as "Miss Porche," and she had thrown silent daggers at me. Here she was again, and now she *was* Mrs. Ali. I had to gamble that she wouldn't recognize me. But there was no choice. I went over to say hello and encourage them to hurry to the dining room.

Even as he took a few steps toward the door, Ali joked that he liked the scenery and he really didn't want to go in yet. Then with a Cheshire grin, he stopped and said, "No one is going to make me."

Unable to resist the temptation and knowing the room was empty except for us, I put up my fists, danced around a little and said, "We may have to call out the Army."

Ali took the bait, perched on his toes and, raising two of the biggest hams with knuckles I've ever faced, growled, "Oh, yeah?" Suddenly, he didn't sound like he was kidding.

Here I was, dancing self-consciously around the East Room of the White House with a guy who could knock down a wall by flinching in his sleep. And meanwhile, at any minute, President Carter was going to make his formal entrance into the State Dining Room and take his seat.

I was beginning to wonder how to get out of this silly situation— and fast—when Veronica came to my rescue. Grabbing Ali's arm, she scolded, "Quit being foolish and get in to dinner."

Maybe she *didn't* recognize me. Maybe she was just being gracious. Whichever it was, I thanked her silently and made a mental note not to joke with Muhammed Ali again about fighting.

Meeting a President for the first time face to face is a truly awesome experience, much like a first parachute jump—incredibly exhilarating, scary and over much too quickly.

The place was the White House.

The date was January 28, 1972, and I had just undergone eight months of intensive interviews with numerous Army and White

House officials. Simultaneously, the intelligence community had been conducting an exhaustive investigation of my background, the thoroughness of which would have made any prospective mother-in-law deliriously happy.

No aspect of my life was beyond their detailed scrutiny. The results had just come back granting me full White House clearance with access to the President. My new title was White House Social Aide.

My first encounter with the President and Mrs. Nixon was at a dinner in honor of Mr. and Mrs. DeWitt Wallace, the founders of the *Reader's Digest*.

I had been in Richard Nixon's presence before, but this was hardly the place or the time to refresh his memory. In 1958, I was that fourteen-year-old little kid in Quito, Ecuador, he had waved at when he made a goodwill tour of South America with Pat. My father, the deputy senior adviser to the Ecuadoran military establishment, was very busy helping to welcome the American Vice President. I was aware that Mr. and Mrs. Nixon were not having a very good time because some people were angry at the United States. On the next stop, Venezuela, a crowd of protesters had even tried to kill Nixon, rocking his limousine and throwing stones.

Years later, I would learn that Pat Nixon said it was the most fearful time of her life. Any mention of that previous encounter would have to wait. The beaming President and First Lady had guests to greet.

As a full-fledged White House Social Aide, I was standing in the Cross Hall that runs the length of the mansion on the State Floor from the East Room to the State Dining Room. As the son of an army colonel, I had been around plenty of brass before, but even the strict admonitions on how to act in front of Dad's boss in no way prepared me for a meeting with the Commander in Chief.

The President and Mrs. Nixon had just arrived on the main floor from their private residence upstairs and were headed for the receiving line in the East Room. Every detail had been checked and double-checked, and during the brief calm before the event began, several of us were caught off guard in the open hall as they emerged from the elevator. Instinctively backing up to make room and consciously trying to become less conspicuous, I found that there was really nowhere to go. My full-dress winter uniform, now adorned with the markings of a military aide to the President of the United States, virtually cried out for attention.

Walking by at arm's length, they turned and looked directly at me, as if recognizing a new face. Both the President and Mrs. Nixon smiled and said hello. From somewhere inside me there issued a greeting that I hoped was fairly natural, "Good evening."

It may have sounded a little strained to them, but they did not show it. They had heard all manner of nervous and quaking voices before from thousands of stunned people and weren't the least bit concerned.

As they continued on to the receiving line, I teetered for a while on legs that were completely unwilling to move. (I literally felt paralyzed.) Fortunately for everyone, new Social Aides are not assigned any significant duties on their orientation visit, for I was frozen to the spot and remained there for some time trying to recover from the strangely pleasant shock of their greeting after they had passed by.

I reminded myself that the White House belongs to *everyone*. That helped a little. I also reminded myself of all the good things I had heard about the job—the wonderful people I'd meet, the fabulous food I would eat at every party—and *that* really brought me back to life.

The evening progressed to the afterdinner entertainment. The Ray Conniff Singers were taking their places on stage in the East Room while the guests claimed their seats. War protests had become a relatively common, almost everyday occurrence in Washington during this era. Everyone was accustomed to the antiwar focus of hatred on the President as the single most identifiable symbol of the government. But no one was prepared for what happened next.

A young Canadian lady living in Los Angeles, Carol Feraci, was hired by Ray Conniff as a substitute singer and had managed to place herself in the front row of the group.

Before Conniff's singers could perform their first number, she reached into her blouse, pulled out a banner and held it in both hands high over her head for the Nixons and all their guests to see. In bold letters it commanded STOP THE KILLING. Several people gasped, and the rest sat staring in shock.

In the perfect stillness, Miss Feraci seized the opportunity to lecture our host. "President Nixon, stop bombing human beings, animals and vegetation. You go to church on Sunday and pray to Jesus

Christ," she said. "If Jesus Christ were in this room tonight, you would not dare to drop another bomb. Bless the Berrigans and Daniel Ellsberg!"

Incredibly, no one moved. After a few moments, Ray Conniff led the group in its first number, which sounded very good under the circumstances. After some polite applause, Ray told the audience, "The beginning of this program was as much a surprise to me as everybody."

Many people including the other singers, groaned and booed, and someone shouted, "Throw her out." Mr. Conniff told Miss Feraci that it would be best if she left. She quietly walked off stage to the waiting Secret Service agents, who escorted her away for interrogation.

Afterward, she held an impromptu press conference in the library of the White House. The Nixons did not press charges, and she departed quietly after talking with reporters for a few minutes and reinforcing her point.

This all happened before the age of metal detectors at the White House. One must wonder how it might have changed the course of history if Miss Feraci had pulled a gun out of her blouse instead of the banner. She could easily have gotten off several shots before someone stopped her, and the effect on the world as we know it could have been enormous. Thank goodness she wanted peace not war.

I was personally intimidated by the surroundings, not to mention the host, the guests and the press corps, and I had no idea at the time of the correct thing to do, so I did nothing. It turned out that doing nothing was not only a good response but also a popular one. No one else made a move either, including the Secret Service detail. Two agents, dressed in black-tie tuxedos just like the other male guests, always sat in the second row behind the President.

Other tuxedoed agents were standing casually along the side of the room with me and several other staff members. Although the situation was an acute embarrassment to everyone, Miss Feraci posed no physical threat to the President. A physical confrontation would have only generated more publicity for her antiwar protest and would have been more embarrassing to the First Family than the protest itself. It was bad enough that she would get enormous press coverage wherein she would be allowed to restate her views in great detail. It would not do to make her a martyr in the eyes of the public by having someone wrestle her to the ground or by taking some other physical action against her.

The remainder of the evening passed without incident, but there was much discussion among the aides of how, through increased vigilance, we could anticipate and perhaps prevent a future similar situation from turning into a catastrophe.

I was exhausted. I was hungry. This didn't seem at all like the kind of fun and entertainment I had expected. And where was the food? Gone.

Well, *better luck next time,* I assured myself.

Next time came just four days later when a quartet of aides was scheduled to work an afternoon reception and tea that Mrs. Nixon was giving to honor American Pen Women. I was told that the Nixons were more generous than some other presidential families had been and that they always gave some little present to their guests at such times as a souvenir of the visit.

Popular gifts of the Nixons' included items with the presidential seal—cuff links and tie clasps for men and pins suitable for a lady's blouse or a man's jacket.

Guests had their own ideas about suitable souvenirs and helped themselves to the cocktail napkins and matchbooks that also bore the seal. These were not intended as official gifts but were put out for their functional value; however, many more disappeared than were needed for any one event, and it was clear that those went home as priceless mementos. Some went home with new and enthusiastic staff members, but most were carried off by the visitors.

This afternoon, each guest would receive a gold-colored ballpoint pen inscribed with Pat Nixon's signature. I couldn't help but marvel at the uniqueness of this gift for the American Pen Women. It seemed so appropriate at the time, but I later discovered that these pens were used, as were so many of the other gifts, for numerous occasions. Like many staff members, I would eventually acquire enough to pass them out to all my relatives and still retain a handful in my box of memorabilia.

My final duty for the day was to get the box of five-hundred pens from the usher's office and to stand beside Mrs. Nixon as she gave one to each departing guest. It seemed like a simple enough task for a new aide, but it turned out quite different from what was planned. Some of the ladies had asked just a few minutes earlier about King

Timahoe, the Nixon's beautiful golden retriever. Since the public is always fascinated with the First Pet regardless of the administration, it was customary to let the animal be seen, particularly when the press was around. Fortunately, reporters were not around this day.

The First Lady had instructed someone on the domestic staff to bring the dog around to the North Portico entrance. She was showing King Timahoe to the guests when I returned with the pens. Approaching her right side with this rather large box of gifts, I noticed that some guests surrounding the dog had their coats on already and were headed out the door. Not wanting anyone to leave empty-handed, Mrs. Nixon hurriedly reached for the pens.

I quickly gave her a handful, and in return she unexpectedly handed me King Timahoe's leash. The thought of being a successful waiter had never occurred to me before, but here I stood balancing a large box of five hundred pens in one hand while this huge, hyperactive dog tugged playfully on the leash in the other.

King Timahoe suddenly made a very excited, high-speed, full circle around me while I held on for dear life, trying to appear nonchalant. The leash was quickly wrapped around my legs before I could react, pinning my knees together. A stiff breeze coming in the door would have blown me over at the First Lady's feet.

I could not have looked or felt any sillier, and Mrs. Nixon's first handful of pens was nearly gone. She would require more in a moment, and here I was doing my level best to just stand up with one hand holding the big box of pens and the other grasping a leash that I dared not release. Timahoe was winning. I felt myself slipping. Another moment and I'd be on the floor. Suddenly I felt a firm hand. An usher had spotted my predicament.

Looking back, I realize it was an hilarious pantomime.

Not a word was spoken as he unwound me, and I continued to assist Pat as though nothing unusual was happening. Did the First Lady know what was going on behind her back? Or was she just too dignified to let on? Or was she afraid that if she looked, *she'd* be the one to fall down laughing. I didn't know. All I was sure of was that aides who proved to be clumsy quickly became ex-aides. That was the word.

Safe at last!

It was over. I had survived without taking a pratfall. But could I survive without food? Well, I mustn't get too excited. There would be plenty of time to sample those great hors d'oeuvres I had heard about.

Next time turned out to be another afternoon affair. My calendar lists my third White House adventure as:

February 3, 1972—Reception for Athletes Involved with Anti-Drug Commercials

I felt elated. Surely the White House knew that athletes were always hungry. I could almost taste those little goodies. The event started out on a high note when the Social Aides were told to drive into the White House complex and park on the North Grounds.

What a plus! I would be entering through the Northwest Gate, used by arriving heads of state. It was truly exhilarating to pull up to the crashproof barrier, show an I.D. card, enter and park in the space nearest the North Portico entrance.

Only a month ago, I was just another tourist walking in front of 1600 Pennsylvania Avenue trying to spot a familiar dignitary. Now, as the massive iron gates were thrown open to me, I was very aware that every passerby craned his neck to see who was entering the White House.

By this time, I had almost completely forgotten—or at least gotten over the shock—that as a Social Aide, I needed to purchase a thousand dollars' worth of otherwise unnecessary dress uniforms. It was almost worth it just for that unique feeling when strangers in public make one feel more important than reality would justify. Who was I to tell them I was just a glorified guide and usher—and oh, yes, ballroom dancer.

As a still very new aide on his third outing, I was given the rather simple job of assisting the Greeting Aides in the Diplomatic Reception Room. Later, there would be plenty of time to mingle and chat with the guests, 350 stars of every major television sporting event.

And there would be plenty of time to get to the reception table. I had been briefed on the routine. I knew what to expect.

Afternoon receptions hosted by the Nixons were treated like cocktail parties. Regular mixed drinks were served by several bartenders, and anything that didn't require an electric mixer was readily available. Hors d'oeuvres of the most extravagant and delicious varieties, aides assured me, were served by John Ficklin, the maitre d', and his competent staff. They had become a staple of life for some of my colleagues, who assured me that we were free to consume as many as good manners would allow.

The rule was that aides had to wait until the appropriate time to partake of the feast. And the appropriate time was after the President and First Lady had greeted the guests, completed the planned speech and photo opportunities, and departed.

At that point, the Social Aide-in-Charge would remove his white gloves as a signal that all aides should do the same. We could then have a drink or two and sample the delectables as we blended into the throng.

So I knew what to do. All I needed was the opportunity.

Everything had gone according to schedule, and I was finally heading toward those beckoning tables when duty waylaid me.

The Department of Defense had just entered the antidrug war, and several senior people had been appointed to lead the various service programs. Most were models of decorum, but one top military figure, a general, was obviously very drunk. I stopped to help. His speech was slurred, and he had difficulty making his points, but he continued to babble on to whoever would stay and listen to him. Many guests were too polite to say or do anything about this general's problem and quickly moved on.

This was shaping up into a first-class disaster. I figured the best I could do was keep him talking to me until the bar closed. Since I was in uniform, he was more than willing to tell me war stories. This worked to effectively limit the damage done by the alcohol he had already consumed and distracted him from getting more.

Other guests stopped to say hello but quickly departed when my new friend gibbered on about the event and the surroundings. Fortunately, it never turned into a major public scene, and I was greatly relieved when he was safely in the hands of his driver at the Diplomatic Reception Room entrance. In the end, I had spent so much time keeping the general out of trouble that I again went home hungry. The guests and my fellow aides had managed to wolf down every last morsel of food.

I was too discouraged and tired to say better luck next time. Would I ever have a personal encounter with party food at the White House? At that moment, I doubted it.

Ah, hope springs eternally. My log shows my next assignment.

March 8—Reception for Delegates to the Young Republican Leadership Conference

Surely the White House knew that youth was always hungry.

It was my first encounter with Tricia Nixon Cox. She had been chosen to hostess this reception because of the similarity in ages between her and virtually all the guests. It was unlikely that very many of the 750 attendees were big-money contributors to the Republican Party but they did spend a lot of time around elections organizing state and local campaigns and appealing to the younger voters.

Tricia would be able to communicate with them on a one-to-one basis, and by meeting her they could more easily identify with the administration. Also, it was two P.M. and the President was busy in his office. He occasionally put these functions on his schedule and attended, but on this day he let his First Daughter carry the ball.

Tricia was only as warm and friendly as the situation would permit. She learned from her parents the practicality of being formal and correct—particularly around people she didn't know.

It's a very effective defense against people's assuming one is too accessible or can be manipulated, and it is a popular defense used by many people in high places. As she shook each hand in the receiving line, she smiled and chatted briefly with anyone who wanted to stop for a word. Many were awed at being there and never got past "hello," but others were prepared with a comment or a question that needed a response. Tricia accommodated everyone equally with cool grace and style. Admittedly, it was a friendly and receptive audience, but how many of us can say something short, sweet and pleasant 750 times in a row and still be gracious to the last one?

As they stood in the long receiving line, the youthful crowd enjoyed the music of the Marine Orchestra playing in the Grand Hall nearby. And after they came through the line, they headed for the refreshment tables. Punch and cookies. Nothing more!

Had the President been the host at the reception, there would have been beef, quiche, little cakes and tarts, and an open bar. Once again I went home hungry and severely disappointed. Glory and pride will carry one only so far on an empty stomach.

I put a candy bar in my pocket as I got ready for my fifth big assignment. My notice to appear and work shows that the President would be hosting:

April 10—National Alliance of Business Reception

I was beginning to feel comfortable with the surroundings. My first observation at this function made me proud of myself for noticing that a lot of these businessmen sported a gold R.N. lapel pin, but at first I wasn't sure whether the men were guests or agents protecting the President. The Secret Service always wore lapel pins for identification, and they routinely changed them for security reasons. That way, as the boss moved from one activity to another, an unfamiliar face could be instantly identified as an agent, and of course, without the proper pin, anyone who did not appear to belong in the area was suspect.

But good grief, how many Secret Servicemen did the President need at this party? There seemed to be no end to them. Almost every other male guest seemed to have a pin with the letters R.N. Luckily, I overheard a helpful staff member tell an aide that the gold R.N. pin signified the wearer had made a political contribution of a thousand dollars or more to Richard Nixon.

Fortunately, I had not embarrassed myself by saying anything to anyone, and in my defense, it had occurred to me that those "agents" busily talking among themselves weren't acting like they had the President's personal safety uppermost in their minds. Ultimately, many of these pins appeared at social functions over the next two and one-half years. Today they are probably worth a tidy sum as collector's items but certainly less than the original donation.

With only guests lingering on, there was plenty of time to taste all the hors d'oeuvres. It didn't take many samples to pronounce them fit for a king—or a president. From strawberry tarts to miniature quiche, they were positively the most delicious edibles my bachelor existence had tasted in Washington, D.C.

I went home with a smile on my face.

2

The White House Game
of Q&A

I was not the kid you would have picked out of a lineup of high school freshmen or even seniors and say, "That boy will one day be dancing at the White House. He's perfect Social Aide material." Hell no! Unless, of course, my mother was doing the picking.

Mother rather hoped I would marry a debutante. Oh, she never came out with a flat prediction or command, but she made it quite clear that it very possibly could happen. I think it was to soothe her own feelings for having birthed a stringbean son with one pointed ear and bad eyesight, who hardly had anything you could call a real date all through high school—a fate worse than death to a woman who looked like Doris Day, had been queen of her high school senior class and had graduated from Stephens College.

Not that I didn't have a crush on a girl. She was the head cheerleader with a red convertible, and for weeks I trembled on the brink of asking her for a date... I spent my high school senior prom night with the rest of the nerds at the local bowling alley.

Now flash ahead to my second year at college. I've gotten rid of my nerd glasses. I'm into contacts and I am indeed dating a sub-deb, slated to have her coming-out party. I must have cared—I was financing our dates by working as a delivery boy for a drugstore at $1.10 an hour.

But was Mother happy? No. Now she was afraid I would get married. Her new theme was "You must not get serious until you finish college. You must not get married until after school."

It was a close call. Serious I was, but marry I didn't. And that's why I was eligible to be picked to become a Military Social Aide at the White House. You *must* be single. That's for starters.

I lucked into it, really. I couldn't have gotten there in a more roundabout way.

The first I heard about the Social Aide program was over dinner one night while stationed on the Demilitarized Zone in Korea. I was already serving as the aide-de-camp to the commanding general, but my desirable and unique job paled in comparison to the world of the White House. We all lived in drafty Quonset huts and, like all soldiers overseas, often thought and talked about the good life back home. Occasionally, we dreamed really big about all the great things we could do when we got assigned back to the real world.

One of the officers there was a friend of Air Force Colonel Don Hughes, then a military assistant to President Nixon. Over several meals, I heard second-hand descriptions of the glamour and excitement of working as a Military Social Aide at the White House.

If we became Social Aides, we would have personal contact with Washington's news makers and power brokers. And, who knows, the opportunity might advance our military careers. That was a plus!

It struck me that if only I could get a job in the Washington area, it would be a fantastic opportunity to do something that most people would never even dream of, while at the same time getting ahead in the service. And what a great life-style. Soirees at the White House!

Of course we wouldn't be paid for being Social Aides and attending White House parties—that was our patriotic duty. Naturally I had seen the posters: UNCLE SAM WANTS YOU. I was comfortable with that. I expected him to want me. He already had me. I just didn't think he'd be needing me for dancing at the White House. Still, I didn't have a closed mind.

Looking at the bleak Korean landscape, I escaped into a dream of dancing at the White House. The colonel had mentioned the fantastic party food and pastries prepared by great pastry chefs. Think of eating what the President ate, dancing with Hollywood stars!

It was a huge challenge. Could I pull it off?

Now that my interest was sufficiently aroused, I only needed to get a posting to the D.C. area. As a captain, halfway around the world in far-off Korea, I would find this was not an easy task. The Pentagon was full of military officers, but infantry captains were relatively few in number. My only hope was an assignment to one of the Army activities in the surrounding area. Recalling a company commander I had served under in Vietnam who had arrived in the war fresh from the Army's ceremonial unit at Fort Myer, I decided to focus my attention on getting into the Old Guard, the President's honor guard.

Getting in appeared to be relatively easy. It was only necessary to ask for the assignment, and without argument or apparent debate my request was approved. What a mirage!

Three other junior officers reported in with me early on a Monday. It was a genuine surprise to find that we had to undergo interviews to be accepted. It was also a surprise to discover that this battalion had two colonels. The commander was a full colonel with a lieutenant colonel for a deputy. We four looked like a parade going from one colonel to the other, lined up outside the offices. My anticipation was short-lived: as the lieutenants came out one by one, the administrative people were helping them get reassigned to different organizations!

For what is normally a three-year tour, they hadn't even been there long enough to have lunch, and already they were sent packing.

Crossing my fingers, I asked one of the officers why he wasn't accepted for the Old Guard. He took off his glasses and said, "I can't wear these on the parade field and I don't wear contacts. I can't function if I can't see, so I'm out."

The second officer had an equally surprising response. "The colonel said I'm too short. Five feet ten inches isn't enough. The minimum is six feet tall."

There was no point in asking the third officer why he didn't qualify. I knew I was already doomed—bad eyes and too short. Anyway, I couldn't ask him because I was suddenly being ushered in.

The battalion commander, Colonel M. E. Lee, was an imposing man at six-foot-three. He had just returned from a ceremony and I noticed his Army dress-blue uniform hung behind his desk. Several rows of full-size ceremonial medals made him look a little like

European royalty. His Marine-style haircut and the wide fireman's suspenders holding up his John Wayne cavalry-style trousers gave every appearance that he was prepared for any eventuality. When he spoke, it was with the authority that comes from a lifetime of leading aggressive combat soldiers and officers.

"Do you know how to march?" he asked.

"Four years of ROTC at Texas A&M," I replied.

"Have you ever used a saber?" He expected me to say no, but I had carried one for my senior year at A&M as a staff officer.

Checking some other details, he was finally satisfied that I had enough decorations, and he noted that I could wear contact lenses to correct for nearsightedness. Colonel Lee explained that glasses reflected sunlight, and the glare was distracting for the audience during a parade, so they were banned in his unit. I wondered if the lieutenant who was reassigned got the same detailed explanation, but I doubted it.

Asking me to stand, he wondered aloud if I was really six feet tall as my records indicated.

I confessed it was a small mistake that had existed in my file for a long time and that it was an honest error that should be changed to five-feet-eleven. However, until now, it had not been a significant issue to anyone since I was well under the prescribed weight limit for my height.

The colonel swiftly replied that I was lucky I had even gotten in for an interview.

By this time, I felt all hope was lost, and I was ready to follow the other officers before me who were already outprocessing, just like lemmings into the sea. After studying my record for some moments, he eventually said he had known an Elmer Bauer at Fort Ord, California, in the 1950s. Were we related?

Suddenly a ray of hope! By quirk of fate, it turned out the colonel was a former acquaintance of my father, and we quit talking about me as the conversation turned to old war stories. After an extensive briefing about the way things were in the Army of the fifties, he finally broke off the conversation and walked me to the outer office. The adjutant was instructed to assign me to the Operations staff. In spite of being an inch too short, I was in and on my way! At this point, I was twenty-seven.

The President's Army Honor Guard is formally known as the First Battalion (Reinforced), Third United States Infantry Regiment—the Old Guard. The other services have comparable but smaller ceremonial units. As the oldest service, the Army leads joint service ceremonies and bears a greater share of planning for joint service functions.

The men of The Old Guard have many unique functions. They guard the Tomb of the Unknown Soldier; they provide the Salute Gun Platoon for all necessary honors; they maintain the horses for official ceremonial purposes in Washington and in particular for Arlington National Cemetery; and as a combat infantry unit, they have to be prepared for a variety of contingency missions in the D.C. area while simultaneously performing necessary ceremonies such as the Army funerals in Arlington Cemetery.

The Old Guard also has the obscure but interesting function of maintaining the official funeral plans for existing and former Presidents and senior government officials. I, for one, participated in the periodic walk-throughs of the Truman funeral plan on site in Independence, Missouri, when his failing health suggested a possible need. Ultimately, most of the plan which President Truman himself had personally reviewed and approved was discarded by Bess while her husband was on his deathbed.

Because the former First Lady had made drastic cuts in the elaborate funeral plans, it was no longer necessary for me to go to Independence when President Harry Truman died on December 26, 1972.

On another occasion, as second in command of the Capitol ceremonial activities, I helped execute the state funeral plan for Lyndon Baines Johnson. It had been read and approved by the former President (as most are), and unlike Bess Truman, who completely rewrote her husband's plan, the family changed little at the last moment. Fate caused some major modifications, however.

The inauguration of President Nixon had just taken place, and the platform on the east side of the Capitol could not be removed in time for the laying-in-state portion. We got the coffin into the Rotunda and out again without slighting either the Senate or the House of Representatives, which was a bit tricky. We brought it into the Capitol on the Senate side to get it to the Rotunda, but we carried it out the next day on the House side. It was a dignified and professional solution, but pallbearers had a very tight squeeze getting through some of those tight turns and narrow hallways.

Sometimes our assignments were a bit mysterious. As a new officer in the Old Guard, I went to the funeral of a retired Army lieutenant colonel in June of 1972. We had advance knowledge that an exceptional number of dignitaries were coming, but no one seemed to know why John Paul Vann rated such a high-powered audience. What drew them together, I learned later, was this one man's impact on the war in Vietnam.

In death, John Paul Vann is now famous as the subject of *A Bright Shining Lie,* by Neil Sheehan. He had an astonishing impact on U.S. war policy in Vietnam from the early 1960s on. Most of us had never heard of him. All of the dignitaries were there to pay their last respects to this man who tried to tell the world that we would never win the way we were going.

Vann said the Army of South Vietnam could not win by simple ground combat. (My father had come home from South Vietnam in 1963 with the exact same message.)

When I see the Old Guard in the news today, I recall the year I spent at Fort Leavenworth, Kansas, in 1949. I was six, and a neighbor boy, Barrie Zais, helped me catch a gopher. I took it home in a shoe box to keep for a pet. It got out and chewed up one of my dad's new leather shoes. When Dad discovered the culprit, we couldn't catch it again, so he got a broom and beat it into submission. Fortunately, Dad was nearly out of breath when he got to me with that broom. The next day, he told the story to Creighton Abrams (the namesake of our Army's main battle tank), who sat next to him in class, and the guys almost laughed him out of school. Barrie Zais is now the commander of the Old Guard.

All officers and nearly all enlisted members of the Old Guard have to get a White House security clearance to perform the full range of their assignments, and this process was initiated immediately for me upon my arrival at the Old Guard headquarters at Fort Myer. Their efficiency was impressive and it was a relief to see my formal clearance process begin.

I was looking forward to performing ultradignified ceremonial duties, but my first weekend in Washington with the Old Guard found me involved with riot control as screaming, angry crowds converged on the White House—and President Nixon—to protest the Vietnam War. It was the end of April 1971, and the Old Guard was on the alert in case the protesters stormed the White House grounds and the police could not handle them. There was no glamour or dignity as I sat on the hard marble floor of a hallway in the Executive Office Building, across the street from the White House—I'd thought I was through with combat zones.

On several occasions, the local police were actually overwhelmed.

The crowd swelled ominously during the week that followed, and the next weekend brought the May Day rally in which hundreds of thousands of war protesters tried to bring the city to its knees and halt all government work. Again, the Old Guard brought in four rifle companies at midnight to bivouac in the EOB halls.

At one point, the intersections on Seventeenth Street, just to the west of the White House, were blocked by crowds of protesters. Police reported to the White House Emergency Control Center that they had no officers to clear them. We gathered up a platoon of soldiers under the command of the lieutenant who led the U.S. Army Drill Team, and got them ready to perform riot maneuvers and clear the area.

Since the National Guard incident at Kent State had very recently resulted in the tragic deaths of several innocent students, all of us had been under strict orders not to load live ammunition, which we believed was still packed in boxes and tied down on pallets with metal bands around them.

Just before the troops went out the door with bayonets fixed (for dramatic effect) but sheathed (for safety), a flying squadron of police showed up on scooters and took control.

While the soldiers who had actually gotten a foot out the door were being debriefed, it was discovered that the lieutenant had opened the boxes of *real* ammo, and every soldier was carrying a live magazine of twenty rounds! These were not just blank noisemakers. A potential tragedy of the most monumental proportions was thus narrowly averted in President Nixon's own backyard.

Another captain turned to me and said, "Hey, Steve, welcome to Washington!"

When the protesters (who included future White House speech writer Peggy Noonan) packed up and went home, I turned my attention fully to rehearsing ceremonial duties. But I yearned for duty as a White House aide. I had gone to a lot of trouble to position myself, on the outside chance I would be tapped.

Two officers serving with me were already White House Social Aides. I envied their good luck as I watched them take off for the White House or listened to them tell of some White House reception they had attended in the line of duty. But I had learned there was nothing one could do to join the White House Military Social Aide program. One had to be recommended by another aide. It was not possible to go to the White House and simply apply.

One day, after I'd been around several months, one of the two aides asked me if I'd be interested in the Social Aide program. I felt like saying, "I thought you'd never ask." My first interview followed shortly thereafter, over the phone, with the senior Army Social Aide.

I told myself, *This can't be too complicated.* How wrong can one be?

Through a succession of interviews, I was passed on for further discussions, and my records were reviewed again and again. After several weeks and numerous stops, including the director of the Army staff in the Pentagon, I arrived at the White House for what I sincerely hoped was the final round.

I had started to think there was no end to it.

The Naval Aide to the President was in charge of the Social Aide program at the time and was the first to see every prospective new aide. Next, because of my service affiliation, the Army Aide to the President wanted to formally interview me. Finally, the Social Secretary to the President personally saw every aspiring aide because she had to work with him or her on a daily basis and she was allowed the final decision.

Each of these interviews lasted at least thirty minutes and some ran more than an hour. In each case, basic and obvious questions were asked about my civilian and military education, previous assignments, hometown, hobbies and family. Questions eventually progressed to more difficult and sensitive areas.

Bit by bit, they squeezed out the story of my life in intimate detail. Who you dated was important. Childhood pranks were important. Everything was important.

"Let's talk about growing up. Can you describe the house of your childhood?"

I had to laugh. "Which particular house would you like to hear about? There were so many of them." Memory flashed to Grandma's big old house in Lincoln, Nebraska, where our main activity as kids was sitting on the porch and spitting sunflower seeds into the yard— the one who spit farthest was the day's winner.

It had a coal chute in the basement that was so dark and frightening that none of us grandchildren ever went alone into the basement at night, for years. That became a rite of passage, and I finally made it at the age of twelve.

"Let me interrupt a moment. You mention other grandchildren. Tell me about your brothers and sisters and where they are now."

"No sisters. Two brothers. My younger brother, Mark—he was born ten years after me—is a computer programmer on the West Coast. My older brother, Richard—Rick was born just fifteen months ahead of me. He now works as a construction subcontractor in Dallas. He was an architectural engineer in college—then a construction engineer in the Army."

"Oh, indeed? So both of you were Army."

"Yes. As a matter of fact, we graduated and were commissioned the same day at Texas A&M. That was because his was a five-year course—so we came out even. And we went to Vietnam a week apart, with him arriving there first."

"That's very interesting. I'll want to hear much more about your military background, but do you mind going back to those houses you lived in growing up as a military child? Where were these homes located? And what was your childhood life like in each place?"

I didn't know how much to tell—memories long buried and irrelevant flooded back. There was the house in Monterey, California, that shouldn't have been wished on any small boy who wanted to blend in and be accepted by the other little boys of the neighborhood. Not only was the house woefully small—it had only one bathroom and two bedrooms—but it was of an unfortunate color—pink!

That vivid color was the cross I had to bear whenever the neighborhood boys taunted me for living in a "girl's house," and yelled, "Pink, pink, you stink," just to reinforce the point.

To prove I was all boy and tough, I organized a group and we dug ditches in the hillside of our backyard, covering the tops with boards to make a tunnel system. We also made Indian peace pipes of large, hollowed-out acorns, smoking dried leaves in them.

Unfortunately, in trying to light these little contraptions one day, my brother and I accidentally set the grass field ablaze. It took two fire trucks to save the houses on the next street, which were directly in the path of the blowing brushfire.

Compared to Monterey, San Antonio was a quiet life in a normal-looking three-bedroom ranch house with a garage and large yard. My most exciting activity each day was to catch enough bugs to feed my captive horned toads, who lived in a large wooden box and begat many more toads.

The house that made the most vivid impression on me was perhaps the one in Quito, Ecuador, because everything appeared so different from America. There were the concrete pillars for fence posts and an iron gate for security. The side fences were actually six-foot-high concrete walls.

There was a lot of security, and we certainly needed it. Even so, my parents woke up one night to find a man standing in their second-floor bedroom. He had just finished stuffing thousands of dollars of jewelry and cash into his pockets.

Before the man got out the front door and vaulted the fence, my dad had his shotgun loaded. He could have shot him but decided not to fire. The fact that the watchdog did not get excited indicated it might have been an inside job.

Anyway, this was a land so poor that many stories circulated about destitute parents who would sacrifice a child to a *gringo's* car for the accident compensation the court would grant them. For the cost of one child, the rest of the family could live well to the end of their lives. While the stories were probably not true, they did serve to cause most Americans to drive more cautiously.

Our maid received what was considered a good salary—$18 a month. As a bonus, she got to keep and sell all the used tin cans, which were then beaten into flat tin or into curved rain gutters.

Our place, which was next door to that of the U.S. ambassador, was anything but a hovel. It was very lovely. Even elegant.

The house itself was a huge white stucco with much wrought iron and so many bedrooms that one was made into a *bodega,* or storage room. That was necessary because we would fly to Panama in a DC-3 twice a year to do our basic grocery shopping—buying by the crate and gross. Each trip we returned home with dozens of cases of food and several hundred bottles of frozen milk.

"Did you have any pets there?"

"The chickens and ducks we raised were my pets." Ten chickens were supposed to lay eggs but refused and seemed unimpressed with the nest eggs Mother used to give them an idea of what was expected of them.

My parents issued an ultimatum to the hens: produce or fry. Every day I checked to see if the imitation eggs had inspired my pet hens to lay more, and each day we got closer to chicken soup. A deadline was set to run out with the last bag of feed. Like a story composed in hen heaven, they laid real eggs the day my mother started searching for her recipes. We got to keep all our pets and had fresh eggs to boot for the remainder of the two years.

"What about sports? Do you participate in any particular one?"

"I do play golf on occasion but I've never broken 100."

"What about when you were growing up?"

"I tried a few." In an effort to join the crowd, I searched diligently for the right one for me. I was too small and mild-mannered for football. Basketball never interested me, though we played it in gym class—anyway, I was too short.

Swimming was a good option, but MacArthur High School did not have a pool, so that was out. Track was too boring. I tried pole vaulting in Quito and nearly hanged myself on the crossbar at a height of seven or eight feet. Only baseball was left. During batting tryouts, I got in line in front of a guy named Jerry Grote. After I had swung at and missed several balls thrown right over the plate, Jerry got up and put out some windows in the school building beyond the center-field fence. He made the team, of course, and went on to play for the New York Mets for many years.

"Do you remember the town where you were born?"

"Not at all." My father served thirty years in the Army as an infantry officer. He fought in World War II, Korea and Vietnam. Moving was a way of life for all of us—though I was born in Albany, Oregon, I was only there about six months before we moved on.

We lived in Lincoln, Nebraska, for a while when Dad was stationed in Italy. That was because the Bauer grandparents lived there. And Mother's relatives lived just across the state line in Kansas.

"Isn't Bauer a German name?"

"Yes. My paternal grandparents were born on the Volga River in the German part of Russia before the turn of the century. They were

raised in the same farming village, and their families immigrated to
Lincoln, Nebraska, before they actually met in the Lutheran Church
there."

"And your mother's parents?"

"The Lortschers were also German, but they came from Speiz,
Switzerland, and settled in Sabetha, Kansas. Ironically, they were
also farmers, so I guess at least I should try my hand at gardening."

After World War II was over in Europe, Mother and my brother
and I went over in a troopship to live with Dad in Milan, Italy, for a
year. We stayed in a beautiful hotel, but I don't remember it well—I
was born during the war, in October 1943.

After that, we came to the Washington, D.C., area and the quaint
little stone house that we lived in, out in Fairfax County. Years later
I went to see it and renew memories.

"Yes, you must have a lot of memories of houses around the world.
Let me ask you, do you smoke?"

I wondered if my interrogator was worried about my blowing
smoke into the faces of White House guests. "No, I don't, I'm happy
to say." I had taken the early cure. How well I remembered when
Mother discovered cigarettes missing from the box on the coffee
table. Though she could not detect smoke on our breaths—we had
covered it with lemon drops—my brother and I confessed anyway.

She phoned my father. When he came home he brought with him
two twenty-five-cent cigars. In 1952, when I was nine, a quarter
bought a *big* cigar. Dad said, "Since you fellows like to smoke, here's
something you'll really enjoy."

We started puffing those things and halfway through, Rick got
sick and threw up on the rug. I could have told him what to do—I
only pretended to inhale and kept the smoke in my mouth so I was not
nearly as sick. But sick enough, and I haven't smoked since.

"And what about drinking?"

Naturally they didn't want drunks greeting the guests at the
White House. "I have a drink now and then when I'm out socially," I
said. "I have never been an excessive drinker."

Drinking was one of the points just about everyone asked about:
"Do you drink?"

"How much and how often?"

"Was there alcohol in your home?" Of course there was. My
parents attended or gave cocktail parties frequently—it was part of

the military way of life. When my parents weren't out, they were home planning the next party they had to give. I grew up thinking all grown-ups went to a party two or three nights a week.

None of us kids considered drinking then, and drugs were unheard of. We would have sock hops for our parties, with soft drinks and snacks—when we asked for a Coke, we meant the carbonated kind.

"Did you have an early experience with alcohol?"

"In a manner of speaking. Just before entering Texas A&M." I told about the night before I left. My brother took me to his friend's dad's quick stop for a beer. I was seventeen and clearly underage but there was no danger of me getting drunk. I could not even finish that one twelve-ounce bottle of Lone Star beer and put the remainder in the trash when no one was looking.

"What kind of mischief did you get into as a teenager—any trouble with the law?"

"Not civilian law—military. With my own father. He was Lieutenant Colonel Elmer Bauer at the time, and we were in Ecuador. I was thirteen and Rick was a little older when we got the idea of borrowing the keys to the folks' new Buick and riding around Quito at night while they went to official cocktail parties, driving the government staff car.

"This worked so well that it got too tame. We borrowed the Army staff car one afternoon, going up and down our own street for practice. Unfortunately, we were just passing the ambassador's house next door when who should be coming out but Dad, his boss and the ambassador. That few minutes of fun blew our entire cover. Severe retribution followed. The only person who benefited from the whole affair was the maid. My parents had assumed that she had been siphoning gasoline from the Buick.

3

Sweating It Out

$\mathcal{N}$ever had anyone sweated so hard to get a job for which one is not paid—that of Military Social Aide to the White House. Some people climb mountains because they are there. Somehow the idea had been planted in my mind that I had to "climb up" and see what life and entertainment were like in intimate detail in the Number One residence of the world. Why? Because it was there.

And if I had to spill my guts about all the intimate details of my own life—from triumphant to dreaded moments—so be it. I would endure the barrage of questioning that was seemingly endless. On their side, I could understand that they couldn't afford to have kooks and oddballs greeting, chatting and dancing with White House guests or in close contact with the President and First Lady.

"Talk a little about the girls in your life."

"Well, I was what you would call 'a late bloomer.' In high school, I didn't really date." My mind flashed back to that awful senior prom night. No date. I had been too afraid to ask a girl and then at the very last moment a girl asked me because no one had asked her. Totally unprepared, I turned her down and spent the evening with the other mavericks at the local bowling alley.

"But when you were a little boy in school, didn't you like girls?"

"Oh, yes. Of course. I think I really started noticing girls in the eighth grade—especially one." Should I tell that I still have something to remember her by? She sat in front of me in class and I started teasing her and poking her and I pretended to dunk her hair in my empty ink well.

She reacted to my crude advances by turning around and stabbing me in the arm with her pencil so hard that the lead broke off. I still have it embedded under the skin of my elbow as a constant reminder of what a smooth guy I was with the ladies at an early age.

"Do you enjoy dancing?"

"Yes, indeed."

"When did you learn to dance? Did you want to learn?"

"Not particularly. I was about twelve and it certainly wasn't my idea." While in Ecuador, some of the parents knew we teens and pre-teens needed help in the all important area of social graces so they arranged for one of the moms to teach us to dance. With absolutely no athletic skill or coordination, I went along with the effort just because the others were doing it and I figured we could all be embarrassed at the same time. We tried several steps that were more a variation of the jitterbug than the current rock and roll. The tune "Rock Around the Clock" by Bill Haley and the Comets, which played over and over, gave us the illusion that we were doing contemporary steps.

There were so few Americans there that we easily arranged sock hops at each other's homes and practiced what we had learned. The group was so small, however, that everyone seemed more like distant relatives after a while than complete strangers. No one dated, partly because we were all around twelve to fifteen years old and partly because there was nowhere to go except each other's houses in groups.

"Would you say you were self-conscious of your appearance when you were growing up?"

"Yes, I was, but with good reason. I wore government issue glasses that made me look like a nerd, I was scrawny and a close haircut like the Marines now wear made my ears stick out."

With all of this—my glasses, the ears, the beanpole look—I was definitely not at ease with girls. In fact, in my high school senior year, I spent a total of two evenings with a girl—the same girl—and it took me the two full evenings to build up the courage to kiss her good night. I was mentally and emotionally exhausted after that episode and took no one else out that year.

Going to A&M was the smartest move of my life even if I did it for another reason altogether—to be with my brother and share his old car.

It turned out that the military regimen of twenty-four hours a day, seven days a week, in the ROTC was just what I needed to build up my self-confidence. That and contact lenses plus letting my hair grow out a bit to camouflage my ears.

My new attitude turned my life around. I discovered that I could walk up to a girl I did not know, strike up a conversation and later call for a date. Not every girl succumbed to this approach, but now I learned not to be too embarrassed about the ones who turned away.

Heaven only knows what made me settle down and date one girl from SMU for two years straight. She was a Pi Phi like my mother and went in for the debutante scene, so Mother really liked her.

By strange coincidence, this one girl, Molly, had her coming-out party in San Antonio the same year as did my cousin, Zelime Amen, who had been transplanted from my dad's hometown of Lincoln, Nebraska. After a while, whenever my mother called or wrote, she would mention Molly and comment on how nice she was but adding I'd be wise to wait until I graduated and got a job before seriously considering marriage.

I waited, but even so, Molly and I drifted apart after graduation. I dated several girls without ever fully committing myself. Some were exceptionally brainy. Some were exceptionally funny. Some were exceptionally good-looking. I just could never find all these ingredients in the same person. I knew I was expecting too much.

The interviewer's questions always came down to the girls I was currently dating or had dated since coming to Washington:

"What kind of girls do you date?"

"What do they like to do?"

"Where do you take them?"

"What kind of people do you run into there?"

"Do you drink?"

"How much and how often?"

Actually, I was not having great luck in dating in Washington. First, because the schedule of ceremonies I had to participate in kept me busy, and second, because of public sentiment. I once again had very close-cropped hair in the manner of all the ceremonial soldiers in the area. There was almost nowhere we could go where people, particularly young women our age, would not instantly recognize us as military men. The antiwar movement was so strong even in the nation's capital that I would be given the cold shoulder by girls.

"I don't date military men," some would say. As a result I often took the unusual precaution of not even discussing my employment. When pressed occasionally, I would simply say I had a sensitive government position and couldn't discuss it at all. The few who stayed around for three or more dates found out the truth and by then it really didn't matter.

"So I presume that means you would have sufficient time for social duties at the White House."

"Yes. That would be my priority."

And somewhere along the line would come the question "Would you mind dancing with little old ladies?" or "Do you have any objection to dancing with little old ladies?"

"Do you know how to waltz?"

No matter what subject we had been on, we always returned to that old standby, "Would you mind dancing with little old ladies?" And its corollary, "Do you know how to waltz?"

"What is it like in the Old Guard? Are you ever assigned to military funerals?"

"Oh, yes. For stretches at a time."

It was not at all unusual for the company assigned to do funerals for the week to go into Arlington National Cemetery from eight to fifteen times a day. We often had several teams working at once to keep up with the normal demands of such a large place as the D.C. area, and the additional pressure of the Vietnam War. Although I eventually got accustomed to the routine of the ceremony for burials, I could never quite adjust to the constant grieving of the families. The worst part was that so many of these servicemen were young casualties of the war. It was always a relief to go for a week of training for anything just to get away from the funerals.

Duty in the Old Guard is unlike any other assignment in the Army. Sure we were a combat infantry unit and we had regular tactical equipment. But we also had the outdated M-1 rifle rather than its replacement, the M-16. The older model was much easier to use during ceremonies despite its greater weight and length. Officers did not carry side arms, but rather were equipped with ceremonial sabers and saber belts.

Only after a newly arrived officer or soldier has marched behind the barracks at Fort Myer long enough to master the use of the long, curved saber or the ceremonial rifle, as required by the Old Guard, is he permitted to perform in front of the public.

Fortunately, I did not have to master the art of tossing rifles and I did not have to endure the excruciating discipline required at the Tomb of the Unknown Soldiers. It takes a special kind of skill which I didn't have. In any case, only enlisted soldiers guard the Tomb of the Unknowns or participate in drill team activities that include rifle tossing.

"Let's talk a bit about your military experiences. I see here that you seem to have an exemplary record in both Vietnam and Korea, a wide variety of experience—parachute, infantry, jungle school. I see you have a Bronze Star. Please recall your Vietnam year. I see it was 1966–67."

In Vietnam, I did typical combat things the infantry did. As a platoon leader I walked through the jungle looking for Charlie— slang for VC or Viet Cong. We were often so close to the enemy before anything happened that there was this constant fear that the world would literally blow up in our faces. And it sometimes did.

A week before I was to depart the country, our base camp at Phouc Vin came under rocket attack. The VC were apparently shooting at the helicopters parked overnight on the airstrip, but it was little comfort not to be the main object. They were such poor shots and the rockets were so inaccurate that they literally peppered us like a Waldorf salad seasoned in Cajun country.

This action started about one A.M. and we all had to roll out of bed, find our rifles and field gear in the dark, and then dash for the bunkers with overhead cover out on the perimeter. It wasn't necessary to awaken the troops. They were way ahead of us. It was just like a John Wayne movie. Every second or third step coincided with another rocket burst nearby or in the tops of the rubber trees above our heads. Only half-consciously drifting away from each explosion, my path was a zigzag of the largest steps I had ever taken on a dead run.

As I neared the bunker area and relative safety, a fiery explosion erupted between myself and a sergeant only twenty feet away. The blast threw me headfirst into a foxhole. When I realized from the pressure on my head that I was upside down, I rolled right side up and began surveying the damage.

I heard moans coming from the next fighting position. The sergeant was mortally wounded. We managed to apply first aid and he was medically evacuated to the main aid station within a matter of minutes but the doctors couldn't save him. The real irony of his death was that he, too, had completed most of his tour and had done so in a conspicuously gallant manner.

As the senior lieutenant in my rifle company, I was appointed executive officer after several months in the field. I took care of the base camp, making sure that all administrative paperwork was completed, that all supplies were ordered and delivered and, most important, that mail and pay came on time.

I even built hot water showers for everyone. We didn't have water heaters, so I borrowed an external fuel tank from a C-123, welded shower heads on the bottom, and rigged a platform where we put cans of fuel oil. Thirty minutes of fire under each tank produced something close to civilized bathing each evening.

Some occasions found me out in the field with thousands of dollars in cash to give to the troops. Most of their money went to a bank account somewhere by automatic allotment, but it was important for morale that each soldier receive some small amount of cash for laundry, soda, poker, and whatever. The cash served as a psychological reminder that life in a war zone could have some semblance of normalcy to it. Since the unit was always on the move during the day, I had to meet the men at their night defensive positions and go from foxhole to foxhole giving each the amount he had previously requested and getting his payroll signature for my records.

This meant I was always forced to crawl to each fighting position in the dark. Approaching each one posed a real danger, despite the use of challenges and passwords. A jittery soldier might mistake me for the enemy crawling up behind him, and if I made too much noise, the enemy might be waiting a few feet away to cash in my chips.

One time I cursed mightily because someone beat me to the only seat on a loaded resupply helicopter. It meant I had to wait five minutes for the next one. We landed in the defensive position minutes behind that first chopper to find the medics surrounding a small area, retrieving objects. The soldier who had taken that first seat had left the chopper and walked directly to my company in a secured area and stepped on a booby-trapped artillery shell. The explosion was so massive that his body disintegrated before it hit the ground. It should have been me.

Several times I moved for one reason or another only seconds before I might have died. I wondered for years why God spared me while so many others were taken.

"Is it correct to say your commission came out of ROTC?"

"Yes, I graduated from ROTC at A&M as a Distinguished Military Graduate (DMG), an honor which gave me the right to apply for a Regular Army commission, just like the West Pointers received automatically."

I had a choice and a decision to make. I did not have to pursue the commission but I knew that I would probably have to go to Vietnam one way or the other, and I thought going as an officer would be preferable, so I was a volunteer. I never considered the Navy, since I always thought I could walk farther than I could swim. The Air Force would have been my first choice, but my eyesight was too bad to even qualify for a career in the infantry, let alone flight school or a cockpit.

Because of my eyes, the infantry didn't really want me either, but I knew that was the place for a career officer, and I had to get there just in case I did stay for twenty years or more. I applied to Major General Ruhlin, commander of the First Armored Division, where I was stationed, and after some interviewing with several high-level officers, including the general, he approved my request for transfer into the Infantry. This would probably not have been a successful effort except for the Vietnam War buildup which was proceeding at breakneck speed at the time.

We all start out as second lieutenants, wearing a single gold bar on each shoulder sometimes referred to as second looeys or "butter bars" because of the color on our rank. Most officers in 1965 were sent to an initial training assignment in the States for a few months and then on to Vietnam.

The Army was expanding so fast then that junior officers were hard to get in any organization outside the war zone. To create more, commissions became more plentiful, and the time to wait for advancement became very compressed. I became a first lieutenant in

Vietnam after just over a year in the Army and then a captain in another fifteen months. Captains were company commanders and were (and still are) always referred to as "the old man." Virtually every one of these "old men" was a kid about twenty-three or twenty-four years old. As was I.

"While you were away, were you in touch with your family—did you write home?"

"You bet. And I even managed to send my mother a birthday gift— a really memorable one." I had gone to Bangkok for R&R—rest and recreation. Shopping there was a real experience, since each store served free Thai beer while we browsed. We had been warned that the beer there was 18 percent alcohol—three times as strong as American beer—but who listened.

During one of these social shopping sprees, I became entranced with the uniqueness of some of the gift items, and I purchased a stuffed cobra locked in mortal battle with a mongoose. I stuck it in the mail with a quick note. Mother got it only ten days belated, but to hear the neighbors tell of her scream when she opened it, she would have been better off not getting anything at all. I made up for that with a pearl ring that was too big for a pro football player's hand.

"And what about Korea? I see you were stationed there 1969–70. But you had returned from Vietnam in 1967. Will you explain that?"

"I left for Vietnam in August 1966 and returned exactly 365 days later. I was sent to Fort Polk, Louisiana, where I stayed those seventeen months. We affectionately referred to Fort Polk as the armpit of the world. I can only say that the tour gave creditability to the joke that the Army must have a two-star general whose only job was traveling the world to find the most remote, desolate and depressing sites to locate new Army posts."

"But why did you go to Korea instead of going back to Vietnam?"

"I wish I could tell you. The selection process for those who went to Korea as opposed to the war in South Vietnam was a complete mystery to the few of us who were there. We served on the Demilitarized Zone and had several fire fights with the North Koreans, resulting in many wounded and a number killed in action but it was much softer duty than Vietnam, by light years."

After returning from Vietnam, I tried to resign my commission, but since I served as a Regular Army officer, my superiors were legally permitted to refuse and in fact did refuse my request, and I was involuntarily extended for eighteen months.

"Was it the leadership that made you want to leave the military?"

"That and the thought that I could do better in private industry."

"Tell a little about your life there in Korea."

I was part of a peace-keeping force of seventeen-thousand men in the Second Infantry Division (plus thousands of other support troops) guarding the fence along the southern edge of the DMZ. We were there to prevent North Korean infiltrators from coming in to collect intelligence, and also to prevent exfiltrators from returning to the North who might have gotten in somewhere else.

This barrier was a ten-foot-high chain-link fence with triple concertina wire on top, just like a maximum security prison. And to those of us stationed there, it felt like a prison. By day, we could observe the fence from sandbagged bunkers built high atop towers, using very few men. At night, however, we had to put two men in every foxhole about twenty to thirty yards apart. This covered the entire division front of several miles. Additional outposts in the southern half of the DMZ were also manned by a squad of ten to twelve men. Staying awake at night, staring at a brush-covered hillside or valley, produced occasional visions of things that weren't really there.

You couldn't afford to take a chance. One night a huge antipersonnel mine was set off because the soldiers thought they were being attacked by North Koreans, but they never fired back, and the next morning, we had a three-hundred pound boar to present to the cooks. Nothing ever tasted better.

Fortunately, after several months in Korea, I became the aid to the commanding general of the Second Infantry Division. Major General Salve Matheson convinced me to change my mind without even knowing about my previous effort to resign. He was smart and hardworking, really cared for the people under him, and, most of all, did not spend all his time trying to make himself look good to his boss like so many others I knew before and since. He convinced me that there was a future for me—and I withdrew my request for release in time to go to advanced military and civilian schooling and on to the Old Guard and, hopefully, the White House extra duty assignment.

"Your father also served both in Korea and Vietnam, didn't he?"

"In Korea, my dad was the senior adviser to the Republic of Korea's Seventh Infantry Division. They saw plenty of combat, and most veterans will attest to the fact that the Seventh ROK was a very good outfit that fought exceptionally well. Again, in Vietnam, he was a senior adviser to one of their divisions for several months.

"He was also the first American commander at Qui Non. Then he ran a Vietnamese training center."

"So I guess your father encouraged you to follow in his footsteps."

"Father never really urged me to become an officer like he was. He simply pointed out the advantages of making decisions as an officer as opposed to taking orders as a private. The choice was obvious."

And so was something else. Eventually I realized that the entire interview process was to see how well one could ad-lib in any social conversation. A wrong answer could certainly get one in trouble, but the important thing was to be interesting and pleasant to talk to—not just provide a preferred response. Candid responses like mine were classed as self-confidence.

A tense moment developed during my last interview when I was asked what book I had read most recently. It sounded a little contrived, and I was immediately afraid it would seem phony, but I had to confess to having recently finished *War and Peace*.

My White House interviewer challenged me to outline the book on the spot. He might have suspected at first that I was trying to snow him but we eventually wound up discussing several of the turns in the plot and almost forgot what we were there for.

Each interviewer interspersed all this routine questioning with a slightly different version of what aides were supposed to do. The inescapable conclusion was that since there were so many things to remember and everything was made to be of "utmost importance," it was impossible to discern the really critical from the merely paramount. A happy medium seemed to be to try and make everyone happy at once, starting with the First Family and working down to the last guest. Clearly this meant different things to different people.

Always, at every level, the conversation came back to dancing. It was not sufficient to show a knowledge of or an interest in the art. The essence of every interview was, "Are you willing to dance with little old ladies?" After being asked this question a number of times, I began to imagine hundreds of diminutive old women wandering around the White House looking for a young man to dance with. One could just picture a tiny and frail but determined lady with white hair suddenly shrieking from a corner, "Here's one! Here's one!" The poor man would instantly be gang-tackled by wrinkles and lace. It began to sound less like fun than before but I was still willing to try it for a while.

The appropriate answer to the question was clear and obvious, but I wonder how many potential aides told the truth and didn't make it past that point. Admitting that you might violate normally accepted rules of etiquette under certain circumstances and drop Grandma in a heartbeat for a movie star would not advance one's career as a Social Aide.

Of course, I always responded that I would indeed be happy to dance with them, just as I was happy to dance with my own sweet grandmother (who, incidentally, was very *sweet* but never danced). It wasn't really a lie because I truly *was* willing, but I confess to greatly exaggerating my enthusiasm.

From the tone of every interview, it seemed clear that I would be accepted. When the Social Secretary said they would call upon approval of my clearance, the doubts evaporated completely. All that remained was that one last hurdle—security clearance—but a major one if the investigators found anything suspicious. There was nothing I could do but wait and hope for the best. And I sat home and waited and waited for the phone to ring. While the security community continued to process my White House Clearance with Presidential Access, I, like millions of Americans, watched the marriage of Tricia Nixon and Edward Cox on television from the comfort of my living room. Having had a choice, I would have found it a lot more fun to be there, but no one works without a proper pass, and the pass only comes after the clearance is approved.

As the security evaluation process unfolded, I became increasingly aware of how thorough the White House is in checking out new employees. One by one, friends and neighbors old and new started asking me if I was in trouble, because federal agents had been around asking questions about me. The questions were even more intimate than I had been asked to my face. They concerned anything and everything that would give a clue to my life-style and habits:

"Did he exhibit unusual or bizarre behavior?"

"Did he have weird friends?" (*They* were talking to my friends.)

"Were the police ever called that you know of?"

"Did he ever advocate overthrow of the U.S. government?"

"Did he give loud parties?"

Eventually, this clandestine activity subsided—or at least the reports from my friends did—and still nothing happened. Several more weeks passed, and finally the call came. The clearance was complete and approved. I could come down to the White House to get my pass immediately, as well as my *Manual for Social Aides* and my aiguillette.

It had taken them eight months.

I was there within twenty minutes.

One of the things I was given to study and memorize was twenty-five pages of photos of everyone who is routinely *in* or might visit the White House. From the First and Second Family members through the wives of cabinet officers to the domestic staff, it tells the aides who they must know instantly on sight. To supplement this rather short list of available pictures we were expected to cut out current shots from the *Washington Post* in case someone made a dramatic change in physical appearance or status, i.e., hairdos, beards, new spouse, etc. If Hollywood or Broadway stars were in town, appearing in some production, it helped to include them in the drill, as they usually showed up at the next big party.

When I got all decked out for a formal White House affair, I looked like something out of a mythical country. White gloves were part of the uniform, but it was the aiguillette that really provided the stunning effect. Uniquely military, it is a gilt cord hung in loops loosely from the shoulder of all military aides-de-camp. Aside from adding a very dramatic decorative touch to a uniform, the aiguillette serves no useful purpose today except to help a general or admiral— or President—pick his personal assistant out of a crowd of uniforms.

There is an amusing history to the aiguillette. In years gone by, when aides were performing their most important function of actually holding the general's horse while he was dismounted, the aiguillette was the rope used to control the horse. It quickly became customary for the aide to loop the rope under his own epaulet when not actually holding the horse.

Besides being a handy place to keep the tools of his trade, this served as a not too subtle reminder to everyone that the aide held on to a large portion of the general's power (his horse). When the horses finally disappeared, the aides cleverly kept the aiguillette for decoration and as a reminder to everyone of their proximity to power.

Incidentally, if you watch the evening news regularly, you'll notice that many countries have adopted this ornate symbol of power. Following the lead of some lowly "horse holder," many foreign generals now wear these fancy gold cords—and of course, the fancier the uniform, the more ornate the rope becomes.

All military aides wear the aiguillette on the left shoulder except the President's aides. Here, too, there is a pecking order, with presidential aides first and everyone else second. Some past military aide to a president, commander in chief, king or emperor, in a stroke of brilliant one-upmanship, decreed that he would wear his aiguillette on his right shoulder. Few people, including most military, ever notice the difference, but the aides know.

There is a postscript. When I started attending the White House parties and looking for those "little old ladies" to dance with, I couldn't find them. I would look back at the interviews and wonder what all the fuss had been about. These ladies looked much too chic and danced too well to deserve that horrible epithet.

4

Behind the Scenes
of a White House Invitation

*A*mericans are not modest about asking to be invited to a White House party. During the course of an administration, literally thousands of people write and ask to be included. Rarely are guests selected in this manner.

So who gets invited? Invitations to attend a social or official ceremonial function are arrived at by a very specific motive of the President, a First Family member or someone on the staff.

An invitation to a State Dinner, for example, can serve many purposes. The guest list is essentially determined by the President and the First Lady based on suggestions from key members of the White House staff, the State Department and principally the Social Secretary. And let me tell you, the social staff at the White House is acutely aware of the power of a presidential invitation and the prestige it bestows upon the recipient.

Besides serving to repay political debts, the invitation list is sometimes designed to smooth political waters. Although vastly outnumbered by the regular guest list of powerful supporters in step with the administration, the political opponents of the President will occasionally be present. But those representing opposing views are normally limited to party leaders and those inclined to earn the President's gratitude by voting across party lines.

While it is unlikely that an official visit to the White House will change a presidential enemy's basic feelings or values, it may soften or temper his or her views. After all, it is harder to be overly critical of someone who has been a host than it is if they had never socialized together at all.

I have noticed that frequent guests often include those who have managed over the years to stay apolitical and who seem to get invited on the strength of their own personality or other assets. The rich, the famous, political and sports figures, and world renowned artists all blend together with ordinary people whose only claim may be that they are "old friends" of the First Family.

But even old friends tend to be well-heeled. It's part of White House lore that Thomas Jefferson once invited his butcher to a dinner and Lyndon Baines Johnson invited a Pakistani camel driver, but that sort of thing doesn't seem to happen too often.

At any rate, the invitations go out in the mail. You'll recognize what it is immediately by the elegant white envelope with the simple return address of THE WHITE HOUSE, WASHINGTON, D.C. in raised letters. And of course, your name and address handwritten in flowing script.

A small card of instructions is also included. After frantically purchasing several possible outfits for the event, most first-timers follow instructions and arrive at the southwest gate to the White House. Those who arrive at one of the several other gates are politely escorted in by a very wary and alert White House police force.

Entering the south grounds, the guest's vehicles pass around the circular drive where family cars are parked along with limousines. The guests then walk up to the last formal security point at the South Portico entrance—the one under the Truman Balcony often seen on the evening news when the President exits his helicopter and returns to the mansion from a trip.

But you're not in yet. Now, as some laughingly call it, it's the White House version of Checkpoint Charlie time.

Just inside the door to the Diplomatic Reception Room, guests present their specially prepared admittance cards, which are scanned under ultraviolet lights to verify their authenticity by the White

House police—officially known as the Executive Protective Service, a supplement to the Secret Service.

Now guests are greeted by a young man or woman in the dazzling uniform of a White House Social Aide. As a harpist plays in the corner—sometimes accompanied by a flute—the Social Aides assist the guests with their wraps. Hats and coats disappear into the safest cloakroom in the world; it guarantees return of exactly what was deposited. For the remainder of the evening, guests will have an opportunity to see only a fraction of the White House's 132 rooms, but the overwhelming beauty of the public areas will make them think they have seen it all.

Duty in the Diplomatic Reception Room—the "Dip Room," as we call it—is the least desirable of all possible activities for a Social Aide. This is partly because the guests spend so little time there, and then only to hang up their coats, and mostly because all the action is going on upstairs. Consequently, only the most junior aides are assigned to the Dip Room, with one of the more senior aides to supervise them.

But the Dip Room aides have an advantage in that they are the first to greet Hollywood stars and other celebrities and sometimes strike up a good conversation while the star is waiting to go upstairs.

Seniority among the Social Aides is determined not by rank, which is customary in the military, but by length of service in the White House. The proper conduct of and supervision over social functions require experience in the Executive Mansion (its official name before Teddy Roosevelt changed it to the White House), and not the lawful authority to issue orders as an officer's commission and rank dictate.

It is, therefore, not at all unusual to find a junior lieutenant issuing instructions for and supervising the performance of captains and majors while running a function. This never presents a problem because prospective aides are warned in advance that they should not even pursue the job if this situation would make them uncomfortable.

Regardless of why they are there, all guests must receive the consideration the President and First Lady would give them if they could personally attend to each at one time. Since they can't be everywhere at once, this task falls to the Social Aides. And since there may be as many as two thousand guests at one time, the Social Aides actually have an impossible job. But we try.

The first thing I was given at the White House was a memorandum containing warnings and cautions for the new Social Aides:

> The slightest social or ceremonial slip or blunder provides the strong possibility of embarrassing the President of the United States, or a foreign dignitary of great rank. Consequently, the Social Aides must at all times be alert to guard against this possibility... You will be required to maintain a personal code of conduct and ethics that is clearly beyond any hint of reproach.
>
> We will place demands on your appearance, conduct and personality even above the high standards required of a professional military officer. On duty, you may be confronted with situations for which there is no written solution, which involves dignitaries of our government and foreign governments with the highest rank.
>
> To react to these unforeseen and usually unprecedented circumstances will require that you react instantaneously with the highest order of judgment, tact and discretion.

A good Social Aide is one who is able to see and deal with any potential or actual miscues or disasters rapidly and discreetly with the least possible embarrassment. The aide creates an appropriate diversion or corrects the situation before anyone realizes what has happened.

For those guests new to the mansion, a short conversation with an experienced Social Aide would reveal some interesting information about the surroundings. One hundred years ago, the Diplomatic Reception Room was a boiler room. In fact, what little existed of the entire downstairs was basement caverns and did not become usable by the residents or public until the 1902 renovation under President Theodore Roosevelt. Later, Franklin Roosevelt used the Diplomatic Reception Room for his famous series of fireside chats. It is no coincidence that it is oval shaped, as both the Blue Room and the Yellow Oval Room are directly one and two floors above it respectively.

What is used as the main coatroom for evening functions is formally known as the Map Room. The name was acquired during World War II when Franklin Roosevelt wanted a top secret war room. He routinely stopped in to check the war's progress, which was posted every hour on a global map. Located next to the Diplomatic Reception Room with an adjoining door, the Map Room currently has only one map on display. This is a priceless 1755 edition of a map prepared by Peter Jefferson (whose son would one day be President) and another man who worked as surveyors to the colonists. When it is not being used as a coat-check facility, the Map Room's rich mahogany furniture gives it a feeling of a very masculine reading room.

Frequently, guests will arrive much too early for the scheduled event, when it would be inappropriate for them to go upstairs immediately. They may chomp at the bit, but the job of the Social Aide is to keep them there.

Sometimes an overeager aide, as I was, can create a sticky situation. On one of my first assignments to the Diplomatic Reception Room, the guests were detained for a few minutes before moving on. To help pass the time, I went over to say hello to a member of Congress whom anyone would recognize from various news accounts. Wanting to appear relaxed and familiar with the surroundings in the manner of a seasoned aide, I cheerily said, "Good afternoon, Senator."

Without a hint of annoyance or contempt, the politician from Massachusetts leaned over and whispered in a very fatherly voice, "Young man, my name is O'Neill, and I'm a congressman."

Of course, I already knew who he was, but the pressure to do well and not appear new at it caused me to stumble over my words. It immediately became apparent that the art of making small talk with national and international figures required considerably more attention to detail than I had thought.

When ready to proceed upstairs, guests step out of the Diplomatic Reception Room into the Ground Floor Corridor and come face to face with a large group of poorly dressed people known as the White House Press Corps. Identifiable primarily by cameras and notepads, they also are the ones with an occasional ink stain on their pockets. Standing behind a velvet rope barrier, they thrust a bewildering array of photographic equipment and microphones at virtually everyone who walks by. This is their first chance to get a story and the visitors' first chance to say something that will be printed in every major paper in America. Unaccustomed to the glare of attention, most guests hurry by the inquisitive press and head for the stairs leading up to the reception area. Others welcome the interview or mug for the cameras.

Few people on their way to the staircase even notice that the walls of the Ground Floor Corridor, also known as the Lower Cross Hall, are covered with portraits of First Ladies. If they pause to look on their way out later, as some do, they will see paintings of Jacqueline Kennedy, Claudia "Lady Bird" Johnson and Eleanor Roosevelt, among others. It was well known that Mrs. Roosevelt hated posing, and so it was a great compliment to the artist, Douglas Chandor, that she actually inscribed on the painting, "A trial made pleasant by the painter—Eleanor Roosevelt."

At the top of the stairs on the State Floor stands a small table with 120 envelopes—one for each guest. A senior doorman, familiar with the regular visitors to the White House and the high and mighty in Washington, is busy assisting the Social Aides in matching faces with names on the cards. As each pair of guests is identified, their cards are handed to one of the half-dozen Escort Aides, who whisks the couple off to the reception area.

Ladies walk to the aide's right while the gentlemen trail along behind. Following etiquette, male aides offer an arm while female aides do not. Introductions to the Escort Aide are concluded in a hurry as all three step out into the Grand Foyer inside the North Portico entrance.

Here, guests are once again greeted by a much larger and better-dressed contingent of the White House press corps. I often wondered if personal appearance wasn't possibly one of the criteria for those in the press who work upstairs and those relegated to the downstairs for a formal-dress social function. Rumors frequently circulated that some press representatives were banished for an evening when they showed up too poorly dressed even to work downstairs. This couldn't be confirmed because no one would admit to being turned away.

Cameras are flashing—especially if Cary Grant or Frank Sinatra or Elizabeth Taylor appears. I have seen important Hollywood stars look wistful as the media ignores them in favor of a flashier name. Some stars of music or acting turn into comedians, shouting gags, hopping around and making faces—hoping their antics will pay off with a picture in the paper or *People* magazine. Females have the advantage, since a star with a low-cut dress is almost certain to be noticed by the cameramen.

Now tension is mounting for the staff. The President and the guest of honor will start downstairs to join the others at exactly 8:12 P.M. and it is we Social Aides who must have 120 guests in their places before the appointed time, escorting them down the Cross Hall to the entrance of the East Room.

Even the way the guest of honor gets upstairs is very formal, very structured. While the others are arriving and are being escorted to the East Room by aides, the guest of honor and spouse are preparing to depart Blair House, which sits almost directly across Pennsylvania Avenue from the White House.

It wasn't always that way. Even in recent history, most guests of honor actually stayed at the White House, and in rare cases some still do. But Blair House became the guest residence of choice due to a chance meeting. It seems as though Churchill was visiting the Roosevelts and had been given one of the upstairs bedrooms. One evening while both Eleanor and the prime minister were having difficulty falling asleep, they happened to meet in the upstairs hallway. Eleanor was suitably dressed, but Winston had on only a nightshirt and was carrying a cigar. The very next morning, instructions were given to establish a guest residence nearby, and Blair House was eventually chosen.

More for security than speed, and to ensure split-second timing, a limousine is used to travel the laughable half block to the northwest entrance. Entering the grounds, the honored guest is greeted at the gate by a cordon of uniformed military personnel from all the services evenly spaced on either side of the crescent-shaped north driveway. This colorful and impressive display of leads to the covered entrance to the North Portico.

The President (accompanied by the First Lady when she isn't entertaining special guests already upstairs) appears and greets the guests as they exit their limousine at 8:00 P.M. The group poses for a few hurried pictures by the small pool of photographers selected for this specific event before the principals disappear upstairs to the family floor. In the Yellow Oval Room, which sits above the Blue Room and two floors above the Diplomatic Reception Room, they will all have ten or so minutes of informal private conversation before making their grand entrance.

That may not sound like much time, but when you start out as strangers and you don't speak the same language or you must make small talk, ten minutes can feel like an eternity.

While the guest of honor is safely positioned in the Yellow Room, the Social Aides continue to escort the others to the East Room. During this short walk, the Social Aide talks to the guests to put the nervous ones at ease and informs them all that they will stop before entering the reception area so that their arrival can be properly announced. At the same time, the aide places in his left hand the two envelopes obtained from the table at the top of the stairs. When the group pauses at the entrance to the East Room, he can hold the cards up near his left shoulder. In this manner, the names of the arriving guests will be in front of the Announcing Aide at eye level so they can be read.

A social or diplomatic blunder of any kind at the White House is serious enough in its own right. A whole new dimension is added when the Announcing Aide uses a public address system. Any mistakes are broadcast for everyone to hear. Errors during introductions come in many varieties, but the most common is to call someone by the wrong name. It is something that this crowd of predominantly official Washington regulars could hardly fail to notice, as almost everyone knows everyone else. Unfortunately, the White House has given the regulars more than one chance to enjoy such mistakes.

Somewhere along the way, a hapless soul serving as an Announcing Aide made the assumption that an arriving couple was married. Only looking at one card, he announced their arrival as Mr. and Mrs. So-and-So. While amused White House regulars knew it wasn't true, the lady wished it were so and the bachelor gentleman was not too happy about temporarily being taken out of circulation by an erroneous announcement.

There was the devil to pay. When the dust settled, the Announcing Aides from then on had firm instructions to read to themselves and carefully study both envelopes before making the public announcement. No wonder being an Announcing aide is considered the second most difficult job an aide can have—the aide who makes the introductions to the President has the hardest one—and only the most seasoned aides are chosen for this assignment.

5

The Protocol Tricks
of the White House Social Aide

*I*t's not easy to get 120 guests stashed away and keep them happy till the time comes for them to sit down in the State Dining Room. The aides who serve as escorts must be nimble of eye, mind and mouth. Picture this.

The Escort Aide, while greeting and escorting couple after couple in fairly rapid succession to the reception area in the East Room and keeping up a line of meaningful chatter with them, must at the same time keep track of everything going on around him, maneuver the couple past the press, and surreptitiously find a faint pencil mark on the lower right-hand corner of each envelope. The clichéd test of being able to walk, talk and chew gum at the same time comes to mind.

The aide must not let the guests know that the little mark is a secret code showing him how high or low each guests is in the pecking order.

The White House is supposed to be democratic, but not all guests are created equal. Every White House guest feels important, and the aide does not want to hurt anyone's feelings. But the truth of the matter is that the little mark will show where each guest belongs while waiting to go through the receiving line to meet the President and guest of honor and their spouses.

The East Room is divided into four imaginary sections, or "sectors," as they are called—and the mark on the envelope is simply the letter "P" or a numeral I, II or III. If you are a "P" you are at the top, in the language of protocol, and you will stand at the immediate left, inside the entrance to the East Room.

P's are principals such as the Vice President, the secretary of state plus the entourage and embassy personnel associated with the guest of honor.

Sector 1 consists of Supreme Court justices, cabinet officers, ambassadors, senators, congressmen, governors and mayors, in that order. This sector is to the left of the center of the room and next to the principals. Sectors II and III consist of the overflow from I, and then everyone else in alphabetical order. The chairman of the board of General Motors, actors, sports figures, the First Children and friends of the President and First Lady all fall into the last category, since they ordinarily have no formal diplomatic status.

Sectors II and III guests are the last to go through the receiving line. It is perfectly natural that someone like superstar Michael Jackson, who earns more in a year—or sometimes in a month—than the President of the United States earns in his term, will end up in a low protocol sector. Even a mayor few have heard of will outrank Michael Jackson.

Without diplomatic status, people in these last two sectors are more or less room-fillers. Even so, any host or hostess in America giving a party would consider it a major coup to have any one of them show up at his or her next social affair. At the bottom of the pecking order here, these people clearly are at the top in any other setting.

With all the excitement generated by the press corps, the pressure of new guests every two or three minutes, announcing and working with numerous Sector Aides, the escorts occasionally forget such trivial things as the names of aides they have known and worked with for a long time. For expediency, no aide ever dares flinch when introduced by the wrong name to a guest. He or she knows that some aide was under pressure and has simply forgotten a name. It doesn't really matter since it would never be an issue, and guests and aides would usually move on to other people rather quickly. Even so, it is surprising how many White House Social Aides are called Smith or Jones.

As dinner guests wait in the East Room for the receiving line to form, waiters in tuxedos serve a variety of mixed drinks from large silver trays. To keep the guests from straying out of their assigned sectors—and out of protocol order—the Sector Aides will explain the evening's proceedings. After opening their seating assignment cards and explaining the dinner seating arrangements, they introduce the new guests to others in their sector. Some guests take the opportunity to inquire about the East Room's rich history.

There are a number of interesting things we tell them:

Dating back to the Executive Mansion's original floor plan and construction, the East Room was to be "the Public Audience Chamber." It was still an unfinished area when the first residents, John and Abigail Adams, occupied the house in 1800, only eight years after the cornerstone was laid.

At this point, some female guest is sure to say, "Oh, yes, this is where Abigail Adams hung her laundry."

We praise the guest for her knowledge of history and continue with other historic tidbits, pointing to the life-size painting of George Washington.

"Is that the one Dolley Madison cut out of the frame and saved when the British burned the White House?"

We tell her she is half right. Dolley Madison had someone break the frame so as not to injure the picture when she spirited it away back in 1814. And when I am doing the explaining, I add that this portrait is the only item currently in the mansion that dates back to the first occupants. And I go on to other things that often raise the eyebrows of the guests in amazement.

During the Civil War, troops bivouacked in the East Room. As the largest room in the White House, it has also been the scene of several weddings of presidential offspring, and all Presidents who died in office except James Garfield have lain in state here.

They want to know about weddings, not funerals. I can tell them that Teddy Roosevelt's madcap daughter, Alice, was married here and that one of her wedding gifts was a hogshead of popcorn. And Tricia Nixon married law student Edward Finch Cox at the White House but the ceremony took place in the Rose Garden. Only one President's son ever married in the White House. That was in 1828 when John Quincy Adams's son, John, married Mary Catherine Hellen. But the President was not happy, because the bride had also been romantically inclined toward the groom's two brothers. There were those who said Mary Catherine just loved the Adams family and those who said she was strong-willed and determined to become a White House bride.

As the last guests arrive and are quickly ushered into the East Room, the Social Aide in charge of the Color Guard prepares to go upstairs to bring the colors down. Like the military cordon lining the drive to the North Portico, the Color Guard is Joint Service, meaning there are members representing each of the armed services.

The Color Guard, as well as the cordon of troops, are from the elite ceremonial units that each service maintains in Washington. They are seen frequently around the capital whenever an official military presence is appropriate. The individuals assigned to the White House ceremonies are unquestionably the best of the best the services have to offer.

The Color Guard is positioned outside the door to the Yellow Oval Room on the Family Floor by the Color Officer. At precisely 8:10 P.M., the Social Aide walks in and requests permission of the President to remove the colors. The flag of the United States and the presidential colors are carried by the Army and the Marine Corps respectively, reflecting the honor accorded to the oldest and second oldest services. The two rifles flanking the colors are carried by the Navy and Air Force, signifying their junior status among the armed services. The Military Aide to the President or the President himself has already explained to the honored guests that they are to follow the Color Guard down the Grand Staircase.

They proceed down the stairs with much dignity—sensitive to the high drama of the occasion and knowing what awaits them momentarily. As they approach the State Floor, the Marine Band in the Entrance Hall plays four ruffles and flourishes while the press corps nearby gets ready for the photo opportunity of the evening.

The Color Guard stops the procession at the bottom of the Grand Staircase and splits left and right. The two heads of state and their spouses step forward, and now, flanked by the colors on either side, the distinguished group is bathed in bright television lights while a staccato of flashbulbs explodes.

Literally hundreds of news photos are taken within seconds. The Announcing Aide heralds the arrival of the two distinguished couples, and the Color Guard closes formation and again steps forward to lead the procession. As it moves around the corner and down the Cross Hall to the waiting guests, the Marine Band plays "Hail to the Chief." The sound reverberating off the marble floors and high ceilings can be heard all over the mansion and is so stirring it would quicken the heart of even the most die-hard political enemy.

With the relaxed confidence that comes from dozens of these entrances, the President and First Lady walk into the East Room with their guests at 8:12 P.M. Just inside the door the Color Guard again splits to the left and right and the heads of state and their spouses step forward and stop just in front of the line of colors. They are, to no one's surprise, conveniently in the proper order for the receiving line, with the President first, the honored guest to his right, the First Lady, and finally the spouse of the honored guest.

The Sector Aides by this time have moved everyone away from the main doors and out toward the four walls. As they back out and away from the forming receiving line, the guests make a half turn to their right. With everyone now facing and able to move in a counterclockwise manner in front of the door, the "P" group, or principals to the immediate left just inside the main door, is already in position at the head of the receiving line.

The Vice President and the secretary of state are the first ones through the line. As the guests walk forward, they meet the Set-Up Aide stationed about ten feet from the President. The aide's primary responsibility is to make sure that the gentleman precedes the lady being escorted. Half joking and half serious, many of the women question why they should follow the men. Western tradition has always put the lady ahead of the gentleman.

I'm sorry if it hurts the ladies' feelings, but this is the White House, where people march to a different drummer, named Protocol.

The only exception to this practice is the relatively rare occasion when the woman is the high official and the reason the couple was invited to the White House, in which case *she* will precede her husband in the receiving line.

Excitement mounts as one approaches the President.

Guests are asked to give their names to the Introducing Aide in the manner in which they wish to be addressed by the President. The reason for this will be explained shortly. Those who have forgotten to put their drink or cigarette down are reminded of the table for that purpose near the Set-Up Aide. Whenever there is an official photographer present (which includes almost all functions), the Set-Up Aide also reminds the guests not to turn their backs on the camera. This request always meets with total cooperation.

During afternoon receptions, when everything is more informal, the Set-Up Aide must also remind guests that they are not to stop and take pictures on their own or to ask for autographs. Aside from greatly slowing down the receiving line, these kinds of interruptions cause very great distress among the staff. In particular, the Secret Service, which stays with every First Family member when they are off the Family Floor, gets very nervous when people suddenly reach into their purse or coat pocket for something.

Most guests comply with the rule with grace. Others flatly defy any rule. Even at the White House.

For some people, the opportunity to get a friend to run out front with a pocket camera for a personal snapshot with the First Lady or President is just too much to pass up. At this point it is too late to say no, so we roll our eyes and redouble our efforts to keep the remainder of the guests from repeating the act.

Standing next to the President is the Introducing Aide. As I've said, this is the most demanding job a Social Aide can perform, as there are no second chances. The aide must hear and understand the correct pronunciation of every guest's name, and as the previous guest moves on, he must repeat the name properly to the President.

When the Chief of Protocol is present, the Introducing Aide will introduce the guest to him and the Protocol Chief then will present the guest to the President. So as not to be distracted, the Introducing Aide always keeps his hands firmly clasped behind his back—thus avoiding handshakes. Nor does he engage in small talk. If something should cause his mind to wander and at the last moment he has forgotten the guest's name, it may cause a major embarrassment to the President as well as the guest.

Sometimes, even using the right name may be the wrong thing to do. Many show business people use stage names which bear no resemblance to their legal names. Also, when the couple is intro-

duced as Mr. and Mrs., any stage name can be easily lost. Miss Anna
Maria Alberghetti (stage name) was once introduced as Mrs.
Guzman (real name). This unfortunate event occurred at a time
when guests were introduced by the name on their seating card
envelopes. The mishap instantly created confusion and embarrassment for the aide, for the distinguished guests and, unfortunately,
for the President. Since that gaffe, visitors have been invited to state
how they wish to be addressed.

No guest coming through the line is exempt from giving his name
to the aide, regardless of how long he has known the host. It is a
standing policy that no matter how many times a visitor comes to
parties, he or she is always asked again for his or her name. This is
primarily to keep the President from making a faux pas.

Once the President has said hello to several dozen people in rapid
order, it is entirely possible that he might draw a blank when coming
face to face with even a close personal friend. A beaming guest who is
sure he has made a lasting impression on the President might be very
surprised—and disappointed—to know that the President doesn't
remember his name, his face or even the circumstances under which
they met several weeks, months or years earlier. But an experienced
politician would never let on to this.

Asking for a name also protects the aide from embarrassment. A
former "Mr." can become a "Doctor" or Miss Jones can become Mrs.
Brown.

Normally, nothing is more acceptable than the guest's own
interpretation of how he or she should be addressed. However,
Introducing Aides must at times and with great care edit what some
guests say. The day after President Carter's inauguration, I was
introducing guests at an afternoon reception when Muhammad Ali
came through the line with his girlfriend. I asked them for their
names even though there was no doubt about who they were as they
had been much in the news. *Washington Post* reporter Sally Quinn
had recently quoted Ali's succinct comment, "I don't want no used
car and I don't want no used woman." After presenting Ali to the
President, I turned to his girlfriend. She made it clear she wanted to
be introduced as Mrs. Veronica Ali.

I had to think fast. Aides must frequently make decisions based on
complete loyalty to the President. Could I let her deceive him? I
quickly turned to President Carter and presented "Miss Veronica

Porche." If looks could kill, I would have died on the spot. She was visibly upset but said nothing. After all, she was standing in front of the President of the United States, and by this time, he was already saying hello to her while reaching to shake her hand. She was in no position to complain either to me or about me.

I could understand her frustration. She had given up her career to be with Ali and his then wife, and in the early days of the relationship, she had subordinated herself to act as their children's babysitter.

Five months after this White House encounter, they were married, and eventually she did return in triumph as Mrs. Ali. I had been amused to read that at his wedding Muhammad Ali had worn white gloves just as I wore at the White House. In fact, everything he wore that day had been white—white tails, white ruffled shirt, white shoes. But in spite of fame and fortune, a huge Hollywood mansion and a second child, the marriage did not last, and Muhammad Ali moved on to a new wife named Yolanda.

As guests approach the end of the receiving line, they should notice a Social Aide standing discreetly several steps away. The Pull-Off Aide is staring intently but politely at the next guest to come out of the line, waiting to make eye contact.

Either because they hate to see the moment end or because they just don't know what to do next, many guests try to hang on and talk. The Pull-Off Aide must catch their attention to start them on their way toward the State Dining Room.

The usual techniques didn't always work for me. I remember the night Ted Turner and his wife came to a State Dinner. It was shortly after he had won the America's Cup in 1977. He already had a reputation for hard work and hard living, and on this occasion he had apparently started the party considerably earlier in the day.

My problem was damage control. There was no way I could tell how many drinks he'd already had—but it was clear to me that he'd already exceeded the limit for such an important social occasion as this. He was laughing and talking with the President.

It turned out that we had the devil of a time getting him out of the receiving line. As he lingered, it caused the predictable chain reaction backup as everyone tried to listen, thus further compounding the problem. But he remained a hero to everyone present, with the possible exception of the Pull-Off Aide.

I think everyone—except Mrs. Turner—enjoyed the fact that he was having such a good time. This was one occasion when it really helped to have the ladies follow the gentlemen. Mrs. Turner gets the credit for getting him out of the receiving line—she almost had to push him—and for making sure no other unusual situations developed for the remainder of the evening.

Upon leaving the receiving line, guests are immediately ushered down the Cross Hall to the State Dining Room, where the maitre d' and the Social Secretary assist them in finding their tables.

Social Aides not involved with the receiving line are free temporarily, but not to do as they please. They are expected to "toe the line" in Cross Hall. We space ourselves evenly along the entire length of the wide red carpet running from the East Room to the State Dining Room with our toes touching the edge. In so doing, we form a military cordon to make the walk to dinner, hopefully, more colorful for the guests. It also keeps the temporarily idle aides from congregating in groups and shooting the breeze.

I never really cared much for being an ornament, so I frequently found a diversion for my attention during this particular ritual. Usually, I managed to place myself across the carpet from a tall, blonde and beautiful Air Force major. She seemed to be a favorite of Henry Kissinger's as he would frequently stop to talk to her. When he did, her five-foot-ten frame, perched on standard Air Force women's high heels, towered over him. She was always afraid to look up while he was there, knowing full well I would be looking at her and trying to make her laugh. She never would admit to dating Kissinger, but several of us kidded her for some time about his persistent attentions.

There was only one way for the aides to avoid participating in this ostentatious display of military uniforms altogether. The two junior officers were always excused from toeing the line so that each could secure a tray of drinks from the waiters to take to the Vermeil Room downstairs. After all the guests were in the State Dining Room and the massive doors were closed, we would head downstairs for our own cocktail party.

6

Look, Ma, I'm Dancing at the White House

*I*t's past nine o'clock. We're bushed.

We've gotten 120 guests safely to the State Dining Room tables with pomp and circumstance and strict attention to protocol. Now they are in the hands of the President and First Lady and the serving crew.

They're happy and we're happy because at last we are going to be fed. It's one of the perks of a State Dinner. A free meal. A fine meal. But not the same meal the guests are eating upstairs. Nor the same fine surroundings. We're too hungry to care. We finish our drinks and hurry to the staff mess situated in the West Wing basement under the Oval Office. We can hardly wait to get there. As someone is sure to remark, "They have to feed us or we'd keel over."

And someone else is apt to say, "*Yeah, our work is only half over.*" The drinks have been tossed down in a hurry, and now we attack our plates, bantering about what has happened to us this night and mentioning some movie star guest we're hoping to meet or dance with later. A little connivance might take place.

It's our patriotic duty to be there and try to make all the guests happy—and our duty to ourselves to have a little fun when possible along the way. We wonder who else is coming and exchange information.

We sometimes have to hurry to meet the new arrivals. About 140 people who could not be squeezed in for dinner are always invited as afterdinner guests. These are usually less powerful or influential members of the Washington scene, or those—such as entertainers— who simply were not available earlier in the evening. Nevertheless, it is still an honor to be invited to the White House, and this generally younger, flashier crowd always begins arriving about thirty minutes before the formalities are scheduled to end upstairs.

Social Aides are again posted in the Diplomatic Reception Room and in particular at the bottom of the stairs. Only on cue of the aides will the guests proceed upstairs. This gives the later arrivals a great opportunity to see much of the downstairs that the dinner guests missed. The China Room is usually the first stop on this impromptu tour.

Next to the Diplomatic Reception Room, the China Room grew out of a collection of dinner pieces from each previous administration. Many of these were gathered by Mrs. Benjamin Harrison from 1889 until her death in 1892. In 1902, Mrs. Theodore Roosevelt reenergized the project, and by 1917, Mrs. Woodrow Wilson was forced to designate an entire room to house the growing collection.

This area, now called the China Room, contains a representative piece from every administration. The public may think it extravagant, perhaps even ostentatious, that every President buys new china, but this collection adds something truly unique to our country's heritage. In recent years, these additions to the collection have been made at private expense.

Next door, the Vermeil Room contains some very beautiful pieces of silver covered with gold. Donated by Mrs. Margaret Thompson Biddle in 1956, some items on display are actually older than the White House itself. Always popular with the ladies, it is no accident that this room also provides access to the women's powder room while entry to the men's washroom is in the Library. The Vermeil Room is also designated to be used by the Social Aides for our own informal cocktail party before our dinner.

The Library across the hall contains a selection of books thought to best represent the heritage and traditions of America. This room quickly became a familiar meeting place for the Social Aides. We always gathered here one hour before the guests arrived to receive our instructions from the Aide-in-Charge. Relaxing on the Duncan Phyfe furniture, I always marveled at the simple beauty of the crystal chandelier which once belonged to James Fenimore Cooper.

Since we always used this area for our planning sessions, I sometimes used the books to hide my copy of the guest list, aides' instructions and the entertainment announcement, expecting that no one would find them there. These items, when stuffed in a uniform breast pocket, created an unsightly bulge in the jacket which, for a military uniform, simply didn't look right. After a couple of dinners where I neglected to retrieve my souvenirs of the evening, I finally concluded that the uniform bulge was worth it, and never left any more.

My original plan to hide these treasures had been so successful that during later visits I looked in some of the more likely hiding places but couldn't locate my booty due to the volume of materials there. But those things may not be lost forever. At some time in the future, a President may go browsing through those books and find what Steve Bauer accidentally left behind. Wouldn't it be ironic if that president's name were on the guest list from an earlier era?

The Ground Floor Corridor itself contains several artifacts besides the First Ladies' portraits. In addition to numerous pieces of antique furniture, the famous bronzes "Coming Through the Rye" by Frederic Remington and "Meat for Wild Men" by Charles Russell are on display. Also somewhat interesting is the vaulted arch over the corridor, which few people notice unless they happen to look up while examining the surroundings.

While the newly arrived afterdinner guests mingle on the ground floor, the Social Aides not assigned to entertain them move upstairs in preparation for the dinner to end. Following the reception and while everyone dines, the East Room is being rapidly transformed by the house staff into a theater complete with a stage and 275 chairs for the guests and the press corps, which occasionally borrows their seats.

Several aides are designated to handle general and VIP seating and to direct traffic when the two crowds of dinner and afterdinner guests converge for the evening's entertainment. Other aides are preparing another receiving line immediately outside the door to the East Room. Just before the afterdinner toasts draw to an end, the newly arrived guests are brought upstairs in a long procession that stops with the Set-Up Aide for the new receiving line.

When the State Dining Room doors open, the President and First Lady quickly take their places and the afterdinner guests are received. Again, the Pull-Off Aide is there to direct them toward the seats in the East Room since the entertainment will soon begin.

Dinner guests filing out into the Cross Hall are lured away from this activity with coffee and liqueurs and into the three rooms that run along the south side of the State Floor between the East Room and the State Dining Room. While the new receiving line is in progress, they can mingle with the guests of honor as well as other guests or admire the history and art on display.

The Red Room, named for its cherry red silk wall covering, has always served as a sitting room or parlor. Furnished today in the style of an empire parlor of the early nineteenth century, it reminds some people of Josephine Bonaparte's Red Music Room at Malmaison outside Paris.

Of all the treasures to be admired in the Red Room, the one I am most fond of is the painting of an outdoorsman with flintlock rifle. I assumed it was Davy Crockett without his famous coonskin cap. I would sometimes challenge others to identify the subject, and they would always incorrectly guess Davy Crockett.

Actually, it is a portrait of John James Audubon, painted in 1828, by John Syme. The rifle simply does not fit in with my lifelong image of the man made famous by his paintings of birds. And evidently, the anomaly has fooled many people.

Two doors in the east wall lead from the Red Room to the Blue Room. The name comes from the blue decorative trim rather than the satin wall covering, which in this case is cream colored. The blue valance which hangs below the cornice circling the ceiling and the eighteen-foot drapes of matching blue have maintained the dominant color in the room since it was first used by Martin Van Buren in 1837. The oval shape, which matches the Yellow Oval Room directly above and the Diplomatic Reception Room below, is what produces the grand bay window in the center of the south face of the White House.

This is my favorite location in the mansion. As one looks out the center window across the Presidential Park and past the Washington

Monument, it is obvious that the trees have been cleared to provide a clearer view of the Jefferson Memorial. Or is it possible that the stories are true? That the trees were cleared so that the massive statue of Thomas Jefferson could look back at the White House and sort of keep an eye on what's happening? A trip to the memorial gives every indication that the statue is gazing into the Blue Room. Perhaps this is the reason that the portraits of the first eight Presidents are hung there.

Further east, the Green Room, so called because of the moss-green silk wall covering, is decorated as a fashionable parlor in the American Federal style that was popular around 1800.

Planned by the White House architect James Hoban as a "Common Dining Room," it now serves as a gathering spot for guests coming out of the East Room next door. Most would probably be afraid to sit down if they knew that the New England sofa on the west wall was once the property of Daniel Webster. Rather than relax, most people, I noticed, simply stand and look for a very long time at the portrait of John F. Kennedy.

Most of the dinner guests have a much higher Washington profile or protocol standing—or both—than the afterdinner guests, if indeed the afterdinner guests have any protocol standing or celebrity status at all. Because of this, it seems rather curious that these late arriving guests get to go to the best seats in the East Room directly from the receiving line. They are inadvertently given this opportunity because the dinner guests usually spend too long visiting in the Red, Blue and Green Rooms.

Only those with the highest social or political profile get reserved seats. These lingering dinner guests are usually the last to enter the East Room and often wind up in the rear seats. On the occasions when I worked the seating for the entertainment, I was never surprised to hear whispered remarks between couples about who got the best seats.

To give everyone a fair chance and also to make sure everyone got situated on time, we often sent aides in to "clear" the three parlors. We didn't want anyone arriving after the principals, and we didn't want the principals to have to wait for the guests. As a Clearing Aide, I could usually get people to move simply by suggesting that they might want to do so. All the aides looked rather officious and imposing in dress uniforms, and most guests responded willingly to our requests since it was clear that we were politely directing traffic at every turn. They had no idea what kind of authority we had for issuing tickets for traffic violations, and that was to our advantage because uncertainty was just about all the leverage we had. It was all based on their willingness to cooperate and their perceptions of our influence.

I recall going to clear the Blue Room one evening when my presence alone in full dress uniform was not persuasive enough. I was in a hurry because just about everyone else had gone in to sit down. A large group of people was in front of the windows looking out on the south grounds and carrying on a conversation. I thought I'd work first on a four-star Air Force general who was standing a couple of steps behind a lady who I guessed was his wife.

He had the pained air of a sportsman standing in ice cold water or a husband waiting for his wife to finish shopping. She appeared to be the focus of attention and was temporarily carrying the conversation in her group. In a conspiratorial tone, I suggested to the general that this would be a good time for him and his wife to go and get a seat for the entertainment. The general turned to me and said, "Young man, I haven't had any luck getting her to move and you won't either."

Yes, he was a sportsman, and apparently had a well-worn license.

Unable to resist the challenge, and in any event required to clear the room in a hurry, I stepped over next to his wife and said in a stage whisper loud enough for everyone in the group to hear, "Ma'am, the President would like to see you in the East Room."

As if bolting for a closeout sale, that lady instantly grabbed the general and almost dragged him to the East Room, and the entire group of people followed to see what was going to happen next. Later on, I avoided both of them. He might have thanked me, but I had a pretty good idea she would have some tough questions for me to answer, and one tall tale was enough. Fortunately for me, I never saw the general or his wife again.

Power struggles with guests were more frequent than you would imagine.

The Social Aides were always operating under difficult circumstances. Their prime objective was to make sure that guests enjoyed themselves completely, but they also had the responsibility to move guests from room to room and activity to activity to keep them in step with the schedule of events. It was important that strict protocol be observed during formal occasions.

However, aides had to exercise judgment, and the ability to react in an appropriate manner to unprogrammed events was the hallmark of a good aide. The experience of having been shot at in combat was most useful in helping me to judge which course of action to take— when to retreat and when to stand firm.

A perfect example of a retreat comes to mind.

During one afternoon reception for some very influential friends of Richard Nixon, we had completed a receiving line exercise and the President had given a short speech to the group. He was in the process of circulating through the room to have a few personal words with some guests while several of us went out in front of him to clear a path.

All the guests cooperated by staying behind the imaginary line indicated on either side of the open area, except for one gentleman. He stood in the center facing in the direction of the President, as if blocking his way and refused to budge. As Mr. Nixon entered the hall and the cleared pathway at the other end, I stepped forward to the man's left side and, gently resting my hand on his arm, urged him to step to the side because the President was coming through. I suddenly realized who he was.

David Rockefeller turned to me and let me know in polite but firm tones that he *was* going to talk to the President. In the moment or two it took for me to decide to retreat, President Nixon had covered the distance and actually hurried up to Mr. Rockefeller, greeting him warmly.

Other guests watched with fascination and ill-disguised curiosity as the two chatted for a few moments, but none got closer than the original imaginary line that they had been standing behind. Seeing the interest the President had in their conversation, I decided it was fortunate that I had elected to withdraw rather than make an issue when one man bucked our system.

On another occasion, I was in charge of seating a whole section of people in the East Room for an afternoon ceremony and speech by the President. We always had specific seats reserved for high-level dignitaries and staff members who were expected to attend. Seating charts were often sketched on paper to insure that every VIP was accounted for. Like everything else at official functions, there was a pecking order for seating, and we could no more violate protocol there than in a receiving line.

We were getting very close to the start of the event and nearly all the seats in my section, which included the Cabinet members, were full. At the very last minute, Roy Ash, then director of the Office of Management and Budget, rushed up front with someone who was not expected in the VIP section and asked that they both be seated together.

I carefully informed him that his seat was right down front with the other members of the Cabinet but his friend would have to sit farther back. To my surprise, he insisted on having two seats where only one was available. I explained with practiced self-assurance that it was not possible to move someone already there out of the section, whereupon he insisted that someone go and get another chair and place it in the aisle next to his.

I realized we were in front of a large number of very senior administration people who could not hear us but were certain that the budget director was having a problem of some kind with one of the hired help. Mr. Ash would not relent in his demand. It was time for me to take aggressive and somewhat perilous action.

Volunteering to seat his friend *temporarily* four seats back, I said I would see what could be done to help him out with another chair. He bought it, not realizing there would be no chair blocking my aisle.

As they sat down, I disappeared to the background. There was comfort knowing, however, that if his solution had stood, either the Social Secretary or the Secret Service would have chewed me out royally for blocking the passageway. Roy Ash did not have his way and it was exclusively my doing, so I was careful to avoid contact with him after the ceremony was over.

The evening's entertainment is always tailored to the tastes of the honored guests. Oftentimes their desires are discovered by the White House staff contacting the local embassy, which will also give any necessary special instructions such as dietary needs, religious taboos, etc. Additional information is also obtained through State Department sources.

If the guest of honor does not understand English very well, music is always the first choice of entertainment. Every effort is made to make the guest of honor feel comfortable and to make the most favorable impression on him or her. Every detail is planned and then ultimately reviewed painstakingly by the Social Secretary. In most cases, the First Lady and occasionally the President also will review the plan at some length to insure that it meets with their personal approval.

Entertainment is one of the keys to a successful evening. The most accomplished stars of stage, screen and television are asked to perform at one time or another. Some of the lucky ones will make several appearances during their careers. Many entertainers who tend to reappear under the banner of the same political party have often been tied to active campaigns for office. A few stars, such as Bob Hope, transcend party lines and are always in demand.

Most guests, with good reason, enjoy whoever is performing. Under the circumstances, almost any reaction would have to be evaluated in the context of the excitement generated by the surroundings. The White House has a way of making even average performers seem great. The very presence of the President and First Lady in a room full of Washington's most powerful adds a lot of credibility and tends to brighten even the dullest performance.

But Frank Sinatra needed no help. He was one of a kind. To my knowledge, no one slept through a Frank Sinatra show at the White House. Other singers have not been so lucky. I've seen men (never a woman) doze off and wake up so rapidly one could almost hear the snap of their necks as they straightened up. It is terribly embarrassing to everyone around them, but fortunately the sleeper and everyone else is always sitting behind the principals. Only the entertainers and those in the back row are in a position to notice.

Very little can be done about sleepers, at least by the aides. A spouse's elbow is usually helpful, but when she doesn't intervene, a periodic pause for applause works nicely too, although the sleepers sometimes wake up so fast that they try to stand at the same time.

What I always thought should work, didn't. Most of these dinners get full press coverage, usually including the major networks and their film crews, who almost always stay for the entertainment. Fear of being photographed making such a social blunder should keep anyone awake, but everyone appears to forget rather quickly that the press is in the room, since, once again, the members of the media are behind the velvet rope barrier which is behind the last row of seats. The press is literally out of direct sight and, apparently, very often out of mind. In spite of all this risk, the nodders and bobbers usually stand revealed just before the show is over.

Stars are just like all the rest of us in many ways. They have their good and bad features, and they probably mirror yours or your neighbor's. We aides must cope as best we can.

John Denver was my favorite performer at the White House even though he sang at a very untraditional event. What made this occasion unusual was that his appearance wasn't at a State Dinner. Betty Ford was having a luncheon for about one hundred ladies and she asked John Denver if he would come by and sing for them at the end of the meal.

He arrived early. Several of us were standing outside the State Dining Room door with him, killing time till lunch was nearly over and he would go on. He tuned his guitar while singing the words to his hit record "Take Me Home, Country Roads." Suddenly, John stopped partway through and started the song all over again, rushing through the first verse. He stopped abruptly again and confessed that he could not remember the words to the second verse.

At first, we aides murmured aloud, wondering if this was a practical joke of some kind, but John Denver was very serious. The gifted composer-singer of a record which sold millions of copies and made him very wealthy had suddenly drawn a blank.

What a place for this disaster to happen—the White House. Clustered around Denver, we all reached for words and the first one to remember was not Denver but a female aide who quietly said, "All my memories gather around me..." All of us let out a collective sigh of relief that was so loud some of the guests craned their necks in an attempt to see what was happening just beyond the door.

John remembered everything after the first few words. He went over the verse several times, genuinely concerned that he might forget the lines again when he performed. We sympathized with him, as we had seen people's memories fail them too often under the pressure of the White House surroundings. I told him not to worry.

"When you get to that part of the song," I said, "all you have to do is turn and look through the door. I will be standing there mouthing the words and you can read my lips."

Denver sang his heart out for about twenty minutes. Everyone was having a great time, enjoying a terrific show which they had not anticipated at all. As John got to the second verse of "Country Roads," he turned and looked through the doorway even though he hadn't forgotten the lines. I mouthed the words with him and he began to laugh as he sang. Several guests, aware that something funny had happened, bobbed their heads around to see better, but no one ever figured out what it was.

White House entertainment has always come in different forms and styles. No record exists of how long either the Chinese wrestling match or the Japanese jujitsu exhibition took that Theodore Roosevelt offered for his guests' enjoyment in the East Room at the turn of the century. Present-day shows usually last from twenty to thirty minutes. At the conclusion, the President gets up and thanks the performers for the program and the guests for coming.

Everyone is then invited out to the main foyer for champagne and dancing. The Marine Corps dance band strikes up a tune on cue, and guests are drawn to the Cross Hall. There they will usually find the two heads of state and their spouses dancing and genuinely relaxing for the first time in the evening. This is the signal for the Social Aides to remove their white gloves and join in.

The Marine Corps dance band is very good and most people join in without encouragement from us, but the real energy for this portion of the evening is usually provided by the afterdinner guests. As a general rule they are considerably younger than the dinner guests. Not coincidentally, having little or no protocol standing, they are less inhibited. Their clothes are flashier and they would probably dance anyway even if they didn't feel like they had to make up for lost time—arriving after dinner when the evening was already half over.

Occasionally, big-name stars are part of the afterdinner crowd due usually to a late performance at the Kennedy Center. Normally, however, these guests are lower-level White House staffers and staff people from the offices of senators, congressmen, Cabinet officers, federal agencies or news organizations. Anyone to whom a favor was owed or whom the administration want to curry favor with or reward for past support could be included. Often enough, to my surprise, names appeared on the afterdinner guest list and the people didn't show.

"No-shows" were conspicuous by their absence because the security guards checked off everyone on a list at the door. Clearly, being an afterdinner guest was not as prestigious as being invited for dinner, but it certainly rated higher than most of the alternatives for a night on the town in Washington.

Guests normally made it back to their hotels the same way they came. Those who parked cars on the South Grounds Drive merely had to walk back out the South Portico entrance to their vehicles and drive out.

Anyone who was fortunate enough to have a chauffeur bring them could be picked up at the door using the "call system." After giving their name to one of the aides in the Diplomatic Reception Room, the guests could relax till their car arrived at the door and someone called them outside. To summon the car, the aide would announce the party's name into a microphone plugged into the wall. The loud-speakers were down at the far end of the drive where the chauffeurs congregated. If the driver was awake, the car would be there in seconds.

On more than one evening, particularly in the cold of winter, a couple would have all the extra time they needed, and then some, to tour the downstairs. The driver would be paged time and time again without any response. Eventually, the White House police would have to go and knock on car windows to wake all the drivers. Sleepy eyed, they would finally show up appear to take their impatient passengers away.

While it was not required or even expected, aides sometimes assisted in seeing that guests who had arrived by taxi had a ride home. This usually, but not always, involved unescorted ladies. No specific guidance was ever given on the subject. We all knew that, as with everything else around the White House, the utmost discretion was required.

As one might expect under the circumstances, several of us aides occasionally wound up dating former White House guests. And aides dated each other, as well. I recall that there was at least one marriage among the White House aides during my six years there.

Part Two

My Life on the Nixon Roller Coaster

7

Pat and Dick and the Shadow...

To be in the Nixon White House was to be ever conscious of the presence of H. R. Haldeman. It was like having a shadow following the aides around.

I remember the first time I became aware of the White House Chief of Staff, soon after becoming an aide. It was at a swearing-in ceremony for a new justice of the Supreme Court in the East Room. The President was the last to arrive, with the Chief Justice in tow.

As is customary, the Announcing Aide intoned on the public address system, "Ladies and Gentlemen, the President of the United States." He followed this with "The Chief Justice of the Supreme Court of the United States."

The extended applause while they took their positions on stage allowed several of us time to squeeze inside the East Room just as the heavy wooden doors were closing. I noticed that the Announcing Aide quickly put down the microphone and the card he had just read from, but he was not able to get in the door due to the standing-room-only crowd. Lucky fellow. Wedged into a corner just inside, I found myself between the very capable Social Secretary, Lucy Winchester, and the coldly efficient White House Chief of Staff.

Because he seldom smiled, no one could tell what mood Bob Haldeman was in until he started to talk. When he hissed at Lucy through clenched teeth, I knew I wanted to be somewhere other than standing directly between them. Unfortunately for me, there was nowhere to go.

"Where the hell did he get that announcement?" Haldeman growled as he leaned in front of me to get closer to her face to emphasize his point.

Lucy didn't answer right away, and even though I had a good idea, I wasn't about to offer any suggestions. The damage had already been done. She was clearly formulating a diplomatic response as Haldeman went on to explain—just in case she didn't understand—that everyone knows the Chief Justice of the United States sits on the Supreme Court and it is redundant to tell anyone that.

Ever so poised and relaxed, Lucy responded quickly in much lower tones than Haldeman had used that the Duty Aide had personally made the change on the announcer's card in the Military Office because the President had decided at the last minute to have Chief Justice Warren Burger enter with him rather than be in place on stage. Haldeman made some more testy remarks about the proper way to announce the Chief Justice, and Lucy volunteered to look into the matter further.

Very calmly, Lucy said that she would get back to him later. Her steady, even response to his attack was successful in calming him down for the moment, but I still wanted simply to disappear.

That evening, I checked my Manual of Guidance for Social Aides and discovered that Haldeman was correct. Even though the press corps missed the gaffe, and no publicity ensued, the Duty Aide for that event was reassigned from the Military Office three weeks later.

We never knew officially what happened to him, but there were strong rumors around that he was hospitalized and possibly confined for severe mental stress. There were no doubt other factors involved also, but Haldeman, Lucy Winchester and I are probably the only ones who can describe the single most significant event in that young officer's career. Haldeman would later write in his book, *The Ends of Power,* "I certainly filled my role as the President's SOB with gusto." No argument there, Bob.

Although this incident added greatly to my personal impression of Bob Haldeman's ruthless reputation in dealing with the lower-level staff members, I was certain that I could stay out of his way and out of trouble.

My education on the functioning of the White House was progressing nicely, but two frequent guests gave me cause for concern. They were often present but seldom talked to any of the other guests. One afternoon, upon completing my assignment of greeting arrivals, I was sent to float through the crowded State Floor on "wallflower patrol," looking for solitary guests either to engage them in conversation or to introduce them to someone they might like to talk to.

Noticing one of these gentlemen standing alone, I attempted some small talk to break the ice before passing him on to someone else. He quickly informed me in a very brusque manner that he worked on the staff and didn't need entertaining. Shocked by his curt response and realizing he had been coming to the parties repeatedly because he *worked* at the White House, I hastily retreated to the other side of the room. He wasn't Secret Service—that I could tell. So who was he?

I reported the incident immediately to the Aide-in-Charge, as we were supposed to do when something extraordinary happened. Even though he was only a member of the staff and not a guest, it still might have reflected unfavorably on the Social Aides, had the staffer complained. And the Aide-in-Charge thus was prepared for any criticism.

Not to have alerted the Aide-in-Charge and then to have had him—or worse still, the Social Secretary, Lucy Winchester—bawled out could have been devastating.

I couldn't have been more surprised when moments after reporting the unpleasantness, the Aide-in-Charge identified the man as a Haldeman special assistant—of whom there were several. One or another of them, he said, was frequently assigned by the Chief of Staff to check on everything that went on at functions attended by the President.

The assistant would then apparently report back to Bob Haldeman on how the Social Secretary and the Social Aides had handled the event.

I was astonished. This was someone from the West Wing of the White House—Haldeman's side—checking on the East Wing staff—Lucy Winchester's side. Yet no one had thought to tell the newer Social Aides. Was it a secret? Or had the more experienced aides become so accustomed to this spy game that they had forgotten the game was being played?

I made a mental note to watch out for the two men who were pointed out to me as Haldeman's gumshoes—Gordon Strachan and Larry Higby—and as time went on, a few other faces were added.

Haldeman's detective that day had been so rude that I had to assume I had offended him greatly and was in danger of getting the old heave-ho from my social duties. My apprehension did not subside until a notice came in the mail two days later scheduling me to work at a State Dinner.

I had survived, but obviously I had a lot more to learn about survival tactics. Haldeman's shadow was felt at every party as one or another of his spies looked and watched and listened in. I had heard that President Nixon was sensitive to criticism and wanted nothing at the White House during his watch to inspire disparaging or sarcastic comments by the picky and prickly press, who never let Nixon forget his famous last words to reporters after an earlier election defeat that they would not have Dick Nixon to kick around anymore.

But did the President actually know how far his Chief of Staff was carrying it?

I decided he didn't, and I grew to like him very much for his friendliness and his wit. Once, I had the opportunity to tell him that I had been in the welcoming crowd in Quito, because my father was a military attaché stationed there, when the Vice President had arrived on a goodwill tour.

The President made a wry face and grinned. I wondered—but did not ask—whether he was remembering his harrowing South American tour when he had faced real danger. He had made a joke of it when he was safely back home and speaking to the U.S. Junior Chamber of Commerce, in Detroit.

Nixon had reminisced about the way his limo had been bombarded with stones—while he was in it. "I got stoned in Caracus," he quipped, "and I can tell you it's a lot different from getting stoned at a Jaycee convention." The crowd had laughed and applauded.

Yes, Nixon was a survivor.

He had survived the goodwill tour and he had survived the threat of getting dumped by Eisenhower even before that—in 1952. Ike had chosen Nixon as his running mate, but during the campaign for Ike's first term, a scandal broke concerning secret contributions—gifts from California businessmen.

Accusers said the money had gone into Nixon's own pocket to pad his income as a senator, but he staunchly maintained he used the money for political expenses and not his own. Eisenhower wanted to wash his hands of the matter by dropping Nixon as the vice presidential candidate. Ike bluntly said he wanted a running mate cleaner than the proverbial "hound's tooth."

Nixon fought back, going on TV to defend the fund—emotionally adding that he'd also gotten a "gift" of a little cocker spaniel that had been shipped in a crate and that little six-year-old Tricia had fallen in love with the dog and named it Checkers. "I just want to say this right now," Nixon said with a choked voice, "Regardless of what they say about it, we are going to *keep* it!"

Nixon left the television studio thinking he had failed. As his limo started to move, he noticed that a big Irish setter was jumping around beside the car and barking, as if applauding. As the story goes, Nixon turned to his wife, saying that at least he had made a hit in the dog world.

But he'd made a hit in the people world, too. Eisenhower got so many telegrams demanding Nixon as Vice President that Ike gave up the idea of dumping Dick Nixon.

It had helped earn R.N. the title of "Tricky Dick" but there was nothing tricky about the way he coped with defeat eight years later when he lost the presidential election to Jack Kennedy. I called it statesmanship. Kennedy had won by scarcely more than a hairsbreadth and there was evidence of voting fraud in various places— enough so that a recount was in order.

But rising above his personal agony over the loss, Nixon decided not to formally charge that the election had been stolen, first, because it would create chaos and delay the orderly transfer of power from the old administration to the new, and second, because it would seriously damage the image of the United States in the eyes of the world and greatly injure our foreign relations.

He even made a joke about losing the election, not wailing that "I was robbed," but going along with the general public, which thought he had lost because of the Kennedy-Nixon debates. Calling himself a dropout from the "Electoral College," he explained, "I flunked debating."

And so I admired the man I served in the White House. I even felt a certain closeness because both of us were survivors. He had been through the war of politics and emerged as President. I had been through the hail of bullets on the battlefield, with men dying beside me, and emerged *alive*.

Only years later would I realize how much of a survivor Richard Nixon had been and continued to be—even rising from the ashes of Watergate to a new life as a semi-public elder statesman.

I even liked the fact that Nixon, a Republican, chose Woodrow Wilson, a Democrat, as the President he most admired and wanted to emulate in finding a way to establish and maintain peace in the world. One of the first things Nixon did when he took office in 1969 was to have Wilson's old desk moved to the Oval Office, where he happily used it—and where I was happy to see it when a secretary took me on a guided tour of the West Wing.

Among his friends and mentors, Nixon talked often, I was told, about wanting to make a mark on history. More than many others who were content just to keep the ship of state steady, Nixon wanted to be a President who would be remembered forever for something special—like bringing permanent peace to the world (a real challenge in view of the Vietnam War).

He would run down the list of recent Presidents and tell why they would always be fondly remembered by the public—Eisenhower for winning World War II, Kennedy for his charm, Johnson for his advances in civil rights. Then Nixon would wonder what he would be remembered for, if anything.

He certainly put forth effort.

He brought our boys home. In effect, admitting the war was hopeless and negotiating a four-party Vietnam peace pact, which was signed in Paris, January 27, 1973, Nixon succeeded in obtaining the release of almost six hundred American prisoners of war, as well as getting all of our troops out of Vietnam by April 1 of that year.

And earlier, in 1972, he became the first American President to visit China and the Soviet Union. The February China trip ended with a communiqué pledging normalization of relations between the two formerly hostile countries, and the May Russia visit ended with what was hailed as a landmark strategic arms pact.

I would say he had done very well. As a matter of fact, I remember the party Nixon gave as part of the celebration of the opening of relations with China. A group of ninety Chinese athletes was the first to make such a visit in more than twenty years—the Shenyang Acrobatic Troupe.

Everyone seemed to be having a good time, but something was clearly wrong. This was a tea, but not one Chinese guest would eat the cookies and little cakes. They drank the tea, but not a cookie did they touch.

Were they waiting to be asked to eat them, or were they afraid the cookies would make them sick? Or was it something about not knowing how to eat them American style? Surely, all they had to do was watch what the other guests were doing.

We tried but we never did figure out what the reason was for this. It certainly wasn't because they were bashful. The troupe chatted happily, then flocked to the windows of the State Dining Room as the President and Mrs. Nixon, having departed the party early, lifted off the South Lawn in a helicopter bound for a long weekend away. The helicopter was the highlight of the function for the Chinese.

And each of them was holding a gift from their host.

As a token of appreciation and to reinforce the memory of the event, the President gave each member of the group a pin with the presidential seal on it. The Chinese in turn presented everyone there with a variety of their pins.

As for the trip to Russia, I remember how excited we all were when we learned that two or three Social Aides were to be selected to go to Moscow to assist with the U.S. embassy dinner there. Dare I hope I would be one? My travel orders were ready and a suitcase as well.

In preparation for the Russian trip, the President and Mrs. Nixon invited three hundred members of the press—theirs and ours—for cocktails and hopefully a friendly send-off. Meeting some of the Soviet press that day—May 19, 1972—was as close to Russia as I would get. I cursed my luck—there but by the grace of a few years experience went I. Only the most seasoned aides were picked.

I was not prepared for the Pat Nixon I would get to know at the White House. From reading about her and the White House social life, I had expected a woman who was a little cool and aloof—even intimidating. But she was none of these. Never was there a person more concerned with others, with the welfare of guests, with making people happy.

Or anyone more proudly Irish. I remember when she invited forty Irish teachers for tea. There were no votes there, yet she lavished as much attention on them as if they had been senators' wives, serving them tea and pastries and sharing stories of their Irish heritage.

It was then I learned that Patricia was not her first name. Her social secretary told me she was awash in names—Thelma Catherine Patricia Ryan Nixon. Her father had chosen the most Irish one for her nickname.

And though Pat Nixon missed being born on St. Patrick's Day by a hairsbreadth, she still celebrated her birthday on that holiday. I was there for her party on March 17, 1972, and was amused at how the President entered into the Irish spirit of the occasion.

It was a very Republican party as well as having an Irish theme, and some 250 guests including congressional couples and Republican party officials and close friends were waiting for the birthday girl in the East Room.

I happened to be standing down the hall in front of the State Dining Room when the Nixons came out of the elevator. One of the doormen, Freddie Mayfield, was also there wearing an absolutely outrageous light and dark green bow tie in honor of Saint Patrick. It would have driven off any snake.

President Nixon saw him and let out a belly laugh that no one would have guessed he was capable of. When they were finished discussing the tie, the President persuaded Freddie to trade ties with him for the evening. As Nixon walked out of the elevator alcove, I complimented him on his distinctive appearance. He smiled broadly and laughed again.

The crowd loved it. Rarely had they seen the Nixons so relaxed and openly having a good time. It just wasn't their style to be so informal and demonstrably funny in public, but obviously they were capable of it. I eventually began to believe that this was close to the real Nixon, and the Nixon everyone else always saw was more of a facade necessitated by the pressures of public life. One could rarely tell it from his public appearances but Dick Nixon was very capable of provoking mirth. Like the time the Opera Society of Washington was performing *The Barber of Seville* at the White House and Nixon invited his barber, Milton Pitts.

Not only was Pitts in the audience, but a grinning Nixon, in introducing the entertainment, pointed him out and joked about how little the poor man had to work with on the presidential head.

And then there was the pixieish way he dealt with Kennedy's vaunted inaugural speech, saying, "I wish I had said some of those things."

Ted Sorensen, who tells the story, asked Nixon if he meant the line that began "Ask not what your country can do for you . . ."

Nixon said no, he meant the line that began "I do solemnly swear. . ."

And now, at his wife's birthday party, he had had his little visual joke and everyone settled down to hear the kind of music, I was told, that Pat Nixon loved.

Country star Merle Haggard, a man who had served time in San Quentin for robbery, sang several songs, including "Okie From Muskogee," and then read a birthday poem to Pat. Two others from the Grand Ole Opry, the Osborn Brothers, also helped entertain by playing bluegrass music.

Everyone clustered around Pat as she shared some Irish stories with her friends. And she shared something else, inviting them to see the living quarters of the White House. I would learn that very few First Ladies of the past and very few of the First Ladies after Pat Nixon would invite any but a select few friends to the family floor of the White House.

Yet Pat did it again and again because she knew it brought joy.

She even did it for singer Ethel Ennis, who had sung the National Anthem for Nixon's second inauguration. Ennis had made the guest list of a State Dinner soon after, but Pat Nixon went the extra mile, spiriting Ethel Ennis and the singer's husband away from the crowd. Then, while the other guests danced, Pat and Dick gave the couple a private tour of the second floor personal family quarters.

That was vintage Pat. It was also vintage Pat Nixon that she decided the public had the right to see the White House gardens.

The entertainment rooms on the State Floor—the Blue Room, the Red Room, the Green Room, the State Dining Room and the East Room—had been open to tourists for years, but for some reason the outside gardens had been considered off-limits.

The timing was terrible. The facts were confusing. There was sleet. A lesser First Lady would have given up and said, "Let's try this another day."

My calendar shows that the first annual Rose Garden Tour was held April 12, 1973, but actually it included the viewing of two gardens, causing confusion among some reporters about which garden was which and what was what concerning each.

Everything about this function was misleading and the only thing that kept it all together was Pat Nixon. First, the Rose Garden located in the West Lawn, doesn't really have roses in it. Although Mrs. Woodrow Wilson planted them in 1913 and gave the garden its name, the roses have long since bit the dust. Though not all in bloom, the so-called Rose Garden was full of tulips, grape hyacinths, crocuses, pansies, geraniums and chrysanthemums. Second, there really wasn't a tour because, on this carefully selected spring day, it was snowing and raining at the same time.

Following the receiving line in front of the Blue Room door, the guests and reporters—at the urging of Pat Nixon—ducked out into the no-rose Rose Garden and back between bursts of snow and rain.

The ceremony to honor several dozen nurserymen and landscapers was held in the East Room rather than in the garden itself. Pat Nixon casually referred to the offending precipitation as "April showers" and kept her audience fascinated by her flower history talk.

But even more fascinating was her explanation of where President Jefferson's horse trough and President Wilson's sheep watering troughs had been located. Wilson had raised sheep in World War I to help the war effort by providing wool for uniforms—or so he hoped.

Reporters also were sent scurrying out to take a quick look at the East Garden, which, to confuse everyone, was better known as the Jacqueline Kennedy Garden.

First developed in the nineteenth century as a lawn area with shrubs, trees and some flower beds, the East Garden was redesigned into a more sophisticated and enjoyable area in 1902 by Mrs. Theodore Roosevelt. The garden was officially designated as the Jacqueline Kennedy Garden in 1965 by Lyndon Johnson, in an effort—his critics say—to win the respect of Mrs. Kennedy, which had always eluded him when he served as Vice President.

The honor was apparently meant to lure the former First Lady back to the Johnson White House, but Jacqueline declined to appear. The East, or Jacqueline Kennedy Garden, continued to be used by First Ladies for their outdoor socials on a lovely day.

A few reporters and guests decided that the Rose Garden should really be called "the President's Garden," since he's the one who uses it—and frequently.

The Rose Garden is not well suited for private family purposes as there are so many office windows opening onto that area. It is instead used frequently as a public meeting place for the President and guests and a State Dinner has even been held there (under tents of course). As one of the most beautiful settings in the White House for a photo opportunity, the Rose Garden is often seen on the evening news. It is an unsurpassed location for heartwarming events—like greeting returning astronauts or prisoners of war.

And it is so convenient for the President. Located just outside the Oval Office, it enables him to step outside in front of the cameras and assembled press, deliver a message and be back at work at his desk in minutes.

Sometimes, when Nixon was greeting people in the Rose Garden, Pat was welcoming another group in the East Room or the State Dining Room or one of the other rooms. They were like ships that pass in the night.

I remember one summer day when *Life* magazine was doing "A Day in the Life of Pat Nixon." One of the things the photographers were shooting was Pat's reception for Army Community Service Women. At the same time this was going on, the President was hosting both Johnny Cash and Golda Meir, and the groups never crossed paths. The diversity of events around the mansion never ceased to amaze me.

Nor did Pat's simplicity and lack of ostentation. It showed even in the things she chose to collect. Not furs or the expensive Chinese porcelains that a later First Lady, Nancy Reagan, would collect. No, nothing pricey. Pat confessed she collected seashells on both coasts— at Key Biscayne and at San Clemente.

She was not given to shopping sprees and she was happier giving than acquiring. She loved giving little gifts, and her face would glow when she did.

She had been a high school teacher. She had worked her way through college—the University of Southern California—and had graduated cum laude.

She had met Dick Nixon when both were cast in the same Little

Theater group play in Whittier and he was a struggling lawyer. They still maintained a bit of a theatrical effect around the White House. I remember the night of a Governors Dinner, when President Nixon took to the piano and Pearl Bailey sang and both told jokes. Their act was a hit.

Pat and Dick brought a little theatrical touch to religion by holding nondenominational Sunday services in the East Room for the first time in history—and having professionals sing the hymns. The two hundred guests, who formed the congregation, were not expected to chime in.

I remember that when Dr. Norman Vincent Peale came one Sunday in March of 1974 and preached a sermon entitled, "The Answer Is Love," the Motet Singers lifted up their voices in two hymns. There was nothing amateurish about their performance—at this point, they had already released four albums of religious music.

Though they were often the ships that pass in the night, there was also a certain kind of teamwork that one was aware of around Pat and Dick. Though Pat never forgot that it was her husband who was the President, and not she, she still was always on the lookout for someone or some group who needed her to right a wrong or an oversight.

That's how it happened that one day I was at the White House helping the First Lady greet about five hundred wives of American diplomats abroad. They were members of the Association of American Foreign Service Women. The date was March 13, 1973. Pat had heard that it was sometimes an embarrassment to these ladies that in performing their social duties abroad they were not able to say they had met either their President or First Lady, and so Pat was correcting this situation.

"At least you can say you've met a First Lady," she told them.

But the President surprised Pat and delighted the ladies by dropping in unannounced to praise them himself for their roles as the wives of diplomats. He thanked them for their countless unpaid hours donated to the various duties they perform, and he went on to say that their lives were even more difficult than that of a politician's wife. He alluded to the physical dangers their husbands often endure and the pride he felt for them.

To say the ladies were charmed by Richard Nixon would be an

understatement. But all too soon he was gone, leaving Pat with her hostess duties.

The receiving line was snaking along at a fairly brisk pace when Pat Nixon had an idea. She had heard that somewhere in that mass of ladies was Mrs. Philip Manhard, the wife of the Foreign Service Officer who had been held captive in North Vietnam but who would be among those released the following week. "I want to congratulate her," the First Lady said to a staffer.

Because I was the Set-Up Aide for the receiving line that day, Pat asked me to please try to find Mrs. Manhard and bring her to the head of the line. I did, and must admit I got a little choked up myself as I watched the emotional meeting between the two women.

Other First Ladies might have waited till Mrs. Manhard arrived in front of them in the receiving line—but that wouldn't have been Pat Nixon, the warmhearted Irish lass. With feeling, the First Lady promised that there would be a big celebration at the White House when all the prisoners of war got home.

But nothing prepared me for how BIG it would be!

8

A Promise Kept—the POW Party

$\mathscr{P}$at Nixon was a woman of her word. My records show that two months after Pat Nixon had rejoiced with the wife of newly-released Vietnam prisoner Philip Manhard and said they would celebrate, the White House celebration began. And it wasn't just a tea or a reception or a greeting from the President in the Rose Garden. No, it was a doubleheader. My calendar says:

May 24—Mrs. Nixon's Tea for POW Ladies; R.N.'s POW Dinner.

No event during my six years at the White House was more thrilling, awesome or satisfying than the celebration held for the just-released prisoners of war. There was so much excitement and happiness around. Everyone wore a big smile, and many alternated between laughter and an occasional tear as emotions overwhelmed most guests with little warning.

This electric mood at the White House went beyond the social staff and the guests to include the domestic staff, the White House Police, the press corps and the usually serious and somber Secret Service, who also sported very happy faces.

The adrenaline was pumping so hard for so long that fatigue did not set in for me until about noon the following day. Considering that this day started with a parade practice at 7:00 A.M. at my regular job of ceremonial officer with the Army's Old Guard, it turned out to be a very emotionally draining and physically taxing experience.

Having completed the parade rehearsal, with I quickly changed into a summer service dress uniform in my office.

Scrubbed up to and including the teeth—even the nonsmoking aides had them cleaned by a dentist every three or four months—I headed for the mansion around noon armed with shaving gear and an extra evening uniform in the car to get ready for the black-tie dinner that followed the tea.

Through force of habit, many of the Social Aides drifted down to the Library for our initial briefing. Someone noted that, for the first time ever, we were supposed to be on the North Grounds for our detailed instructions, so we all trundled back out into the beautiful morning sunshine that seemed to break through the rain clouds just long enough to welcome the POWs. All these neat haircuts, beautiful uniforms and spit-shined shoes of ours would have been more appropriate in a limousine, but in no time we were unceremoniously loaded on a bus where we got our orientation and detailed assignments.

Half of us were going to work Mrs. Nixon's tea for all the ladies, and the others were going with the President to organize the meeting with the former POWs. All this was happening at the State Department, so it was necessary for us to be bused over, as parking would be nearly impossible for all our cars.

The ladies' group was an unusual lot. The majority were devoted wives of the POWs who, by all indications, waited faithfully for their husbands to return. Mixed in with them were women of all ages who were linked in some way to a POW—a sister, daughter, mother or girlfriend.

Some men were single when they went to war, others were left widowers while imprisoned in North Vietnam, and a number of POWs were divorced or abandoned by their spouses. Any POW who did not bring his wife was permitted to bring someone else, but it had to be from the immediate family. Those who were legally single were allowed to bring dates, and some did, while others opted for a family member. One brought a recent *Playboy* Playmate-of-the-Month which caused a hell of a stir among the Social Aides.

While the ladies gathered on the eighth floor of the State Department for tea, the six-hundred-plus former POWs were meeting downstairs in the auditorium to be briefed by President Nixon. Having been free men for several weeks, they were by now aware of many of the details concerning the printing of the Pentagon Papers and the Ellsberg and Watergate burglaries and of subsequent investigations which appeared to tie these events to senior White House people.

This partisan crowd of POWs cheered vigorously for a long minute when Nixon criticized leaks which damaged national security, but no mention was made of "the Plumbers." (Nixon created this group within the White House to plug such leaks, and now they were under investigation for possible unlawful surveillance activities.)

Some of the Social Aides were nearly as overcome by emotion as many of the POWs were when the President said he had never addressed a more distinguished audience.

I knew from conversations with him that President Nixon felt nothing could surpass the sacrifice made by those men who died in battle or were captured by the enemy.

Most of the men there had been severely mistreated, and reports showed that many prisoners had died at the hands of their captors. Many survivors were crippled and malnourished and had to use crutches and wheelchairs when the prisoner exchange took place.

A great number of artificial supports were in evidence at the party, and some men would probably never escape them. Several tried valiantly to walk upright and naturally, but many a limp gave testimony to the inhumane treatment the POWs had received from the North Vietnamese.

Nixon asked the POWs for their support in educating America's youth to the need for a strong national defense and hoped the former prisoners would assist him in rebuilding the nation's faith in itself. The men reacted with instant support and loyalty to their Commander in Chief. It was an enthusiastic ending and set the mood for the evening's festivities which turned out to be the greatest party the White House had seen in its 173-year history—with the possible exception of Andrew Jackson's inauguration when an overflow crowd swarmed in and out of the White House windows and stood on chairs to hear over the din.

May 24—POW Dinner

Anyone planning a dinner must consider how large the dining room is. At the White House, that normally limits the guest list to 120. An overflow crowd of 30 more can be accommodated in the Red or Blue Room and on rare occasions is, but even this unusual arrangement very much limits the number that can attend. So how do you seat fifteen hundred guests for dinner? Easy. Just create another room. A very big room.

And Pat and Dick did.

For this event a 100- by 180-foot tent complete with chandeliers was erected on the South Lawn with its center approximately where the President's helicopter usually touches down. Larger than the main area of the mansion itself, it held not only 126 dinner tables but a large stage as well.

And the Nixons did something else. They invited a flock of Hollywood stars who they were sure would gladden the hearts of the POWs. But there is only so much man can do—even if that man is a President.

As one guest put it, "God must be having a long, long cry for the POWs." It had rained all afternoon and all the previous night, and it was still raining. The ground under the tent was thoroughly soaked, and each step produced a squishy ooze of mud. Burlap runners were placed everywhere in the aisles and helped to keep people's feet free of mud. The runners, though, would not stay dry, because the water soaked through in many places, and in several spots there were outright puddles.

A canopied walkway was installed from the South Portico entrance sloping downhill to the tent entrance. A ramp was included to accommodate those in wheelchairs. Unfortunately, nothing could be done to stop the table and chair legs from sinking slowly into the turf. Ladies in spiked heels also grew progressively shorter the longer they stood in one spot. Not surprisingly, there wasn't a complaint from anyone.

With this addition to the house in place, attention turned to the food preparation. Yes, the White House has a fabulous kitchen...fabulous for up to 150 guests. To accommodate sixteen hundred meals (they always made extra), it was necessary to import Army field kitchens, which were also located on the South Lawn out of view. Very large Army refrigerator vans were placed on either side of the tent to hold the appetizers (supreme of seafood Neptune) and the desserts (strawberry mousse) prior to their being served. Roast beef and vegetables were done in the kitchens.

John Ficklin, the White House maitre d', and I had been joking about this evening for some time. The White House was insisting on finding matching china on which to feed the POWs. It was a White House tempest in a teapot. The thought did cross my mind that the guys probably couldn't care less whether their plates matched. They had been buried in holes in the ground and locked in bamboo cages with rats and mice and cockroaches. They would have been happy to eat standing up or sitting on the floor of the White House with a rice bowl—and here we were worrying about matching china.

I kept needling John about this, offering to bring in my matching china service for twelve. He kept telling me to do just that and keep it handy in my car trunk. He ended up borrowing china from every government agency. And though the fifteen hundred place settings didn't match, at least those at each of the 126 tables were perfectly uniform.

On the night of the party, just before everything officially started, I walked down the ramp to the tent entrance and found John surveying his masterpiece of a layout. I facetiously told him that my china was still in the trunk of my car if he needed to use it, and all pieces matched. We stood and joked about it for several minutes, not realizing that we were standing in front of a Public Broadcasting System camera with its red light on and that we were on national television live.

The guests arrived at the East Portico in buses from several hotels nearby. Rain continued to fall at the slow steady pace it had all afternoon, but fortunately, the first hour was planned as cocktails and an open house on the three main floors of the mansion.

No one had to venture out to the tent area for a while yet. Nor did they want to. Again, warmhearted Pat had opened the living quarters to the guests, who were delighted to view such things as Lincoln's bed. The POWs had the run of the house, and almost anything was permissible.

White House Police and Social Aides placed around the three floors to answer questions spent most of their time taking numerous pictures for many groups of guests with their own cameras. The

POWs may have been away for a long time, but they were not distracted enough by all the attention they were receiving now to fail to make a photographic record of a memorable event.

An unscheduled appearance by the Nixons created a stir on the third floor, where they said hello to everyone lucky enough to be there. Several ladies thanked the Nixons for their corsages, which they knew were provided by the White House. None probably realized that they were paid for personally by Richard Nixon. Hollywood stars such as Vic Damone, John Wayne and Jimmy Stewart circulated through the crowd giving autographs and being photographed by the multitude of unofficial cameramen as well as the few official ones present.

Cabinet officers and senators were less well known and didn't receive much attention, with the distinct exception of Henry Kissinger. Every POW knew how hard Henry had worked to get them all released, and each one wanted to thank him in person.

For a guy who enjoyed the limelight and seemed to work hard at getting attention from the media, Henry Kissinger was strangely uncomfortable at the effusive outpouring of gratitude.

Wives of POWs kissed and hugged him with tears of joy. The men pumped his hand or slapped him on the back or both. It was an unforgettable sight to watch Henry Kissinger greatly embarrassed by unbounded praise and adoration. Never again would I see him that way.

Wandering through the crowd, I found the beautiful actress Joey Heatherton in a sizzling dress with no back, standing all by herself. Here was my chance to establish an acquaintance that should have been made several years earlier. I explained to Joey that I wanted to say hello this evening because we had missed meeting in South Vietnam six years ago—"and I've been kicking myself ever since."

I refreshed her memory about how, when she was traveling with the USO and entertaining the troops, a First Infantry Division general named Hollingsworth invited her to fly around with him while he visited field command sites in the countryside to give instructions and inspect defenses. She agreed to go, and with virtually no warning—as usual—the general landed his helicopter at my company commander's location. I had departed with my platoon on "cloverleaf" patrol only a half hour earlier. We were deeply engrossed in finding Viet Cong and had no time to be concerned about the arrival of some VIP aircraft. Except that this one had an incredibly beautiful round-eyed blonde on board.

The news moved faster than a new second lieutenant with a swarm of red ants on his head—not an uncommon sight in the jungle. Quickly, every soldier in my platoon heard about what he was missing. Security and safety deteriorated rapidly. It was my responsibility to make a command decision on whether to continue the mission with totally distracted troops or to try to make a successful abort. Either action would be difficult and dangerous.

I did the only thing possible under the circumstances. Calling the infantry units to our left and right and the artillery fire coordinators, who all thought we would be somewhere else in a few minutes, I notified them we would be retracing our original route to return to base camp at high speed.

The distance which took us thirty minutes going out required only ten minutes or less coming back. We arrived just in time to see the cloud of red dust rise as the chopper lifted off with its precious cargo—and I'm not referring to the notorious General Hollingsworth, who never said five words without cussing.

Joey said she remembered the trip and the general very well, and then and there I got a big hug and a kiss. It had been a long time coming and would have been more appreciated six years earlier, but it certainly was worth the wait.

The thought occurred later that she might have mistaken me for a POW—but who looks a gift horse in the mouth.

With so many guests present and scattered all over the mansion, Mrs. Nixon was understandably concerned that she could not be a good hostess or even meet them all, let alone entertain them.

Phyllis Diller, who was standing with her, said, "Don't give it a thought. A good hostess is one who can convince her guests that caraway seeds are supposed to have legs," and she cackled her famous laugh.

At the appropriate signal, the Social Aides moved everyone out to the tent for the meal. It took a considerable time to get fifteen hundred people into their seats, but no one seemed to care as the minutes slipped by. The dinner was served by waiters borrowed from everywhere, just like the dishes. We Social Aides disappeared for a quick bite to eat and returned in time for the entertainment.

Bob Hope was introduced as the master of ceremonies by President

Nixon. He did a few one-liners and then introduced several other entertainers. John Wayne got a big round of applause when he complimented the POWs for their fortitude and said, "I'll ride into the sunset with you anytime."

But the greatest applause came when the thirty-five-member chorus of POWs, which was formed secretly in the prison camps, sang a hymn which they had written under the noses of the North Vietnamese. There were not many dry eyes in the room, and one POW, an Air Force sergeant, was so overcome with emotion he sobbed uncontrollably. With one leg missing, he was one of the few who could not stand even with help. His only leg was heavily bandaged.

The POWs toasted the Commander in Chief and Irving Berlin led everyone is singing "God Bless America." All remaining dry eyes in the room overflowed. It was the culmination of years of agony, not only for the POWs but also for the families left behind. Now the worst had ended at least for those in the room. Few people forgot that other families still waited with dwindling hope for the sons, husbands and fathers who had not returned.

President Nixon announced that the dancing, which usually ended at midnight, would be extended to 2:00 A.M. or later for those who cared to stay. He went to bed around midnight while everyone else stayed and danced and danced and danced.

Joey was not the only stunning attraction that evening. Equally as startling was a *Playboy* centerfold named Micki Jo Garcia. She had a face, a dress and a figure that matched every guy's idea of what a Playmate should be. Her date was an Air Force officer who never let go of her. I suggested that one of the very attractive female aides ask him to dance, and without a moment's hesitation he flatly refused.

As prearranged, I was standing by so Micki wouldn't be left alone, but that situation never arose. They were inseparable and started walking away as I watched, wistfully.

My teammate said, grinning, "Well, what do you think of her?"

All I could think of to express it was, "She *is* outstanding." I stood there just repeating it over and over, and lo and behold, the *Washington Post* reporter standing nearby picked it up and printed it the next day along with Micki's picture as proof.

I danced with partner after partner. I do not know when the last guests went home. My rifle company had to be in Arlington National

Cemetery at six in the morning to help place miniature flags on each of 260,000 headstones for Memorial Day. I left about 4:45 A.M. and went straight to my office at Fort Myer to change into a fatigue uniform. I was back to just where the previous day had started. It was not possible to sleep even if I had wanted to. There were at least a dozen guests still there after 4:45 A.M. I know of no other White House party that went on that long.

But then no other group of guests at the White House ever had better reason to celebrate.

9

That's Entertainment!

Only a Hollywood mogul or a President of the United States would get to meet such an array of people—the heads of state, the famous, the glamorous, the powerful, the colorful, the bizarre. Yet here I was rubbing elbows with them, too, simply because I stood in the shadow of the President and First Lady.

It felt good to be needed. In my white gloves, dressed to the hilt in my military uniform, with gold braided aiguillette hanging from my shoulder, I was there to do whatever was necessary to make each White House party a smashing success with no glitches. As were the other twenty-three White House Social Aides.

The job excited me. It was worth the hours, the exhaustion. The rushing from my day duties as a ceremonial officer to my night duties as something of an assistant host for the President. I was like a guest, yet not a guest. I mixed and mingled and filled in as escort. I danced with some and stood chatting with others, hopefully amusing them with little anecdotes and listening to their stories.

I answered countless questions about the White House from "Can you take me to see where the President sleeps?" to "Where does Congress meet?" It was amazing how many people—and not only foreigners—did not know the difference between the Capitol and the White House. Or have respect for the President's privacy.

But tact was the keyword. Tact and preparedness. Guests would have been surprised if they had known what I was carrying in my pockets. Social Aides were always prepared for routine and unique emergencies. I considered all of the following as absolutely necessary equipment for every function: a book of matches, extra brass clasps that hold ribbons and decorations in place on uniforms, two safety pins, breath mints, change for pay telephone calls, business cards, two pens and note cards, a spare shoelace, a couple of paper clips, and several rubber bands. Anything might be necessary in an emergency.

And there was something else in there. One of the most unusual items every Social Aide carried was a set of official military travel orders in miniaturized, laminated card form, designed to fit in a wallet. Known throughout the government as "blanket" travel orders because they were issued for an indefinite period of time and any official event, they would allow us to depart on a moment's notice to do whatever the President or First Lady required anywhere in the world.

No two parties were quite alike. No two guests were quite alike. I was there to do whatever the President would do if he had the time. And why didn't he have the time? Because he was busy taking care of the honored guest and because there were just too many guests—120 for a sit-down dinner and sometimes a thousand or more for a reception.

With so much glamour around the military Social Aides, it was a good thing we, by tradition, were unattached. In view of all the media attention focused on the White House at every party and the multiple opportunities for embarrassment to the administration, a married aide might have gotten into real trouble.

After all, the military services from which the aides are drawn are populated with red-blooded men and women, not saints. So the White House, in all its wisdom, selects only single officers to become Social Aides and perform intricate and sometimes delicate social duties. Then, if a hot romance develops involving some Social Aide, at least he—or she—is not married, and that narrows the possibility of a messy scandal that reflects on the White House.

Still there was at least one embarrassing incident that I can remember. That was when a First Lady happened upon an aide and another White House staffer in a compromising situation. She graciously rose above the incident, and the aide was not dropped, but the couple kept their romantic liaison out of the White House from then on.

Had either person been married, it would have been a different matter, and I'm sure *that* Social Aide would not have been seen again at White House parties.

I cite this merely to show you may think you have a problem solved but you can never think of everything. Nor can the White House. Anyway, when I started attending White House parties as a Social Aide, romantic liaisons were not high on my list. I just wanted to survive and experience the presidential—or at least the White House—way of life.

Having already worked several daytime events and the formal dinner for the founder of the *Reader's Digest,* I very much looked forward to my first international social function, a black-tie affair for the twenty-three members of the Organization of American States. But something was wrong. As I approached the White House, it struck me as a little odd that the twenty-four Social Aides working this evening would be parking on the South Grounds.

That was where the guests traditionally parked. We aides usually parked somewhere else to be out of their way. I knew that the White House did not break with tradition lightly—there had to be a very good reason.

When I arrived, I learned that no one could park or even enter on north side. Eight hundred war protesters had marched into Lafayette Park, right across the street from the north entrance to the White House, and the district police had taken unique but proven defensive measures.

Previous experiences with mobs had taught the District of Columbia authorities to maintain a healthy respect for their capabilities. To prevent the crowd from surging across Pennsylvania Avenue and over the White House fence, the police parked thirteen city buses end to end along Pennsylvania Avenue. With both ends being flat vertical surfaces, the buses made a very effective barricade which even a thin man could not penetrate. Since the buses blocked the north gates, the Social Aides and the invited guests all arrived at the southwest entrance. The uninvited guests who never entered the eighteen-acre White House grounds went home later that night after two-hundred were arrested. The date was April 15, 1972.

The evening was fascinating for me as a newcomer but otherwise uneventful. I noted that the most popular man at the affair was a Dr. Guillermo Sevilla-Sacasa, the ambassador from Nicaragua under Somoza. Although a short, stout man, Sacasa seemed to grow in stature as he quickly moved through the crowd.

One of the other aides explained that Sacasa was receiving all this attention and deference because he was the dean of the diplomatic corps, and thus the most important man there. It was an eye-opener for me to see that in the world of diplomacy and protocol, a little country like Nicaragua could outrank the giants like England and the Soviet Union.

The entertainment was a bit too highbrow for me.

Birgit Nilsson, the Swedish diva, performed parts of five operas to the delight of the assembled guests. I enjoyed it in part but also looked forward to more popular entertainment.

I didn't have long to wait. At my very next event, just six days later, I listened to college kids singing on the South Lawn on a beautiful spring day.

There were seven hundred young guests from sixteen colleges representing sixteen countries and five continents, all milling around, partaking of punch and cookies, singing and trying to shake Pat Nixon's hand. Pat was as patient as a pastor at a church door on Sunday morning.

But this was one time the First Lady was not the focus of attention.

The spotlight that day was on an attractive American girl who brought some of the 1970s culture to the White House. She wore bright red pants and a see-through red crocheted top with nothing underneath.

She might as well have been topless! Needless to say, she got *top* attention not only from the male guests, the Social Aides and the White House Police, but curiously enough, even the other girls—especially those from foreign countries—showed an unusual interest in this fascinating display of decadent American charm.

If the famed Marine Corps Orchestra, which always plays for the presidential parties, played a note out of key here and there, it would not have been noticed. What I did notice was that even some of these seasoned and sophisticated musicians were too distracted by this daring young female to keep their eyes on their music sheets.

Pat Nixon was not the only White House hostess to have to cope with an exhibitionist female guest. If it was any comfort to her, this wasn't the first time there was a little nudity at a White House social gathering. Back in James Madison's day, Elizabeth Patterson Bonaparte—she had married Napoleon's brother—showed up at the White House in a transparent Grecian gown. The hostess was speechless and guests were gasping.

First Lady Elizabeth Monroe did not have the young woman thrown off the premises, nor did First Lady Pat Nixon. Pat Nixon, always the lady, acted as if there was nothing unusual about her guest, but I had to reflect on how hard it is for the White House to have a plain, simple everything's-fine-and-dandy event.

Nor was it only those of the female gender who were guilty of displaying themselves. Lyndon Johnson liked to swim in the nude at the White House, and the story goes that he didn't care who saw him. And come to think of it, an early President—I believe John Quincy Adams—was caught in the act of swimming in the nude in a tributary of the Potomac River behind the White House. The female reporter who spied him is said to have sat on the President's clothes until he gave her an interview.

More recently, President Kennedy's dogkeeper revealed that JFK did a little skinny-dipping in the White House pool in mixed company in the early 1960s. But those were private occasions. It's a lot different when it happens at a White House social function, such as the Nixon's South Lawn musicale.

Pat's lawn party, that spring day in 1972, had been a fun party but, socially speaking, it had been a flawed party. By now, I had been attending these White House events for several months and I had still to see the perfect party with a household-name guest and no glitches—the kind of party you'd expect to see on a movie screen. And finally, it happened.

June 15—State Dinner for President Luis Echeverría of Mexico

There is little to compare with the excitement of a State Dinner at the White House. Contrary to what one might expect, the visiting head of state is not always the reason everyone enjoys an evening such as this. In fact the guest of honor—in this case the President of Mexico—is seldom the driving force that creates a successful party.

It is usually the presence of some Hollywood superstar or sometimes the entertainment which electrifies the evening and helps make it a memorable event. Tonight would be a combination of both, and my greatest expectations of White House social life would be realized.

Perhaps the warm feelings of friendship were established earlier in the day when the two Presidents bear-hugged at the arrival ceremony on the South Lawn. This was a rare display of emotion for Richard Nixon, who was not known for such grandly warm gestures in public.

It may have been prompted by the fact that President Luis Echeverría did not speak any English and this was a most effective method of communication. The guests at the State Dinner exhibited the same warmhearted emotions, and the relaxed atmosphere allowed all there to really enjoy themselves. In a departure from the normal dozen or more round tables, guests ate at an E-shaped table. This may have made it easier to accommodate the interpreters which both President and Mrs. Echeverría required. It did not make it easy for the violinists who walked through the room during dessert. Unable to pass between the tables, they were obliged to circle the guests like a wild West show.

Jack Benny was so much like his television character that he could be easily found throughout the evening by simply following the sound of laughter. True to his entertainment background, he stopped to chat with the Marine Corps Orchestra, and before he left the entire group was howling with delight.

President Nixon fell into the Jack Benny style of delivery by complaining that he'd asked Jack to entertain but "Benny forgot to bring his violin." As everyone laughed, some guests applauded and one called out, "Send him back for it," and got an even bigger laugh.

The best Jack Benny story around the White House concerns his run-in with the Secret Service, who were reported to have asked him on one of his visits what he had in his violin case.

"A machine gun," said Benny.

"Good," said the Secret Serviceman. "I was afraid you had your violin."

After dinner, the entertainment had to be musical because of the language barrier. The Nixon's choice turned out to be none other than Pete Fountain, who set all twenty presidential toes to tapping.

I noticed many heads were craned as some guests got in the act and tried to follow Pete and his eight backup musicians while they played some of the best jazz music ever heard anywhere. The finale, "When the Saints Go Marching In," raised goose bumps everywhere. The guests were so charged up that if the President had gotten up and marched around the room, the entire audience would have followed like a great conga line.

Other guests included Richard Zanuck from Hollywood, Leon Hess, the oil man, astronauts Thomas Mattingly, Charles Duke and John Young—who gave an Apollo lunar mission memento to President Echeverría—and Major General Alexander Haig. I had not seen Haig since we served together in Vietnam. He was then a lieutenant colonel and I was a lieutenant in the First Infantry Division.

We laughed as we recalled the time we were both stationed at the First Brigade Headquarters camp at Phouc Vin and the officers in my battalion would visit his battalion officer's club during our short returns to base camp. His unit, the Twenty-Sixth Infantry, was known as the Blue Spaders and they had a breast pocket patch shaped and colored to match the name. Their traditional drink was a shot glass full of Drambuie, which, when lit, burned in the shape of a blue spade.

The trick was to drink it before the glass got too hot (courage), and to not spill any on oneself during that frightful gulp (skill). If the residue in the glass was still burning but no drops of liquid would pour out on the bar, one became an honorary lifetime Blue Spader. Both General Haig and I had achieved that noble wartime distinction.

Throughout our conversation, I marveled at how, in just five short years, Alexander Haig had risen with three promotions to the rank of two-star general. Later, I was in for a bigger surprise at his next promotion, when Nixon skipped him to four-star general and made him White House Chief of Staff, succeeding Haldeman.

The evening produced another historical figure from Southeast Asia. Near midnight, as one of the most junior Social Aides, I was stationed in the Diplomatic Reception Room to assist guests in retrieving their wraps and securing their rides home, when I noticed a petite Oriental lady sitting quietly alone near the door.

I introduced myself and asked if I could help. To my profound surprise, she turned out to be Mrs. Anna Chennault, the Chinese-born widow of Lieutenant General Claire Lee Chennault of Flying Tigers fame. A descendant of Robert E. Lee and Sam Houston, Chennault was also the man who conquered the "Hump" from India to China over the Himalayas—flying in supplies in World War II.

This exotic and lovely lady was given a great amount of credit for having gotten Richard Nixon elected President in 1968, beating out Hubert Humphrey, Lyndon Johnson's choice as his successor.

Even President Johnson had accused the "Dragon Lady," as some called her, of manipulating American politics. The story was that to help Humphrey, Johnson, five days before election, announced a bombing halt and gave the impression that the National Liberation Front and the South Vietnamese government would appear together to negotiate a peace in Paris.

Candidate Nixon got Anna Chennault to convince her longtime friend, President Thieu of South Vietnam, to turn down President Johnson's offer to attend the peace negotiations. If LBJ's plan had worked, it might have tipped the balance of public opinion in favor of the Democrats, but it backfired. The enthusiasm across America for the Democratic Party and its candidate, Hubert Humphrey, quickly deflated when Thieu indicated he would not attend such negotiations.

Nixon won the presidency, and now the lady whom history credited with a good part of the success sat quietly and passively on a small sofa against the wall waiting for her car. After two or three calls, her driver finally appeared and whisked her away into the night traffic. She was gone, but not before I discovered that in spite of fame, she was not haughty, but just a quiet, dignified—even reserved—lady who seemed somewhat uncomfortable in the White House atmosphere.

The senior Army Social Aide called one day and asked if I would like to work the upcoming Halloween party. The only condition was that the aides would have to arrive extra early to dress in an appropriate costume. Having worked quite a number and variety of functions already this year, I elected to pass this one on to a newer aide. I had turned down my first White House party, and it gave me a certain feeling of control and self-confidence that had eluded me to date.

As reelection time drew near, White House parties took on a political flavor, and I do not doubt but that the reception for the ethnic press scheduled for October 27, only a week before the election, had some direct bearing on the President's massive victory. This particular reception was clearly scheduled for a purpose, and the purpose was well served.

I noticed that Haldeman's staff man and sleuth with whom I exchanged the unhappy words had not been seen for several functions. I ruled out the possibility that he had dropped in and found everything perfect, because another of Bob Haldeman's boys, Larry Higby, was there and was becoming a regular. In fact, we never again saw the other fellow until the Watergate hearings, and then he was on television.

Just having a Haldeman spy around was enough to make me uncomfortable at the ethnic party. But there was someone else who also caused a certain nervousness among the aides. That was Bill Gulley, who seemed to be billed as the big bad wolf. Any time some negative or unpleasant instruction was given to us—such as, "Don't ask for a White House VIP tour pass except for your parents and immediate family" (what could we tell an old friend?)—it was blamed on Gulley.

Next to Haldeman, he was the most feared. I'd heard a lot about this guy, but he was almost never around the parties at the White House. In fact, I am unable to find a guest list on which his name appears, even though every other senior staff member shows up at least once, including the President's secretary, Rose Mary Woods.

Gulley had enormous influence because he controlled most of the perks available to the rest of the staff. He decided who got a car and driver and when, who got to use special military aircraft and special communications devices such as secure telephones, who ate in the White House mess, and who used the yacht *Sequoia*. There should be no doubt in anyone's mind that these very visible and useful status symbols were highly coveted. One's power and influence in the inner circle could be gauged by the perks available to that person.

Gulley's title was Director of the Military Office of the White House. When someone used his name to emphasize a point, people like the Social Aides listened very carefully. Anyone could take issue with his instructions, provided they were at a level which would permit them an audience for an appeal. But few people below the sub-Cabinet rank would even consider it. I think it really ticked off a lot of powerful people inside both the White House and the Pentagon that a retired Marine Corps sergeant major was entrusted by the President to wield so much power. No one could say or do anything about it but the President himself.

So as long as the Commander in Chief was happy, Bill Gulley was secure in his job. I wished I could have felt as secure in mine. There were so many opportunities for mistakes, I had a vague uneasiness that each White House party might be my last.

Christmas was coming—my first at the White House—and I wanted to enjoy the ambiance there, but I couldn't shake off that uneasy feeling, in spite of the fact that I'd been helping at the parties now for almost a year.

I concentrated my attention on the stunning White House decorations.

As if to complement the national Christmas tree on the Ellipse across the street from the South Lawn, another nineteen-foot tree was placed in the Blue Room looking out on the South Grounds and across the Mall. Because of the tree's size, it was necessary for the already overburdened staff to have the antique French chandelier removed each year for the holidays, and it was then reinstalled in January. Ornaments for this tree were now traditionally provided by some ladies' group, and it was always the most beautiful attraction in the house during the holiday season.

In the Cross Hall, the gleaming floor-to-ceiling pillars were wrapped in bands of red velvet, making them appear as gigantic candy canes. Holly branches decorated all the walls. Long flowing curtains of crimson red cloth hung from ceiling to floor. The most unusual decoration was the poinsettia trees. Wrought iron stands, wide at the bottom with terraced levels coming to a point, had dozens of potted poinsettia plants on them. In full bloom they looked like solid red seven-foot-tall Christmas trees.

In the State Dining Room on a special table was the gingerbread house provided every year by John Ficklin's very capable culinary staff. Roughly two feet tall, one and a half feet wide, and two and a half feet long, the house is entirely edible. Because of this and the fact that it was so attractive, on certain occasions it was actually necessary to place a guard beside this tempting delicacy when children were there—and even the guards could scarcely cope!

Come with me to the wackiest children's party ever. Oh, it wasn't wacky to start off with. It just ended that way. At first it was very elegant, very proper and even very diplomatic. That's what it was—the diplomatic children's party, of December 18, 1972.

With the White House elaborately decorated for the Christmas season, a number of social functions were scheduled that included a wide variety of guests. This particular party was planned expressly for children. And what better way to improve U.S. relations with other countries than to invite the offspring of the foreign diplomats?

First Lady Jacqueline Kennedy initiated this affair back in 1962, and it had become an annual event that seemed to grow each year. To assist in this project, the White House asked The Hospitality and Information Service—called THIS—of Washington to help. Designed specifically to aid Washington-based foreign diplomats, THIS was easily able to arrange for nearly a thousand children of the ambassadors and other senior embassy personnel from eighty-two nations to come for an afternoon of fun.

Due to the unusually large size of the group, the parents were asked to wait with their embassy cars or not come at all. Crowd control would be a lot easier.

Besides, we could not possibly cope or be concerned with the needs of dozens of ambassadors or their wives and still focus our attention on the children, whose party it was. Viewed from the child's standpoint, the little ones would not have to compete with grown-ups for attention.

Everything was ready for the party early, as usual, and the senior Army aide, Major Bob Banning, and I had gone outside on the walk in front of the Diplomatic Room entrance where the children would arrive. Although only a light snow had fallen the night before, Julie Nixon decided that the children would enjoy seeing a snowman on the South Lawn when they arrived. She called Joni Stevens, the secretary in the Military Office, and asked her to take care of the project.

Joni recruited a couple of people who dutifully went out with her and scraped up enough snow to construct Frosty. Arms were added when Joni got some sticks and carefully trimmed them to give the appearance of the famous Nixon two-handed V's for victory. The only concern was which way to put the face on. Eventually they elected to have him facing the Mall and the fence where all the tourists stop to look and take photographs of the Mansion.

When Major Banning and I arrived later, everyone else had

departed and left the snowman alone. At the time we did not notice the symbolism of the arms that indicated it was supposed to be the President.

Bob pointed out to me that the children would get out of their cars behind the snowman and would not be able to see his face, giving them the impression that he had none. We set about creating another image of eyes, a nose and a mouth on the back side of his head so they might enjoy it as though it were directed at the house.

That snowman was eventually seen by hundreds and probably thousands of people from outside the fence or from the door to the White House. Very few would have ever realized that it was (innocently and accidentally) a two-faced imitation of the President, except for the *Time* magazine article and photo that appeared shortly thereafter.

But as I've said, at the White House, no matter how hard one tries, one can never think of everything.

As the children arrived on this particularly cold afternoon, they were as eager as if they were at the opening of a Toys 'R' Us sale. They were in a hurry to get to the party and the food, but we insisted they pause long enough so that the domestic staff could hang all coats and jackets in the very large cloak room on the ground floor and tell each child the number of his or her coathook.

Then kids rushed up the stairs to the State Floor where the good times rolled.

Everything was great. Each detail delighted the children, whether or not they knew about Christmas, American style. The tree with many of the decorations and toys down at their eye level was almost hypnotic. The huge gingerbread house in its place of honor with every color of frosting on it and every spun-sugar window glistening, was deliciously enchanting!

Any available Social Aide watched over the treasures of the tree but it took a tough Marine aide to safeguard the gingerbread house. The White House had learned the hard way that a child's hand is faster than a Social Aide's eye. Walls had fallen in and chimneys disappeared in the past and, well, kids just have more respect for a Marine.

The "New Zoo Review" characters, looming larger than life, were superb. Everything Freddie the Frog, Charlie the Owl and Henrietta the Hippo did or said evoked a big response from this discriminating crowd, whether the kids understood the words or not.

The punch and cookies were delicious in any language. Santa was tops, handing out toys and leading the children in singing "Jingle Bells," which sounded very good and almost understandable as it was rendered in the accents of some eighty nations.

Mrs. Santa was also outstanding if you didn't mind that she looked like she'd gone on a Nutri-Slim diet and had given up her "fat and jolly" look. But even if she wasn't certifiably chubby, Pat Nixon Claus was jolly and she hugged the children and sat among them, talking and laughing and communicating in the language of love.

Suddenly it was over and the rush to the cloakroom began. Bob Banning and I preceded the first group downstairs to make sure everything went well and the young guests departed safely. We turned to the first children and asked which coats were theirs. Blank stares greeted us.

Questioned again, they responded in their native tongues. But of course we didn't understand, so after a little sign language they walked over to where they thought they saw their coats. We let them look around and split up to help more children who by now had begun to back up at the door.

This distressing and tedious experience was repeated time and time again. Other aides came to help, but the room only held a few of us, including children, at one time. How we wished a mother or two had violated the ground rules and shown up. One or two members of the domestic staff were also present but it was a little late to quiz them about the wisdom of helping the kids hang up their coats and then expecting them to remember which numbered hook they were on.

In all fairness to the house staff, no one could have anticipated the mountain of clothing these children would bring with them, but a better system had to be devised.

Eventually we discovered that fully two-thirds of the children did not speak sufficient English to communicate with us. Social Aides are required to have many skills but they are not required to be linguists. Even if they were, the few of us there could not possibly have covered all the languages represented. By the time the last child left, we had spent an hour and a half in the coat room, and we had completely lost our voices.

Not only that, when the last little guest departed, several coats remained as a reproachful reminder.

The next children's Christmas party was different. With typical military zeal and a good memory of the prior year's fiasco, we Social Aides volunteered to run the coatroom ourselves. Hundreds of diplomatic children again arrived on schedule without parents, and they were immediately sent to hang up their winter wraps. The holiday spirit was once again in great evidence and the children were very animated. One could be sure by the happy faces in this crowd that Santa Claus was coming soon.

To solve the previous year's cloakroom problems, we gave each child a stick-on nametag as they arrived, writing his or her name phonetically, country of origin and the number of the coat hook.

If children couldn't speak English, we could return their property by giving them the coats on the hook number on their tag. They could easily identify their own garments, and in the worst case, if that wasn't the correct coat hook number, it was probably the next one over.

That done, up the stairs the happy children went, and we Social Aides were feeling pretty *good* too as a result of our simple approach to solving the previous year's problem. In self-congratulation, we sobered up long enough to make sure that the guards were once again placed on the Christmas tree and the edible gingerbread house. We were all set for a quick getaway following this party.

The "Sesame Street" gang put on a terrific show. The auspicious assignment of guarding Big Bird's behind as he walked around the rooms greeting the little guests fell to lucky me. The show manager's experience had been that, given the opportunity, children would pluck Big Bird's pretty yellow feathers for souvenirs.

Kids knew enough to go for his tail feathers, where Big Bird couldn't see what they were up to. As a result I performed a pleasant clean-up detail picking up the few feathers that fell out naturally. These and some finger puppets of Oscar the Grouch—from Santa's souvenirs—were a gift to my cousin's little girls the following week.

Later, as the children were enjoying cookies and punch throughout the main floor, I couldn't help but notice that some of them were playing with their nametags. I watched uneasily as kids pulled them off and then reattached them, each time with less success than the last.

And just like their diplomatic parents as they met new friends, they all felt the urge to give a gift. What did they have that they could part with? Why, their nametags of course! Each child gladly gave up his own tag to obtain a souvenir of new friendship. It didn't take long for other children to see this happening before they too joined in.

Since we didn't speak the same language, it was impossible to explain to them that they would need their own nametag to retrieve their winter wraps. Saying no to them or shaking a head or finger in disapproval was not the answer either, because each was moving too fast to understand which of their actions was inappropriate. The last thing we needed was a diplomatic flap with a child.

At this point, it didn't really matter much that some would even exchange their new souvenirs for still newer ones. The damage had already been done by the time we noticed it.

One child was not participating in the exchange. He took all the nametags offered to him but refused to give one in return. After a while he got bored and handed me a stack about two inches thick that he had collected. Whether the children knew what they were doing wasn't clear but those little rascals were certainly having a good time, and the Social Aides were destined to pay the price.

When we got to the cloakroom, it was a disaster rivaling last year's. It appeared that only one in ten kids had the proper nametag, but we didn't know which one.

Passing out coats ended up taking longer than the whole party had. We went out and gathered the few mothers we could locate in their cars to come in and help find coats they recognized, as well as translate where possible.

Eventually all the coats were returned to the proper embassy, but it took more than a week to accomplish. One can only imagine the stories going around the diplomatic circles as to how incompetent the White House staff is when dealing with children. They had us dead to rights on that one.

10

Once in Love With Mamie

I will never forget the party that was the turning point of my White House career.

December 16, 1972—Cabinet Christmas Dinner

Washington was covered with snow the day I received a fistful of assignments to work several White House parties for the holiday season. For this dinner, the aides were to wear a very formal mess uniform with black tie. Without a visiting head of state and entourage, it looked like it would be an uneventful evening.

As the seventeen military officers began to gather in the Library on the ground floor of the mansion, it was easy to distinguish the newer aides from the old hands. The more experienced members of our group relaxed casually on the beautiful caned Duncan Phyfe furniture. The newer aides, unaccustomed to the easy familiarity one eventually acquires with the surroundings, seemed frozen in the center of the room around a large octagonal library table perched on a pedestal of three legs. They often stood as straight as the fresh cut flowers, perhaps fearing a crease in their immaculate uniforms.

Had that been me eleven months ago? I'm afraid so.

No one else concerned with the function had arrived yet. The Social Aides were always at least an hour ahead of the guests, beating even the Washington press corps to the event. One senior aide, designated in advance as the Officer-in-Charge, arrived even earlier and had been in the Social Secretary's Office with Lucy Winchester, receiving detailed instructions and last-minute changes of schedules, sequences of events and special assignments.

When he developed a complete plan of action, he would pass out specific instructions to the other aides, along with a copy of the guest list and a booklet describing the entertainment for the evening. These booklets were generally three and one half by seven inches with a beautiful textured paper cover embossed with the Presidential Seal. The insert page, held in place by a color coordinated soft cord binding with a tassel, announced the event at the White House.

It also provided a biography on the entertainer, and gave a detailed program indicating each part of the performance. Copies of the booklet were provided to each guest and they were never left behind. We each studied all this material and made notes on small cards for easy reference.

The Officer-in-Charge, an Air Force lieutenant colonel, bounded into the room and everyone fell silent.

The general outline of the evening's events was followed by some specific instructions for several of us. When he barked my name, the adrenaline started pumping. Would I mind escorting an elderly lady for the evening? It was a deceptively simple question and caution was in order.

Suddenly I felt like I was back in some general's office a year ago being grilled when I was earnestly striving to get into the White House Social Aide Program.

It was almost a conditioned reflex that I once again responded affirmatively. Of course, it wasn't entirely true but his plan was clearly set and it would be easier on everyone (especially me) if I was a volunteer.

Only then did he announce that the special guest was Mamie Eisenhower. My body shifted into adrenaline overdrive. It occurred to me that the last year of hard, dedicated work had been truly noticed and tonight's escort assignment would be my reward.

Some rapid-fire directions brought me back to my senses. I was to go up to the private residence immediately to meet Mamie and then escort her downstairs later. She would be the guest of honor, and it was my job to make sure that she did not miss a cue.

Elated, I could have floated up the stairwell to the private quarters but used the President's elevator instead, just to get familiar with the buttons. It would not do to bring her back down and wind up in the basement.

We met in the Yellow Oval Room, where hundreds of world leaders (including Mamie) had experienced countless private moments. It was absolutely stunning. Yellow was everywhere, punctuated in every significant wall space by a masterpiece of art. Two red armchairs graced one side of the fireplace. The remainder of the furniture a bright yellow which actually matched perfectly was the carpet and the walls. It looked as if perhaps when a sofa had to be reupholstered, that the walls and the carpet had to be redone also to make sure they would be in perfect harmony.

When I introduced myself to Mrs. Eisenhower, she smiled broadly, repeating my name to make sure she had it correct. She never forgot it. I had no idea what to expect, but she sensed my nervousness and immediately put me at ease with her genuine concern.

I didn't find some little old lady who needed a strong arm to lean on and be shielded from the press or other guests. What I found was an alert and perky woman who not only was very much aware of her surroundings but was actually eager to step in and exert her own special influence on them.

Her hair was done in the same style she had worn at the White House. Yes, Mamie still had those famous bangs. They suited her image perfectly. She had established her place in history and to attempt to look overly trendy would have only confused her admirers. Her dress was simple but elegant. Her eyes were very sharp and penetrating and I simply could not turn my attention from her because of the strength of her personality. For the moment, I needed more help than she did.

It took Mamie only an instant to notice the crossed rifles on my uniform. She expressed great delight at the prospect of spending the evening in the company of an Infantryman. Pleased at the compliment, I was truly surprised that she recognized military insignia, despite her background. Apparently General Eisenhower had in-stilled in her a great admiration for all soldiers and especially those who did most of the actual fighting.

Mrs. Eisenhower wanted to be briefed on the evening's plans just as if she had never been there before. This was a pleasant surprise. Some regular White House guests are more inclined to tell an aide what they want, where they will stand and what they will and won't do. Some don't tell in advance at all, and just go and do it, regardless.

As we linked arms to go downstairs, I sensed that we were depending upon each other for an enjoyable evening. Following the custom with elderly guests, I offered the use of the elevator to go downstairs. Mamie gave a confident laugh and said she wanted to use the Grand Staircase.

She said that was the way all Presidents had brought their guests down to a party, and she wanted to relive some old times. Soon it became apparent that this was her first visit to social Washington in quite a while and she intended to enjoy it to the fullest. Each step was a treat. She commented on the position of each portrait as we descended, and I was amazed at her ability to recall the wall decorations of this staircase from many years before. She was in her own element again and was relishing every minute of it.

As we entered the East Room, we were immediately surrounded by a throng of Mamie's admirers. I attempted to step back a few feet and let the mass of dignitaries greet her but she would have none of that. At my first evasive move, Mamie tightened her grip on my arm, and out of the side of her mouth, she said, "Don't leave me."

As each guest welcomed her back to Washington she would interrupt them and introduce this "fine, young Infantryman, Ste-phen Bauer." Confronted by the top men of the administration—Caspar Weinberger, George Shultz and George Bush—I knew I was turning beet red as they graciously responded when she told them how proud she was to have such an escort.

After all, what the hell could they say?

Later, in a touch of irony, she introduced me to Haldeman and I felt like saying that the man probably knew me better than I knew myself—from his spy reports.

It was a good night as far as the party was concerned. It was a bad night for the aides because H. R. Haldeman was present. The hapless aides practically quaked in their shoes when Haldeman was in attendance. He ruled the roost in the Nixon administration and was endlessly critical.

My break came when Mrs. Eisenhower finally accepted my offer to get her a drink. I retrieved a bourbon and soda from a waiter and held it for her so she could greet guests. During the next hour or so before dinner, she drank about half of it. She was later to drink half of a crème de menthe frappé after dinner. This is mentioned only to dispute stories that Mamie was a heavy user of booze. It disturbed me to hear occasional references to her "drinking problem."

History has shown that many people in and around the White House have had difficulty with alcohol, but Mamie was not one of them. As we sneaked off to the Green Room for a few minutes of rest, she explained that she suffered from Ménière's syndrome. This was a malfunctioning of the inner ear which had serious repercussions.

She lost her sense of balance frequently and sometimes suffered nausea and tinnitus. The problem had plagued her for twenty years, she said, and so did the rumors. She was very hurt that people assumed the worst of her, since she hardly ever drank at all, but she did her best to put on a good public show of indifference. That was my idea of a first-class First Lady.

We returned to the East Room just as President and Mrs. Nixon arrived. Mamie stood between them as they began receiving guests. I managed to back out of the line, much to my relief. Checking her table seating assignment in the State Dining Room, I noted the names of the people with whom she would be dining. After the last guest passed through the receiving line, the President, Mrs. Nixon, Mamie and I had to wait a few minutes while everyone else walked the wide red carpet that runs the length of Cross Hall and found their seats in the State Dining Room. Several portraits of former Presidents and First Ladies along the way cause everyone to pass slowly from one end to the other. I had time to brief Mamie on her seating arrangements.

Suddenly I realized I was standing with the President and the First Lady and I didn't know who would be joining *them* for dinner. Panic! Being in mid-sentence, I continued my explanation to Mamie as calmly as possible while my stomach churned.

After covering everything, I turned to the Nixons and apologized for not knowing who was seated at their tables. (The President and the First Lady do not ordinarily sit at the same table. This allows them to meet and entertain different guests.)

I was sure that this time I was through—I had committed a grievous error. Never mind that it was not my assigned duty. A really seasoned aide would have anticipated the situation and known. To my profound relief, the Nixons seemed unconcerned, and anyway, the Duty Aide, Lieutenant Colonel Bill Golden, appeared a few moments later with the information.

Mamie and I went ahead of the Nixons so she could be at her seat when the President entered. Protocol dictated that the President and Mrs. Nixon make an entrance, but tonight it would be different. As Mamie walked in, the room erupted into applause which continued through the Nixon's entrance. Mamie was a little embarrassed but managed a smile while quickly taking her seat, and I slipped out the side door to go down and dine with the other aides.

Following the normal format and schedule, the dinner and toasts lasted well over an hour. All the aides were back in position outside the doors when everyone emerged into the Cross Hall. The staging and seats for the evening's entertainment had been set up in the East Room while everyone was eating, and the afterdinner guests were already arriving downstairs. The President and Mrs. Nixon were obligated to stand in the hall and receive them as they arrived.

Mamie, however, was a guest and she was clearly fatigued from all the attention she had received. She wanted to get away and relax for a few minutes, so we slipped into the Green Room again to avoid the commotion out in the hall. The stream of people leaving dinner collided with those newly arrived as they exited the receiving line and all headed for the best seats in the East Room. A few wandered into the Green Room but politely kept going when they saw us talking quietly.

Mamie was still friendly, flirtatious and utterly charming. She wanted to talk and I wanted to listen. I learned a lot about her life from her but I also later discovered from a relative of Mamie's dentist just how friendly she could be. He had been Colonel Alfred E. Toye, head of the dental ward at Walter Reed, and when he showed some interest in a piece of jewelry Mamie told him about, she brought her whole collection for him to see on her next dental visit.

Very soon, Mamie and I learned we had something in common. Wistfully, almost sadly, she told me she had been a "golf widow" even at the White House, because Ike had been on his putting green instead of with her. Golf had been his life.

I told her golf had been my mother's life too. "I was a golf *orphan*," I said. "I was required to learn to play golf at the age of ten and either played or caddied every weekend thereafter for what seemed like forever."

The former First Lady laughed delightedly. I continued, "For a time there it was a toss-up whether my brother, Mark, would be born on the fairway or in the hospital."

Again, Mamie Eisenhower's tinkly laugh rang out, "And which way did it go?"

"He was born in the hospital, but just barely."

"And how is your golf today?"

"Not so good. I *very* rarely play."

"Oh, I understand," she said, and I was sure she did.

Mamie asked about my background. Explaining that I was an Army brat, I mentioned some of the many places our family had lived in but that San Antonio was the favorite and one that we enjoyed for many years. Her face beamed. She and Ike met on the parade ground there at Fort Sam Houston when he was only a second lieutenant.

It was love at first sight at the main flag pole and she was only nineteen. Her father, however, did not approve of her seeing an Army man, even if he was an officer. Before he would allow them to marry, Mr. Doud, her father, forced Ike to refuse an assignment in pilot training. Ike had just been notified to report for flight school training and he wanted the assignment very badly.

Mamie knew that Ike loved her when he agreed to give up a career of flying for her.

She laughed as she told how, as a bride, she had moved into Ike's bachelor quarters and had nowhere to put things such as Ike's field gear. Employing her creative talents, she simply dumped these items behind a piano placed diagonally in the corner. One of the few luxuries she accepted from her wealthy parents, the piano performed a very basic function by providing a suitable storage area.

To help make ends meet, Ike helped coach local football teams, for which he was paid a trifling sum. We were both laughing at Mamie's memories of their lean years when suddenly she became sad and asked me about my war experience.

Since this was a wintertime black-tie formal, I was wearing an

Army Mess Blue uniform complete with miniature medals and decorations which indicated that I had served in combat in Vietnam. Mamie asked if it had been a difficult tour and I replied that I had been particularly fortunate but many others had not been so lucky.

As an Army combat veteran's wife, she was very interested in hearing more about the war, so I described briefly the surprise and terror involved in fighting an enemy at exceptionally close range in a jungle. She had apparently given the subject considerable thought and expressed her sincere hope that it would all end very soon.

She gave me the distinct impression that she had or would discuss her feelings with President Nixon. Coincidentally, Henry Kissinger had recently returned from the Paris peace talks, having announced that peace was "at hand," and then no agreement had been reached. We spoke to him briefly earlier, but he was understandably not in a good mood and the conversation was very short.

People continued to walk through the Green Room, but Lucy Winchester, the anxious Social Secretary, came specifically to check on us and to see if she could get the star attraction to mingle with the crowd.

Mrs. Eisenhower quickly made it perfectly clear that she was happy right where she was and she was thoroughly enjoying the company of "this fine young Infantryman." I gave Lucy a sheepish grin of embarrassment and resignation and she quickly retreated from the room. Within seconds all the doors to the Green Room mysteriously closed from the outside and we were alone.

The evening became ever more unbelievable. Here I was with a wonderful lady who was already a significant part of American history. The President of the United States, the Vice President, the Cabinet, all their ladies and all the other leading Republican figures in Washington were out in the other room looking forward to talking with her. But Mamie Doud Eisenhower wanted to sit quietly with me while we talked about what military life was like in today's Army for junior officers and their wives.

Apparently, not much had changed in the intervening forty years of Army life because the Eisenhowers had very similar experiences to my family's. She had moved more than thirty times to get from Denver to Gettysburg, and they had to spend a great deal of time apart. It was not a complaint, but rather a statement of empathy for the young men and women in the service today.

Mamie wanted to know what my father had done in the Army. I said he'd been an Infantryman for thirty years and retired as a colonel in San Luis Obispo, California. She once again affirmed her admiration for the Infantry. I suddenly realized—and a later check confirmed—that my selection as the former First Lady's escort had more to do with my Infantry background than my aide performance the past year in the White House.

I was stunned by what she told me next. She said that when she and Ike lived in the White House, they invited some of the Military Aides to play cards in the private residence on Thursday evenings. They occasionally threw parties for the bachelor aides and sometimes even invited them for dinner. I had to be truthful and report that those practices were no longer observed except that we were able to eat in the Staff Mess during formal dinners.

She did not seem too impressed. We were laughing aloud as Mrs. Nixon entered the room.

I was facing the fireplace, seated on the small New England sofa, once owned by Daniel Webster, and Mrs. Eisenhower was in a chair to my left. I stood as Mrs. Nixon came straight over and sat between us on the sofa next to me. She motioned me to sit where I had been, and quickly picked up the conversation.

I was rather surprised to see Pat Nixon pull out a cigarette. Thankful for something to do with my hands, I quickly lit it for her. It was not until months later at an impromptu party at Trader Vic's Restaurant that the press discovered that Pat smoked.

She continued the conversation by telling us stories. There were several obvious punch lines and each time we were supposed to laugh she reached over and slapped me on the left thigh with the back of her right hand. I was beginning to relax and have a good time so I probably would have laughed anyway. At least this way it was certain that the laugh came on cue when the First Lady so desired.

We enjoyed ourselves for about ten minutes and were all laughing when the President entered. I got up to move away so that he could sit with Mrs. Nixon, but he asked me to please sit down again.

The President was standing across from us in front of the fire. Mrs. Eisenhower was still seated in a chair to the left of Mrs. Nixon and me. We were in front of her husband on a sofa that suddenly seemed extremely small. It crossed my mind that perhaps during the flurry of excitement, I might have inadvertently crossed the boundary of familiarity with the First Family.

It was a basic aide rule never to try to get too cozy with the First Family. But it occurred to me that I was starting to feel like part of this family—everything was so natural. Pat had taken out her compact and was checking her makeup and the President was showing that he knew what each of my medals and badges represented, adding that he was particularly proud of me and every other Vietnam veteran.

Mamie took this opportunity to repeat to the President all the extravagant things she had told others about me—and adding a few—when I was saved by the arrival of her son. John and his wife stepped into the Green Room and exchanged greetings with us but did not come to the center of the room where we were.

Instead, they stayed by the door to the East Room and were rather quiet—almost withdrawn. Very shortly an aide came to seat them for the entertainment and they quickly disappeared. Lucy Winchester entered to tell us everything was ready and we rose to leave. The President offered Mamie an arm as she got up, but I had instructions to escort her. Not wishing to correct the President but also aware of Haldeman's penchant for order even in social functions, I stepped over to Nixon's right side out of his way but still in his field of vision.

There was no doubt about it. We Social Aides were much more afraid of Haldeman than we were of the President, whom we viewed as a good guy. Nixon was a pleasure to be around—always friendly with us, interested in us and full of little quips. Haldeman could best be described as a storm cloud waiting to rain on someone's parade.

Mr. Nixon saw me and recognized my dilemma at once. He apologized and said it would be better my way as he placed Mamie's hand on my arm. It was a small gesture but perfectly typical of President Nixon. He was unfailingly courteous to all the staff and no one in the Nixon White House, with the possible exception of Pat, was more decent and civilized in dealing with us.

Perhaps he was making up for the way he knew some of his lieutenants treated subordinates. I don't know. But it was most fortunate for me that the President followed my lead, since Haldeman was like a hawk that night, replacing his own sleuths, and personally watching everything.

Mamie entered the East Room to a hearty round of applause from the afterdinner guests who had not yet seen her. Since the rooms in the White House tend to be on the cold side in the winter, I had arranged for another aide to place Mamie's white fur stole at her chair.

She had used it at dinner and now she again slipped it over her shoulders. Curiously, I had been cautioned by her to "keep an eye on it" and wondered if she were really concerned about security!

I sat beside her and the Nixons in the East Room during show time. Fred Waring and his Pennsylvanians performed beautiful Christmas music which all the guests seemed to enjoy very much. After the performance, a tired Mamie wanted to escape the guests who would surely crowd around again to visit with her. She and I and the Nixons were quickly ushered out to the hall, where they mingled for only a few necessary minutes before retiring upstairs.

I followed behind with Mamie as the Nixons walked to the elevator. Mamie took my hand and thanked me for one of the loveliest evenings she had had in a long time. She said goodnight, and stepped into the elevator with her host and hostess.

I watched the floor indicator light rise then suddenly reverse itself. The door opened and out stepped the President. He also thanked me for Mamie's wonderful evening. Then, to my complete amazement, the President of the United States threw me a salute!

Surprised beyond words, I'm sure my mouth dropped open. He said, "Thanks a lot, we really appreciate your help," and disappeared again into the elevator. I walked into the party feeling like a kid on the Fourth of July.

I arrived at the mansion the next morning in time for White House Christmas worship service and had to take a lot of ribbing from the other aides about my "date." They were clearly envious of my good fortune. When the Officer-in-Charge walked in and announced that Mamie had asked for the same escort again, it brought forth a cascade of whoops and laughs from the other aides which must have carried up to the main floor.

I was to meet Mamie in the Family Living Quarters.

Mrs. Eisenhower walked out of the Yellow Oval Room with Julie in tow. They were chatting gaily and greeted me warmly by name. For eleven months, I was just another face on the staff and now Julie actually knew my name. We headed downstairs together as Julie repeated many of the things I had shared about myself with Mrs. Eisenhower the prior evening. Obviously, they had discussed the events in considerable detail.

The Archbishop of Philadelphia, John Cardinal Krol, spoke and and the Obernkirchen Children's Choir of Germany sang Christmas hymns. There were three hundred guests crowded into the East Room to go to church with Mamie.

There was one more surprise for me. Mamie pulled a letter out of her handbag and gave it to me. She wanted to thank me formally for the previous evening with a special remembrance of her. I was speechless. Many guests had enjoyed their evenings at the White House enough to write and thank the President and they occasionally included very favorable references to the Social Aides. To the best of my knowledge, no one had ever written to an aide.

Mrs. Eisenhower next visited the White House for Nixon's inauguration on January 20, 1973, but I could not attend any of the functions as originally scheduled because my unit was called out on alert at the last minute due to war-protest demonstrations. It was a compliment to find out later that she had asked for me as an escort.

I've thought a lot about Mamie since that encounter. Everyone imagines from time to time what it would be like to change places with someone famous and to perhaps have a significant place in history. Mamie was quite an amazing lady, but in her shoes, one would also have to suffer jealous insults from those who envied her. So being a part of history, I was finding out, was not a bed of roses.

All I know is that her visit changed my whole attitude. From that moment on, I was at ease in the White House—and anyplace else.

11

My Two Worlds

$\mathcal{A}$s I left my Army unit each time I was called to attend a White House function, it felt as though I was passing into another world. While my lieutenants continued the sobering task of burying servicemen in Arlington National Cemetery, I got all scrubbed up and went downtown to have tea with the President's wife. Or to personally introduce a hundred guests or more to the President.

Actually, I never knew exactly what I would be assigned to do until I got there.

It was a Hollywood touch that as a rifle company commander in the Third Infantry, I had an orderly—a specialist fourth class—who took care of my military wardrobe. But he was a necessity because we changed several times a day depending on the various ceremonies and training activities and there was often no time between functions for a key officer such as a company commander to maintain several uniforms himself and still make every required appearance.

It was a good thing that the Old Guard had so many duties. One week of funeral service and constant bombardment of family grief was all that the men could stand, and we would then be switched to a week of practicing squad and platoon tactics or map reading. Anything for a little relief.

And whatever the duty, we were dressed for it. Besides taking part in ceremonial services, guarding the Tomb of the Unknown Soldiers and providing the Salute Gun Platoon for all necessary honors—such as the arrival of a visiting head of state—the regiment is a combat infantry unit which must be prepared for a variety of emergency military situations in the D.C. area, such as an attack on the White House.

The Old Guard is even responsible for taking care of the trained horses that march along with empty saddles and boots facing backward at a presidential funeral.

I would arrive at my office at Fort Myer in Arlington before seven every morning. But the day before, I would have told my orderly, "Smith, I need a dress blue uniform for a funeral at 8:30 tomorrow morning and another one at lunch." Unless I was saved by a call from the White House, I might officiate at two or three Arlington Cemetery funerals in the morning and sometimes as many as five or six before the day was over.

The end of the day might find me getting ready for a White House party—but without the help of my orderly. He never touched my White House uniforms. I would polish and set up the brass, place all the ribbons properly, see that my white gloves were spotless, hang my gold aiguillette in precise position from my shoulder.

Nobody let an orderly do it. It's too important to leave to someone else. Even my shoes got special treatment. I would spray a little Pledge on my black patent leather shoes. Somehow they didn't seem to shine properly unless they smelled of lemons.

Even a minor case of lint was serious business, so we always used two-inch-wide masking tape rolled backward around the hand to dab it all off. It looked like an aboriginal rite with a bunch of guys standing around patting each other all over with sticky fingers. Imagine explaining that exercise to a stranger.

We were always in the limelight. Regardless of whether it was day or night and no matter where the Social Aides went, we were under bright lights and intense scrutiny. If not the scrutiny of Haldeman and his spies, or the Military Office of the White House, or the Social Secretary's staff, or the press, then the public could be counted on to examine our every action. It wasn't as if they watched for us. One would have to be certified blind not to notice Social Aides in full dress regalia.

I laughed when a girlfriend said we aides all looked like Emperor

Haile Selassie—or at least it passed as a laugh—but I had to admit it was a reasonable comparison, and it hurt. However, the parties were so exciting, any sacrifice was worth it.

But in spite of how hard we tried to look perfect and be perfect, not all White House parties were perfect. Things happened. Even when the President entertained important guests away from the White House, untoward things happened. I can remember very well the visit of Soviet Premier Leonid Brezhnev in the spring of 1973.

When the Soviet head of state visited, he was treated to a very special tour of the United States, which included stops at Camp David and the Western White House at San Clemente. Eyewitness reports in both locations reveal that the Soviet leader had some basically human characteristics.

What we learned was that for all his criticism of western decadence and life-styles, he was apparently not reluctant to join in when the opportunity presented itself. Brezhnev traveled in his own aircraft complete with staff and stewardesses. At Camp David, the Russians were put two to a cabin, with the notable exception of one particular stewardess. There was a nonnegotiable demand that she have her own cottage. After dark the first evening, two KGB agents were seen escorting her to the Soviet Premier's quarters.

When the Brezhnev group went to Nixon's summer home at San Clemente on June 22, similar sleeping arrangement demands were made for the stewardess. As the old saying goes, the dirt hit the fan.

Brezhnev was staying in Tricia's room just down the hall from the Nixon's bedroom. Mrs. Nixon came out unexpectedly and as she turned up the hall saw two agents again escorting the stewardess toward the Premier's bedroom. Pat beat a hasty retreat until they passed and then went the other way.

That version was recounted by a male staffer, some years later. But I have no doubt this incident occurred, because I got a similar report from a young lady on the White House staff. She dated one of the Secret Service agents who was on duty in the Nixon's bedroom area. Her friend said that at about 6:00 A.M., Mrs. Nixon came out of the bedroom on her way to the small kitchen area for juice or coffee. At that moment, both the Secret Service agent and the First Lady saw several—not just one—Aeroflot stewardesses come out of Brezhnev's room and head down the hall.

Whichever account is more accurate, it seems quite obvious that the Soviet Premier was no more self-disciplined than the bourgeois westerner he often criticized.

As my sources told it to me, Brezhnev was not the only visiting Russian with a roving eye. The White House staff which normally traveled with the President was accustomed to using the San Clemente Inn as a temporary headquarters while in California. It was the closest, most convenient spot short of being in the main compound itself. One of the young female staffers told me what happened when Brezhnev and his entourage visited the Western White House.

Everyone was booked two in a room, including the Russians. This was done routinely for reasons of economy and efficiency as well as because there were only a limited number of rooms available in the inn.

My lady friend had already checked in with her usual female roommate on these junkets, and they were half unpacked when the call came. The Russians did not want two in a room. Several in their delegation insisted that they should have their own private lodging.

It was obvious that the Soviet staffers were all charged up and had high hopes of finding a willing California girl to entertain for the evening. So, privacy would be essential because they only had a limited amount of time before they had to return to Russia. The Soviet Premier was their leader in every respect and they were apparently only following his example.

The demands of the Russians were met, but no one is sure who approved them. Nevertheless, my friend and the other lady were instructed to pack up and move out to the next-best lodging area. The fact that this happened to be several miles away caused these two considerable grief. When their participation in planning or decision making was required, even at odd hours of the day and evening, they would have to travel an extra distance to get there.

Annoyed at the reason for their inconvenience, the ladies decided to strike back as best they could. Recalling college days, they pulled the beds apart and then remade them with only one sheet. The single sheet started at the top, went half way down the bed and then doubled back to the head to look like the top sheet folded back. With a blanket and a bedspread everything looked normal, but only a midget could sleep comfortably in a short-sheeted bed, and none of the Russians qualified.

Next the two took their cans of hair spray into the bathroom. Wash cloths and towels of all shapes and sizes were laid out but the ladies felt that the foreigners might not feel comfortable with all the American water and fabric softener products. They proceeded to hair spray all the towels stiff as boards to give them a distinctive feeling of being at home in Russia.

In the continuing spirit of a frugal staff within the Nixon White House, these ladies traveled with transparent plastic wrap so they could keep some leftovers around. This provided the means for the most unique trick of all. Returning to the bathroom, they carefully wrapped the entire top of the toilet in perfectly clear plastic. When the Russian staffers arrived, any liquid that might be poured into the bowl would splash off in all directions.

Everything carefully unpacked was thrown unceremoniously into suitcases and they hurriedly left the room, anxious at that point to get out of the area. Let the Communists enjoy a little decadent American humor. If they still had the inclination to chase girls, they would at least go a little slower.

At the White House, problems were unavoidable. It would take a soothsayer to predict who would be involved in the next one. Still, a glitch here and a glitch there helped to keep us on our toes.

It was soon after the Brezhnev visit that I was assigned to damage control at a State dinner for the Shah of Iran. But it wasn't the Shah or his beautiful wife, the Empress Farah, who caused the White House concern, it was our chief entertainer, the romantic ballad singer Tony Martin.

Before the entertainment began, Martin was in the Blue Room waiting to sing while the afterdinner guests arrived. Several of us were alerted to a special requirement from the Social Secretary. "Don't let Tony Martin have another drink!"

We went in to distract him and keep him busy until he went on, but he repeatedly asked for another drink. It was clear that he didn't need another one before going onstage. A promise that a waiter was coming stalled him for a while. Annoyed, he pressed the issue rather insistently, so I agreed to get one for him.

There was nothing else I could do. I gave specific instructions to the bartender and finally returned with something any nondrinker could have handled. With a couple of drops of alcohol floating on top of a tall glass of liquid, the drink hopefully would taste reasonably good on the first sip. He took a drink, looked at the glass and said nothing. It seemed like a good idea for me to disappear then so someone else would have to explain the second sip.

Teamwork did it and eventually, we were saved by the curtain call.

And he was saved by the delay technique.

During the East Room entertainment, Tony's singing was great. No one would have suspected that he had had a lot to drink. The audience loved him. But between songs he gave himself away when he tried to be funny. He didn't get much response and I think we were all thankful that he wasn't asked to do a comic act.

Tony Martin had been a guest at the White House a few months earlier when the guest of honor was West German Chancellor Willy Brandt. On that occasion he had not been the entertainer, but a perfect guest escorting the most popular woman of the evening, his wife, dancer Cyd Charisse, an utterly charming and beautifully slim lady.

No, that night it was actress Mamie Van Doren who caused an incident of sorts. Naturally, when we aides saw the ravishing Mamie arrive in what could best be described as a super-revealing dress and radiating pep and good cheer, we were not surprised that Henry Kissinger was paired with her for dinner.

Some of us hoped we would get a chance to chat with the voluptuous lady, but Washington's top bachelor was monopolizing her.

After dinner, Henry left Miss Van Doren alone in the Cross Hall for a few minutes. Seeing her by herself, one of the Army Aides made a beeline over to talk with her and within two minutes, he was red as a beet. We couldn't hear what she whispered in his ear, but it embarrassed this combat-tested infantry officer to the extent that he disappeared for the evening shortly thereafter—and alone.

Asked later what had transpired, he refused to tell. Though we tried to break him down, we failed and it remains one of the evening's little mysteries.

On the night of the Iranian State Dinner, besides Tony Martin, our attention was focused on the ever-present Kissinger.

Kissinger was not a handsome man, but he had personality and bounce. He always had some little quip or story to tell and, I swear, he must have conducted half his business in the receiving line because he never stood still. He was here, he was there, buttonholing people—especially those with whom the President had some business at the time.

And yet, somehow, he managed also to bring smiles to women's faces at the parties with his flattering attention and sweet talk. This night was no exception. "Henry the Kiss," as Nixon's National Security Advisor was euphoniously referred to behind his back, especially by the ladies of the press, was in high clover. He was paired with Christina Ford, one of the most beautiful and sexy women to come to the White House. It was said that President Nixon got a big kick out of seeing to it that his then-bachelor aide was always seated beside the most dazzling female in the State Dining Room.

Nixon liked to tease Kissinger about his women and part of the joke, according to White House scuttlebutt, was to place him next to temptation. This night, Christina was so stunning when she walked in with her husband, Henry Ford II, that an aide commented, "Here comes Kissinger's dinner partner."

He was right, of course.

The two reigning beauties of the party, Christina Ford and Empress Farah, looked so much alike in physical appearance, hairstyle and dress that they could have been sisters. And they seemed to be vying with each other in the matter of ornamentation.

The Empress Farah had chosen well from her vast collection of jewelry and was draped with a spectacular necklace. But Christina was one up on her and won the sparkle contest. She had an even greater number of gorgeous gems draped around her neck—and with Christina's plunging neckline, there was more room to display it.

I cannot say whether Kissinger expressed the desire or whether President Nixon actually tipped the social staff off, but somehow he was always sitting next to beautiful women at White House dinners, and an inordinate number of those dinner partners had low-cut dresses.

If not responsible directly for the presence of the dazzlers at his table, Henry certainly did nothing to deter this effort on his behalf. And those ladies who couldn't sit next to him were waiting for him after dinner was over.

I remember after one dinner when press people complained to me that they couldn't get near Henry to ask a question because of all the female admirers swarming around him. When asked privately, some of my female friends confessed that they had a strong attraction to him but it was more of the appeal of a powerful intellect rather than the traditional Hollywood good looks variety. Whatever the reason, the result was the same.

Before the year was over, Kissinger's life-style had changed by virtue of his becoming Secretary of State. No longer could he simply be paired with the most sultry or beautiful woman in the room. I see by my log, for example, that on December 4, 1973, at the State Dinner for the President and Mrs. Ceausescu of Romania, Henry sat with that country's First Lady and the Romanian Ambassador's wife.

Not that they weren't attractive—they just weren't his usual movie star or fashion pacesetter. Afterward someone dared ask Kissinger what he had found to talk about with these ladies and with a twinkle in his eye, he said, "We talked about Count Dracula, who was also a Romanian, and I learned some things."

Marriage finally put the crimp on Henry's style and I recall more than one White House party where Kissinger was complaining plaintively that nobody paid any attention to him anymore—"They want to talk to my wife."

Nancy Maginnes, the lucky woman who finally captured him, was reputed to be as brainy as he, and worked for the Rockefellers. The wedding took place March 30, 1974, when Watergate overshadowed Henry's love life as a sub-rosa topic of conversation at White House parties.

When tragedy strikes someone with whom we aides have come in close contact at the White House, we feel a special sadness. I remember when King Hussein of Jordan arrived with great fanfare for a State Dinner on February 6, 1973, bringing his bride.

The King had divorced Princess Muna and had only recently married Queen Alia. It was her first official visit to Washington and she was a big hit. Everyone was very impressed with her beauty, poise and charm. An old friend of her father at the United Nations, George Bush, who was then, I believe, chairman of the Republican National Committee, made her feel much more at home this evening with his genuine interest and his knowledge of her country.

The next year would find Bush more deeply involved in the Eastern world, when he became Chief of the U.S. Liaison Office of Peking, the People's Republic of China.

Several years later, Queen Alia was killed in a helicopter crash and

I felt as badly about it as if it had happened to someone in my hometown. I was surprised again—but this time happily—when Hussein married an American girl, Lisa Halaby, the daughter of Najeeb Halaby, former Pan Am president and then head of the FAA. Lisa became Queen Nour. She, too, eventually came to the White House, but by then I was no longer a Social Aide.

Relatives have given more than one President cause for concern and even embarrassment. It cast an aspersion on FDR, for example, when his son Elliott was accused of ordering a low-ranking military man to be bumped from an airplane during World War II to make room for his (Elliott's) dog, Blaze.

Such a thing could never happen with the Nixon daughters, who were among the most considerate and best-behaved girls I have known.

However, though the Nixon children were ideal, the President did seem to have trouble with other relatives and not all in-laws of the family were well mannered.

I recall when the White House press was lying in wait for the President's brother, Donald Nixon, because there was a rumor that the White House Secret Service had wiretapped his phone. Donald did not show up for the State Dinner to which he had been invited, and later Haldeman revealed that President Nixon had indeed ordered the taps to keep track of his brother's activities.

The in-law trouble involved Tricia Nixon Cox's new sister-in-law and presented me with my first serious problem with a guest. It was at the time of Nixon's second inaugural and all the family had gathered for the inauguration ceremony. On January 21, a special party was given at the White House for them.

The highlight of the party was to be a family hurrah for the man who had scored a landslide election victory. All the guests understood that, and what was expected of them, and all cooperated with staging it at the scheduled time.

Only Tricia's sister-in-law seemed determined to be a spoilsport. The moment approached when the Nixons would make their entrance into the State Dining Room and we Social Aides were signaled to gather all the guests for a unified family cheer. Everyone responded to our request to join the assembly and each individual was genuinely pleased that he or she had not been overlooked, with the notable exception of Ed Cox's sister.

I had the responsibility of gathering people from the Red Room, where Ms. Cox was talking to a group of four or five people. Approaching them quietly, I stopped and waited patiently within her field of vision for her to acknowledge that I had something to say.

It is reasonable to assume that under any circumstance, no interruption of a guest would ever occur unless it was very important, but the presence of a uniformed member of the staff was not enough for her to stop before she had made her rather lengthy point.

When she finally did pause and look at me, I announced that everyone was wanted in the next room for the President's arrival, which was expected at any moment. As though she had heard nothing and I had never been there, she turned back and resumed talking to the group.

It was astonishing that anyone, let alone a guest or relative by marriage, would so cavalierly and openly ignore, if not flout, the wishes of the President of the United States. Pausing for a few moments, I considered making another appeal but decided it wasn't worth the effort.

I reported the incident immediately to Lucy Winchester and she agreed they should be left in the Red Room if they didn't care enough to cooperate.

Later, *after* the President and Mrs. Nixon had made their entrance to the cheers of everyone else, Ms. Cox and her small group walked in and joined the rest of the guests. Whether it was a result of this incident or not is unknown, but I never again saw Ed Cox's sister in the White House.

12

You Meet Everyone, but Everyone, at the White House

I thought that any star of the music or acting world, invited to entertain at the White House in front of the President of the United States, would of course be very nice, very polite and on his or her best behavior. Wrong! Some were and some weren't, and I had to learn the hard way who was nice and who wasn't.

Johnny Mathis was. Frank Sinatra wasn't.

I greatly admire the talents of Frank Sinatra. I just wish I could admire his disposition as well. There was one particular occasion where he lost his cool:

April 17—State Dinner for His Excellency Giulio Andreotti of Italy

Everyone covets an invitation to the White House and those who would be choosy want one to a State Dinner. If ever there was a night when veteran Washington socialites wished to be at a formal presidential dinner, it was tonight because word had gotten out that the entertainment was to be Old Blue Eyes himself. During the course of the evening, and unlike many of the guests who failed, I had a chance to chat with Frank Sinatra briefly in my role of friendly White House Aide.

I discovered him to be very much like the boorish character in the press accounts of his latest run-in with some unfortunate person somewhere. He didn't seem happy, wasn't willing to smile or even pretend that he was enjoying himself, and I quickly retreated to more pleasant company.

But I told myself that it was not important whether a Social Aide liked him but whether the guests did. And the word was that even the Prime Minister of Italy was looking forward to seeing the master showman perform.

And perform he did. More than half a dozen of his most famous hits really charged up the audience as it walked down memory lane. One and all were on the edge of their chairs, tapping their feet and bobbing their heads.

At the end of his act—or what everyone including the President assumed was the end—the applause was thunderous as all the guests stood to pay their respects to Sinatra. He had not sung publicly for almost two years and he had just delivered a solid performance.

Very contritely and quite unlike his normally aggressive style, Frank told everyone about his boyhood and what a privilege it was to be performing not only for the President of the United States but also the Prime Minister of Italy. He said for a kid from New Jersey who looked forward to the day he got a glimpse of the mayor, this was the greatest honor he could have. A patriotic encore of "The House I Live In" followed, and I think everyone, including me, was genuinely touched by what seemed like a new Frank Sinatra—how could I have so misjudged him!

In praising the singer, Mr. Nixon said, "Once in a while there is a moment when there's magic in the room—when a great performer, singer and entertainer is able to capture us all. Frank Sinatra did that tonight."

Sinatra was so moved by the praise that he actually stepped around the side of the bandstand with tears in his eyes. It was a touching moment, and at that point, I was convinced the man had mellowed out completely. Shortly he would demonstrate how wrong this assumption was. As the President escorted the honored guests to the door, the reporters followed Sinatra into the Green Room where I was standing. Someone asked him how he selected the songs which produced such a magical evening. His answer was anything but mellow.

"How else could I put a program together?!" he hissed with a sarcastic grin, adding a few more words of annoyance before turning away. Even the press stood stunned for a moment as he abruptly stalked out of the room in a huff. And I heard one reporter ask another—"What happened? What did we say?"

None of us aides saw Sinatra again that night.

My conception of the singer, formed over several years and based on numerous accounts, was fully confirmed that night. Frank Sinatra is a great entertainer on stage, and off stage he is a very unattractive public personality. Granted, it may be only the media that set him off in public, but in this case he was surrounded by many fans and admirers and he was also in the President's home.

He could have done himself a lot of good that night because the press was trying to praise him. I determined, if at all possible, to stay out of his way.

It set a bad precedent that at my first White House party, as mentioned previously, one of the Ray Conniff group of singers— Carol Feraci—had chosen that event to berate the President about the Vietnam War in front of more than a hundred people in the East Room. But I chose to look at this as the exception to the rule and attempted to make certain that never again would an entertainer be rude in the White House. It didn't always work.

Most *were* nice, but I recall the run-in I had with one of The Carpenters, who entertained for German Chancellor Willy Brandt. Karen Carpenter was bristling and emotional and seemed to be preoccupied with the audio equipment.

I asked if I could be of service and if she had found everything satisfactory when she checked the equipment setup. She made a sarcastic and obscene remark about what I could do to fix it, if necessary, to which of course there was no answer expected or given. Her performance and that of the group passed without incident and to substantial applause. My only regret was in not appreciating that Karen had a very serious problem.

The fact that she died not long after that at the age of thirty-two of heart failure brought on by anorexia nervosa caused me to reconsider my harsh judgment of her that night. That she did not seem to enjoy herself or the surroundings to the extent that most guests and entertainers do, became perfectly understandable.

By the time I met Johnny Mathis, I had become a bit leery of big-name stars off stage, thanks to the unpleasant encounters with Frank Sinatra and Karen Carpenter. Therefore, I made sure to approach Johnny Mathis with deliberate care when he was standing alone in the Blue Room. To my surprise he turned out to be a very warm and friendly personality. There was no self-indulgence or ego here, just a relaxed, casual guy who was himself a bit awed at being in the White House.

Though Johnny Mathis now sits on top of the music world, he was born in a basement, which may have been the reason he was chosen as the entertainer for President William Tolbert of Liberia on this night of June 5, 1973.

Tolbert, the honored guest, also had come from humble ancestry—his grandfather was an American slave freed by Abraham Lincoln's signature in 1862. At the dinner, Tolbert marveled at how far his family had come in just a few generations of freedom.

Johnny's natural curiosity about the surroundings was very much like that of the average White House tourist or visitor for an afternoon tea. He could not have been a better guest before, during or after his performance. Incidentally, he put on an absolutely splendid show for the President of Liberia.

And Johnny Mathis did not stand alone on the nice-guy list.

There was beautiful Mary Costa. What a trouper! She had sprained her back in a fall and was in such pain she was unable to come to the White House to sing on the night of the State Dinner for British Prime Minister Edward Heath, and the Army Chorus from Fort Myer filled in.

The Metropolitan Opera star, who, incidentally, was the voice of Sleeping Beauty in the Walt Disney classic, was given another chance to sing at the White House a few weeks later when Prime Minister Lee Kuan Yew of Singapore was the guest of honor.

In spite of the fact that she was still in considerable pain, Mary Costa came and performed brilliantly. She told us that she *had* to come because her mother had told her that if she didn't make it this night, she would never be asked to return.

Her mother might have been right.

I never got jaded meeting names in the news—from the names

encountered in *The New York Times* to the *National Enquirer*—and whenever time permitted, I would strike up a conversation with them. Some were exactly like they were on TV or big screen—Ozzie and Harriet were—and some were altogether different—like Frank Sinatra.

Now and then I would think of how hard it would be to recognize some of these famous people if I saw them on the street. I met Glenn Ford and Edgar Bergen at a dinner for the prime minister of Singapore. I would have pegged Ford as a nice-looking businessman and if I'd seen Bergen without his famous dummy on his knee, I'd have guessed he was a small-town banker.

Some names I saw at the White House only once. Some came so regularly they felt quite at home around the White House. I recall it was a stellar night for celebrity hunters when Prime Minister Edward Heath was the guest of honor.

Cary Grant made one of his frequent visits, and understandably he was the center of attention, wherever he went. It was mostly women who sought his attention but a few men were there as well to say hello. He was a good sport as usual, and later, when everyone sang along, his voice could be heard above the other, shyer guests.

It was almost as if he were an assistant host, helping the entertainment and encouraging others to sing out. I had the thought that it was too bad he was a movie star because he would have made a great Social Aide. He was one of the easiest guests I ever talked with—interested in everything and, miracle of miracles, even modest.

I remember the Heath dinner for another reason, as well.

This evening the aides benefited from one of the perks of working at the White House. Arriving a half hour earlier than normal, we all assembled in the East Room to pose for our annual Christmas photograph with the President and the First Lady. Every year we got two Christmas gifts from the Nixons. The first was an oversized version of their greeting card, which was sent to a very select group—close personal friends, the White House staffers and us Social Aides, among them.

Each year, the Nixons used, as their Christmas card, a different painting from among those of former Presidents which hang in the mansion. The large reproductions of the Presidents that we received were suitable for framing.

Included with the reproduction was a small plaque to be attached to the card's frame after it was mounted, giving the subject, the year of the gift, and the fact that it was from the Nixons.

The second Christmas present was the photograph of the twenty-four Social Aides with the President. The amusing thing is that the Nixons never got around to posing for our Christmas photo until the holidays were a vague memory and the large group photo did not arrive until weeks after that—sometime in March.

I was too delighted to quibble and I hurried to get the giant Christmas card greeting and the large group portrait framed and hung, since the only other thing decorating the walls of my bachelor apartment was a pair of temple rubbings from Bangkok.

This year we were having our Christmas photo session rather early—February 1.

The staff had set up small foot-stands like a choir uses to raise the back rows. This was important for the shorter aides because we were not arranged by height. The more senior the aides were, the closer they stood to the First Couple. The two most senior of our group flanked them with the position of honor next to the President.

To test everything before the Nixons arrived, we got in place and Lucy Winchester and the head of the Ushers Office, Rex Scouten, stood in for the First Couple while the photographer took a few practice shots.

These were also valued mementos because we worked so closely with these people on every event. Rex was one of the most experienced hands in the house, having begun his service there with the Secret Service in 1949. More recently, he has served as the White House Curator, and is responsible for every object in the mansion as well as the building itself.

When the President and the First Lady arrived, they each thanked us for our efforts over the past year, saying their parties could never be done without the Social Aides. It was an odd feeling because I had been around them so much for so long, it had become second nature to have them in the same room. Ordinarily, we were more or less nonchalant about their presence but this time they were there specifically to praise us and thank us for our support. Being the object of their undivided attention even for a few short minutes was a heady experience.

Incidentally, Christmas cards were a major undertaking at the White House each year. And still are.

Normal-sized Christmas cards were sent by the Nixons to around 100,000 people, including the most famous Hollywood and TV stars, sports figures and leaders of business and industry. Their list also had the names of many political contributors as well as just good friends. And some reporters and other media people who did not get large cards received regular-sized ones.

Volunteers—club women—come in droves to do the addressing. The ladies are recruited for this grueling task from organizations around the Washington area such as the various Officer's Wives Clubs and political party organizations. These ladies spend several days getting the cards addressed under close supervision from the White House Correspondence Unit in the Executive Office Building. Their reward is to be invited to a tea at the White House for a personal "thank you" from the First Lady.

And the lucky ladies get *their* reward *before* the Christmas decorations are gone.

It's difficult, if not impossible, to get a gift delivered to the President or First Lady, and the White House security involved might seem a little ridiculous until you realize this is the age of the letter bomb, the car bomb and every other kind of bomb.

It's also not easy for an enterprising eager beaver to get publicity for a gift and it's not even easy to find the right gift—something wanted or useful.

The White House has almost everything imaginable, so it seemed somewhat odd that it lacked something as common and ordinary as a record collection. Not wishing to let this newly discovered opportunity pass, the Record Industry Association of America offered to assemble and donate a suitable library. Five members got themselves appointed as commissioners by Mrs. Nixon and spent two years in preparation for this day.

"This day" refers to the day of the presentation when the group hit the jackpot with publicity and even a party in their honor. My log reads:

March 20, 1973—Record Library Reception

Having various expertise, each commission member was in charge of a particular area of music, but all shared the responsibility for selecting rock-and-roll albums. Perhaps that is the reason the Mothers of Invention made it and the Beach Boys did not.

Receiving two thousand albums took only a few minutes. The press corps and 350 guests looked on as the best possible publicity for the recording industry unfolded. The White House routinely receives all manner of gifts. Many are unplanned, but some, like these records, are announced in advance. No matter, the records were still treated like any other gift that arrives at the White House.

All presents are carefully screened by the Secret Service—this includes X-raying them when appropriate—and they are then cataloged by the White House Gift Unit. Most gifts are set aside indefinitely until someone, usually the First Lady, can take the time to go through them. Rarely does someone get the opportunity to make a presentation directly and to have it covered by the media.

In the case of the record collection the donor felt well rewarded to have a media event and the White House received an extensive library of albums along with several thousand dollars' worth of stereo equipment.

There are tricks in every trade—even for the volunteer work of the Social Aide. One is getting guests to leave when they refuse to believe the party's over.

Evening parties seldom present a problem with guests hanging around too late. The entertainment normally goes till midnight, and Presidents seldom stay very long to dance. Some of the guests are regulars and could care less about lingering at the White House and dancing. But protocol says they can't go till the President leaves.

As soon as the Chief Executive departs, several dozen couples almost rush the exit. Others follow suit, thinking it is the appropriate departure time.

But some simply rejoice that there is more room on the dance floor.

At midnight the band takes a break. Things get quiet and dull enough for ten minutes that many go home on their own. Only diehards remain for still more rounds of dancing. Eventually, very few people are left in the cavernous room, and the vast emptiness and the late hour usually drive the rest out the door.

Afternoon functions are a little different. It is still part of most people's workday, and energy levels are relatively high. Heavy hors d'oeuvres are served, but few people (except perhaps the experienced staff and Social Aides) eat enough to counteract the effects of the hard liquor served in copious quantities to whoever is interested. (This practice has apparently been carried on for a number of administrations. I always laughed at the thought of that famous radio blunder where someone referred to an administration official as "a high White Horse souse." It turned out that White Horse scotch had been replaced by 100 Pipers in the Nixon years, but the result was often the same.)

Even if the First Family has departed, some energetic guests are reluctant to go. Good food, good booze, and the chance to linger in the most famous landmark in the nation make virtually every late afternoon social event last longer than intended.

The French have an interesting way of putting guests on notice that a function is drawing to a close: they serve orange juice. The guests know that's the signal to depart. At the White House, we moved the guests with a maneuver called the "Turkey Trot." Social Aides would place themselves on the far side of the room with the guests between themselves and the doors.

Generally, no further hint would be needed. Just the line of military aides in full-dress uniforms would be sufficient to move the guests toward the door. No one had to tell them to go. Body language did it. But not always.

In some cases, getting guests moving in the right direction called for extreme measures. An aide, while chatting quietly with someone, his own back to the guests, would slowly back pedal till he bumped into one of them. When the aide turned to apologize profusely to the guest, their faces would be only inches apart, but the Social Aide would not move away. The natural reaction of the guest was to step back, not realizing he or she was moving toward the door. The aides then switched positions so that another close encounter or accidental bump, if one was required, would be with someone new.

Soon enough, part of the room would be completely cleared, and the other part crowded with guests who had been herded like turkeys toward the door. The sections were separated by a line of military uniforms trying not to look like a line of military uniforms.

Other aides or doormen would occasionally close the very large wooden doors to the side rooms with an accidental crash. Questions would immediately arise as to whether or not it was time to go. The

Social Aides always assured the guests they were welcome to stay longer while all their senses and some of the other guests said, "Go before your ride leaves you!"

Another trick we had to learn was how to get guests to dance with each other.

Wallflower patrol was a delicate game. The object was to see how to get the shy or inhibited guests to enjoy themselves without being too pushy. One maneuver that worked well but took some planning went like this. A male and female aide would each find a bored looking guest and simultaneously ask them to dance.

After a few moments either one or both of the aides would confide to their dance partner that they had promised to dance with the other aide and would they mind changing partners? Of course the guests always agreed and when the switch was made, the aides paired the guests off with each other and then danced off together to the other side of the room to find some more shy or inhibited guests.

Sometimes, the entertainer can inadvertently cause embarrassment to the First Lady, as happened when British Prime Minister Heath came to dinner. The Army Chorus of Fort Myer was in the middle of a Three Dog Night rock version of "Joy to the World." The major contribution for this song was from one of the soloists.

As this fellow sang, with ardor, he moved along the front row from one member of the audience to another, each time making eye contact for a few beats of the music. This is a common technique used by all stage performers because it personalizes the presentation for individual members of the audience. Unfortunately, the Nixons never sat for the rehearsal, and by some accident the singer trained his eyes on Mrs. Nixon no more than five feet in front of him when he sang "and I'm going to make sweet love to you."

I could feel the tension around me as others were clearly as uncomfortable as the First Lady was and squirmed in their seats. Pat Nixon remained as cool and unruffled as always, but for a moment or two, she did stop smiling.

I could have told the singer he had the wrong technique or the wrong First Lady for this intimate nightclub-style approach.

Still another problem, very occasionally, is that the White House has invited too many people. President Nixon himself once acknowledged that formal dinners were "overbooked"—because there always were a few guests who weren't able to accept. This brought the number of attendees down to the maximum that the State Dining Room could hold.

But one night the theory backfired and caused an emergency. Everyone accepted. That was March 1, 1973, when it seemed everyone wanted to dine with Prime Minister Golda Meir. What to do? The emergency was met by moving furniture out of the Red Room and putting tables in there.

The evening was a brilliant success. Henry Kissinger, who had not attended many parties for some time due to the Paris peace talks, was in rare form, and the entertainment the President had chosen was outstanding.

Van Cliburn put on a masterful performance. He might not have done so well except for the fact that he refused to eat with the rest of the guests as many performers do. Instead, he practiced downstairs for a full hour before the show. And he didn't just rehearse on any old White House piano.

Any musical artist will tell you that using one's own instrument is a tremendous source of self-confidence even if the substitute offered is of better quality. Because of this preference, pianists have a particular problem in this regard—they're not Superman.

But this did not stop Van Cliburn. He shipped his own piano down from New York just for the occasion when he discovered that the one at the White House was about to undergo substantial repair. This was not as unusual as it might appear. Many artists went to extraordinary lengths for a twenty-minute performance at the White House.

There is no more favorable publicity than a good review from the President of the United States. It matters not in the slightest that the performer receives no pay for an appearance. Indeed, who might not be willing to pay for the privilege of being there? Publicity like that is just not available at any price.

It is probably thanks to Chuck Robb that the White House did not frown on Social Aides discretely dating persons they met at the White House.

Marine Captain Charles Robb probably has had the highest profile of any Social Aide. Falling in love with and marrying the daughter of the incumbent President quickly elevated him to a status quite a bit above the other aides as well as all the other staff members. A unique situation perhaps, but the experience shows what can happen when carefully selected young officers are placed in dazzling uniforms among the social and political elite of Washington. Virtually any scenario is possible under the circumstances.

And there are several versions of the story of how Robb happened to fall in love with Lynda Bird Johnson, the elder daughter of LBJ.

This much can be safely said—before Robb, Lynda Bird had been dating an Army captain. He had been in a class ahead of me at Texas A&M and by his senior year had achieved the highest position in the thirty-two-hundred member corps of cadets as the corps commander.

Unconfirmed, however, are the many stories told by Aggies about how the White House had the captain flown from various military assignments to a particular social function in Texas or Washington to escort the President's daughter.

Probably it was the President who finally had him assigned to the White House as a Military Aide. Not too long after his arrival, however, he met another girl there and his attraction to Lynda Bird waned.

Lynda Bird was suddenly trapped in the lonely White House, continuously under the scrutiny of dozens of reporters. She no longer had a steady date. It didn't help that Lynda's younger sister was the life of the party, whose uninhibited dancing earned her the nickname of "Watusi Luci" and who beat her big sister to the altar—with an East Room wedding reception, August 6, 1966.

The situation was even more embarrassing for someone in Lynda's position since it could be assumed that everyone knew it was not a circumstance she desired, but rather one that the captain had created.

Like so many other "private" subjects in the house, some people really knew what was going on and others only thought they knew. However, enough of these tales eventually came true that the White House watchers were willing to overlook the minor inconsistencies.

Who came to lonely Lynda Bird's rescue? The Social Aides of course, but it wasn't by accident or their own design. The story goes that, needing an escort for a trip to Rehoboth Beach, Delaware, Lynda Bird asked the White House Military Office to send up the album of pictures of all the Social Aides. She picked out Chuck Robb as her escort that day, and boom, it spelled romance.

Eventually came the White House wedding—December 9, 1967. It is clear now that Lynda Bird got the pick of the litter among the group of aides because Chuck went on to be both the governor of Virginia and U.S. Senator from the state.

13

In the Creeping, Crawling Days of Watergate

$\mathcal{T}$he sadness of Watergate began with such little things. I look back and I think if this and if that, it never would have happened. If he hadn't been surrounded by the wrong people. If he hadn't tried to be so loyal to various men on his staff. If he hadn't been so desperate to be reelected by a landslide. If he'd cleaned house among his staff sooner. If he hadn't let it escalate. If he had come forward early and apologized to the people...

First, the break-ins...

May 29, 1972

At 1:30 A.M., the first of two Watergate break-ins began at the headquarters of the Democratic National Committee. Several telephone taps were placed and numerous documents were photographed. The intruders escaped without incident.

They were not street-gang types or international spies. They were your everyday ordinary office types who worked for CRP—affectionately referred to as CREEP—the Committee to Reelect the President.

All they wanted was to see what Democrats were up to, what

damaging material the Dems might have that would hurt the campaign to reelect Nixon. Or so they said in justification.

Their boldness may have been related to the fact that, only days earlier, J. Edgar Hoover was found dead at home in his bed. Many stories suggest that with his passing went a wealth of confidential and very embarrassing information on many of Washington's political elite. They were *gung ho* to help their man.

The very fact that Hoover was gone must have given people like G. Gordon Liddy, who worked for him in the FBI at one time, and was now the general counsel to CREEP, a feeling of new freedom to pursue the same type of background intelligence data on the Democratic opposition. Liddy took the credit for planning the Watergate break-in.

Success made CREEP bolder.

June 17, 1972

Because the listening devices or "bugs" placed in the offices of the Democratic National Committee on May 29 were not working as planned, the team again entered the Watergate complex to place new listening devices and to photograph additional documents.

Entering through the stairwell from the parking garage, James McCord from CREEP placed a piece of tape over the lock on the door to each floor to permit quick opening if a hasty retreat became necessary. The tape was placed horizontally, leaving a small piece showing on either side when the door was shut. Had it been applied vertically, we probably would never have heard of Watergate.

A security guard, Frank Wills, noticed the tape on the ground floor door. Thinking the cleaning crews were once again taking shortcuts and defeating the security system to facilitate repeated entries, he merely pulled the tape off and forgot about it. The cleaning crews were supposed to use their keys.

McCord approached the door a short while later and noticed the tape was gone. After having his expert pick the lock again, he replaced the tape in the same horizontal manner. Frank Wills came by again, saw the tape had been replaced, and decided to call the police.

During the next twenty-six months, the Nixon White House would make a very great effort at conducting business as usual. In the social arena, they would be largely successful, until they virtually ceased such activity altogether just a few weeks before the President's resignation.

Newspapers in general used only small stories about the Watergate break-ins—all except the *Washington Post*. The *Post* gave it a large amount of space and hammered away at it from day to day. The word was that Nixon was much annoyed with the *Post*, causing the first escalation.

At a party on December 15, *Washington Post* reporter Dorothy McCardle was excluded from covering the White House event. Such parties are covered by a small group of reporters known as a pool and the *Post* is always represented.

McCardle wrote her story for her paper from materials she got from her colleagues. The next two White House events on the 16th and 17th also were covered by pools, with Dorothy McCardle excluded.

Washington correspondent Helen Thomas of UPI then ran a national story reporting that the *Washington Post* had been cut off from covering White House social functions. She linked the event to the *Post's* heavy coverage of the Watergate break-in in which the Democratic National Committee headquarters had been bugged. Nixon's Press Secretary, Ron Ziegler, refused to comment on the reason for the exclusion of the veteran social reporter for the *Post* or the conclusions drawn by Helen Thomas.

At the next opportunity, the reporters took the issue to the highest level, questioning Mrs. Nixon repeatedly on the subject. Pat was forced to declare, "I don't have anything to do with pools. I'm not an ugly person. I don't discriminate against anybody. There's nobody in the world I dislike."

New guidance for the Social Aides was issued shortly and we took on a whole new attitude in dealing with the press. Our efforts to protect the First Family from being badgered by the media were redoubled. Because of or in spite of Watergate, it would never be the same again.

I did not realize that I was rubbing elbows with men who would be deeply involved in Watergate matters and only later could I see that I had served at the White House during a turbulent period of history.

February 2, 1973—Swearing-In Ceremony

Five cabinet and fifteen high-level administration figures and their friends gathered for this relatively lengthy event. Chief Justice Warren Burger administered all twenty oaths, one at a time, despite lingering flu symptoms. What President Nixon referred to as his "peace cabinet" included the first woman counselor to the President, Anne L. Armstrong. Others participating who have resurfaced repeatedly over the years were Elliot Richardson, James Schlesinger, William Simon, Frank Carlucci, William Casey and Donald Rumsfeld.

Notable among this group being sworn in was Egil Krogh, the ex-Plumber who engineered the break-in of Dr. Lewis Fielding's office in California in search of anything of value in his files on his patient, Daniel Ellsberg.

Krogh eventually was to spend six months in prison for this escapade which did not produce any tangible results. In the meantime, he needed a job after the Plumbers were disbanded so he got himself appointed as an Undersecretary of Transportation.

April 30, 1973

President Nixon went on national television to accept full responsibility for Watergate. Haldeman, Ehrlichman and Kleindienst had just resigned and John Dean was fired. Gordon Strachan, Haldeman's spy at previous parties, had been moved out of the White House some time earlier—perhaps to put some distance between those most likely to cause embarrassment to the administration and the President.

Now he had resigned from his position at the U.S. Information Agency. His last official ties with the White House were finally eliminated. Larry Higby, who also played sleuth for Haldeman at a number of social functions, had not been to any parties for quite a while. Apparently he had been spending an unusual amount of time helping Haldeman with the Watergate cover-up and the two decided to just let us do the best we could. Somehow we managed.

The next day, West German Chancellor Willy Brandt was scheduled to be guest of honor at a State Dinner, and it was an embarrassing situation. Such things are planned far in advance and cannot be cancelled for any reason short of death or calamity.

The chancellor himself did the diplomatic thing after becoming aware of the planned announcement of four major administration resignations the day before the arrival ceremony. He simply arranged to be on a fishing trip in Maryland that evening while all the unpleasantness was going on.

Then, at the dinner, in his formal afterdinner toast to the President, Brandt did make reference to his host's "serious problems of a domestic nature," without saying the word Watergate.

In fact, nobody used the "W" word, but the guests did something else.

Sensing the President could use a boost to his morale, those seated in the East Room for the entertainment gave him and Pat a standing ovation when the First Couple entered.

But the tide could not be stemmed. By May 10, just ten days later, the toll of Watergate departures from the White House had reached eighteen, as Egil Krogh resigned his post of Undersecretary of Transportation.

Unaffected by all this were the White House Military Office and the Social Secretary's staff—and of course, we twenty-four Social Aides. Parties continued as usual, but several of the old familiar faces were gone. The President probably missed them, but the social staff didn't. It was a relief no longer having to run into Gordon Strachan at White House parties—the chap who had been such an unnerving presence at one of my first functions.

But suddenly we had a new problem as the Vice President, Spiro Agnew, came under siege. We aides were expected to help him and his wife, Judy, get through, as best they could, White House functions at which his presence was mandatory. Such a party was the State Dinner on September 18, 1973, for Prime Minister Bhutto of Pakistan.

The full resources of the social staff would be required this night to keep the press away from the Vice President. We would not be entirely successful but we did minimize the potential damage.

The Social Aides are frequently reminded, in crucial times, not to let the press corner and badger a member of the First Family or a guest. With dozens of reporters wandering around during a major function, it is absolutely impossible to prevent them from asking questions of any one person, let alone a select group of three or four.

No one really suggested that a question or two was unacceptable. What the staff desperately wanted to sidestep was a scene where a family member or distinguished guest would be trapped with no graceful exit when he or she wished to avoid answering a barrage of questions or to cut short a controversial conversation that would probably be in most newspapers the following day.

Our job was not to hinder the press but to extricate those buttonholed persons from an uncomfortable situation. It was a delicate line to walk between freedom of the press and the rights of an individual.

Getting out of an awkward discussion required finesse. The actual process of moving from one portion of the evening to another can terminate any conversation. It is always possible to be "behind schedule" and have to move on. Since only the staff knows the real schedule, it always was a convenient excuse. The careers of staff members depend on their taking good care of the boss, so everyone accepts it at face value when an aide says, "We must go."

This approach has tactical applications everywhere, and we used it quite frequently at all social functions. Anytime anyone looked trapped, no matter who he or she was, we aides came to the rescue with an invocation of "the schedule" or "you're needed" somewhere else.

It is important that the person being saved really want to be. I misjudged one situation and rescued the Social Secretary from a perfectly innocent conversation. Fortunately, Lucy appreciated the thought even if my conclusions about the tenseness of the discussion were wrong. She promptly turned around and went back to finish the dialogue I had interrupted.

This evening we would apply all our skills in saving the Vice President and Mrs. Agnew. The papers had been speculating that Agnew would resign rather than face court charges of financial malfeasance involving tax evasion on money received from Maryland contractors while he was still governor of the state.

The press was waiting, but upon the Agnews' arrival at the North Portico a few minutes ahead of the honored guests, the Vice President and his wife nearly ran to get inside and upstairs past numerous reporters. Later, instead of preceding the heads of state down the Grand Staircase and stopping to witness their descent, they went straight to the East Room for the receiving line and left behind several dozen reporters who at that point had to remain within the velvet rope barrier till after everyone was seated for dinner.

Following dinner, we closed off the Blue and Green Rooms to everyone but the principals—including the Agnews—and the honored guests. To my knowledge this was never done before or since, but it effectively prevented anyone from probing the now-defensive Vice President.

While this select group was relaxing in privacy, the remainder of the guests were being seated for the entertainment in the East Room. A quick step through the Green Room doors and up the aisle was all that was necessary to get the Vice President in position for the entertainment.

It was a great plan except for one thing—no one had been designated to clear the path. Consequently, what could go wrong did. The Agnews stepped out and ran straight into a reporter who got a couple of good questions off to both of them. When Agnew flatly refused to comment on "stories from undisclosed sources," the reporter left the two alone. I'm sure the Vice President cussed the White House staff for that mistake, and it was deserved.

But days later, he was again facing the White House news gang— this time at a State Dinner for Prime Minister Norman Eric Kirk of New Zealand. Using a different approach, protocol was again changed and the Agnews entered the East Room to the booming announcement over the public address system, "Ladies and gentlemen, the Vice President of the United States and Mrs. Agnew."

The partisan crowd reacted in unison, and the roar of applause in support of the beleaguered Mr. Agnew actually drowned out the announced arrival of the new Secretary of State, Henry Kissinger.

In a rather strange and abrupt turn of events, it was not considered necessary for the Social Aides to run interference for Agnew. Somehow he had established a story that deflected further questioning from the media. Nevertheless, many of us continued to keep an eye on him, but no one had to rescue him this time.

Other events also helped to make the evening different. There was no scheduled entertainment. Guests would simply go out and dance after dinner. Without a scheduled entertainment program to introduce, President Nixon had time to take Pat out on the dance floor for a turn. No one had seen them dance in years and everyone was delighted at the impromptu performance. They danced quite well together in spite of the obvious lack of public practice, and the other guests gave them a solid round of applause.

In a few more weeks, there was no more need for charades at the White House on Agnew's account—the Vice President had resigned, October 10, 1973, pleading *nolo contendere*. As new Vice President, Nixon chose the House Minority Leader, Gerald Ford, who was a popular guest and known as "Mr. Nice Guy."

By a strange set of circumstances, I had inadvertently become aware of taping going on in the White House. I was simply doing a good deed. I was certainly not playing detective. I had enough problems as Announcing Aide, responsible for heralding everyone's arrival over the public address system.

I remember how carefully my version of the pronunciation of each name was rehearsed, double-checked and approved well in advance by Lucy Winchester. The announcements proceeded without a hitch but would cause considerable distress to my nervous system before they were over.

One hundred people reading some honored guest's name will come up with at least one hundred different versions. In this business though, only one pronunciation is acceptable; at the White House it should sound as much as possible as the person would say it himself.

For many announcers there was a moderate level of nervousness as each individual's name was called. When the President and the honored guest arrived, I would feel a very real danger. The possibility of tripping over one's own tongue or even being stricken with temporary amnesia was significant.

To prevent social or diplomatic blunders, the full text of what is to be said as the dignitaries arrive is written out on a card. Names like Houphouët-Boigny are done in phonetics, but even those are subject to interpretation.

I felt amply rewarded those nights because I got to meet and hear some of the great entertainers such as Johnny Mathis and Frank Sinatra and chat with stars such as Jack Benny. Learning of a bugged White House was far from my mind.

What happened is that a White House staffer called and asked me to obtain a copy of a recording of the United States Army Band playing the annual concert at the Watergate amphitheater. This performance, available to the public free of charge each summer and attended by thousands of people, always concluded with Tchaikovsky's "1812 Overture" accompanied by the Salute Gun Platoon from the ceremonial unit at Fort Myer. The assistant bandmaster quickly agreed to part with a copy of the tape when he found out that someone at the White House was requesting it.

An assistant on the White House social staff was sent to retrieve it and asked me if she could possibly get a copy also. We sat and drank wine while making two extra copies: one for her and one for me. During the conversation, she informed me that all State Dinners are tape recorded by the White House Communications Agency. Could I get a copy of one? Of course, she could do anything if her boss approved.

In exchange for Tchaikovsky's masterpiece, performed by one of the finest musical ensembles in the world, I received a taped copy of some State Dinner entertainment and felt more than repaid with this White House souvenir.

I was amazed. I distinctly recall thinking at the time what a unique discovery it was to me that a taping system was being used. Numerous visits over nearly two years had never even given a hint of a recording system and the technicians weren't that obvious in the back of the room. They appeared to be taking care of the lighting and microphones only. Apparently no one else had given it a lot of thought either.

Having made that relatively innocent discovery by accident, I was even more shocked to hear Alex Butterfield, deputy assistant to the President, reveal that there was also a taping system in the Oval Office. I had walked down to the President's office more than once with a young lady from the staff (there are a lot of young ladies on the staff). And it is only fair to assume now that I have been recorded for posterity as a voice on the famous Nixon tapes—hopefully, an inaudible one.

The Nixon taping system was voice activated. When we entered and said something, the tape started automatically. *If* this had not been the case, there probably would not have been sufficient incriminating evidence to force President Nixon out of office.

I was away from the mansion but still working as a Social Aide on the night of the next escalation of the Watergate affair, the so-called "Saturday Night Massacre" of October 20, 1973. Only at the time it was billed as "Thirteenth Annual United Nations Concert and Dinner."

But much more was going on at the White House than a lovely night of celebration of peacekeeping. President Nixon wanted Special Prosecutor Archibald Cox fired, and Attorney General Elliot Richardson refused to do it. Richardson then was asked to resign. The Deputy Attorney General, William D. Ruckelshaus, also refused, and he was asked to resign as well. The next official in the chain of command, Solicitor General Robert Bork, cooperated with the President and fired Cox.

While these historic events transpired at the White House, a few of the Social Aides and I were assisting the United Nations staff at the Washington Hilton. It was the U.N.'s thirteenth annual dinner and concert and it was also the twenty-eighth anniversary of its founding.

Also assisting were about thirty young ladies from one of the local girls schools. Since everything was relatively informal, we got most of the crowd to their seats right away. That left the remainder of the evening for about five or six of us to entertain all these girls. We danced our feet off, and of course the girls weren't the least bit tired since they outnumbered us completely. In the spirit of cooperation, I volunteered again the following year anyway.

The next Watergate escalation did not happen until early the next year—March 1, 1974—when again, two events were taking place at the same time. One was a party with the accent on youth, the "Reception for the Young Republican Leadership Conference," that took center stage at the White House.

But while Julie and David Eisenhower personally welcomed the fifteen hundred young Republican achievers who were being honored for their work of the past year, some older Republicans were attending a different kind of *party* at a federal courthouse nearby.

Seven of President Nixon's former campaign and White House aides were being indicted for their parts in the cover-up of the Watergate burglary. Haldeman, Ehrlichman, Mitchell, Colson, Mardian, Strachan and Parkinson were accused of being part of a conspiracy to "corruptly influence, obstruct and impede the due administration of justice" in the Democratic National Committee Headquarters break-in and bugging case.

Meanwhile at the White House, when the guests weren't pursuing David and Julie, the press was. I find it fascinating that the news corps will ask virtually any famous person what he or she thinks about a breaking story just to get a printable quote. Surely no one would seriously believe that Julie Nixon Eisenhower had any relevant knowledge of what was going on in a federal court down the street, but because it concerned her father, perhaps the press expected her to say something defensive that might help sell papers.

Evenually, I even heard a story claiming that David Eisenhower was the "Deep Throat" who was leaking Watergate secrets to the *Washington Post* reporters, but I didn't believe it for a minute. The theory was that, as a serious historian, he wanted to set the record straight. I'll let historians deal with that one.

All during the Young Republicans reception, the Secret Service solemnly stood nearby watching everybody closely while we Social Aides tried to help Julie and David cope with the reporters and the eager crowd. Throughout an hour and a half of this pressure, the two did not once lose their cool.

As a postscript to this day, I was not surprised when charges against one of the seven original co-conspirators indicted this day were dropped: Gordon Strachan, the man who had been a thorn in my side at White House parties. Considering how busy he was kept checking on social functions for Haldeman, I couldn't envision him having a very substantial role in Watergate. He wouldn't have had the time.

In March of 1974, Vice President Ford seemed to be a little more prominent around the White House. At a farewell dinner for Melvin Laird, who had been Secretary of Defense and a presidential counselor, and who was moving on to private industry, Nixon and Ford shared honors. Both gave speeches in praise of Laird. And the funny thing was, the dinner party just wasn't necessary by convention or by precedent. Nixon could have easily gotten away with a simple ceremony somewhere and a gift but this was a full-blown formal dinner.

By May, the mood around the White House was increasingly glum. My calendar records:

May 29—Reception—International Neighbor Clubs

This reception is unique only because it was to be my last big routine social function with the Nixons before they departed the

White House. No one really guessed that they were leaving even though some signs were evident.

The number of parties had decreased markedly. People now discussed the Watergate affair in hushed tones even at White House functions. And the President was regularly inviting conservative congressional leaders to dinner cruises with him on the *Sequoia*.

Even in these dark days, the staff could find something to amuse themselves. An often repeated story made the rounds. It seems that the President was out on the *Sequoia* with several guests when trouble struck. The engine stopped just before the yacht reached the dock. Nothing would get it started again, so the crew arranged to take the guests off one at a time in a rowboat.

Nixon waited impatiently for his rescue. Having been to this dock many times before, he was well aware that several sunken pilings were nearby. Taking aggressive action, as he often did in a crisis, he stepped out of the boat and walked along on the pole tops just below the water's surface, leading his guests to the safety of the dock. It looked for all the world like Nixon could walk on water, and had the power to make others walk on water too.

Reporters standing on shore observed the entire event. Next morning the *Washington Post* headlined the rescue: NIXON CAN'T SWIM!

The incident gave everyone a much-needed respite from grim headlines. Nixon White House staffers could laugh at this joke over and over, even though the storytellers sounded more and more desperate as time went on.

While talk of impeachment was really only wild speculation among the public and the press, Mr. Nixon appeared to be taking no chances. His guests included those Republicans and Southern Democrats who appeared to be most likely to back him up in a congressional showdown. On one such trip down the Potomac, the beleaguered President took along his Chief of Staff, Al Haig, for good measure. It obviously wasn't enough, as the daily revelations in the Congress, courts and news media drew the circle of responsibility and accountability tighter and tighter around the Oval Office.

August 8—President Nixon Announces His Resignation

In spite of all the clues, we just didn't see it coming. Admittedly, the Social Aides are not privy to the behind-the-scenes policy and the decision-making process at the White House, but we did hear a lot of things second and third hand. While not always reliable by reporters' or lawyers' standards, these stories did indicate the general areas of concern among the staff and sometimes told exact accounts of what had happened or would happen.

No one seriously suggested resignation. It was an absolute shock that it could happen so quickly without a hint of a rumor floating around the lower-level house staff members. We got our information by way of the television announcement along with the rest of the world. Some of us were called later that evening and told to be at the White House at midmorning the next day.

I consider myself fortunate to have been one of only eight Military Social Aides asked to be present for the Nixon's farewell to the staff and the swearing-in of the new President to follow, although my instructions for the August 9 events were not even postmarked to me until August 15. Washington often works in mysterious ways, but in the atmosphere of confusion that reigned behind the scenes, it is surprising that the Military Office got the notices out at all.

August 9—Nixon's Farewell to the White House Staff

The Cabinet officers and all available staff members began assembling in the East Room around 9:00 A.M. It was an extraordinarily somber crowd. Anguished looks on virtually every face reflected how deeply everyone felt about what the Nixons must be going through personally. There was also a measure of sorrow for the presidency itself and how the highest office in the free world was being embarrassed by the greatest scandal to rock the institution in the history of the nation.

Some felt bad for themselves as well. Who would stay and who would go?

The short notice that everyone had—including Vice President Ford—saved all some agonizing over the numerous possibilities and also prevented power struggles and special deals. It was just about as close as one can get to a come-as-you-are change of the presidency. While some could not avoid thinking of their own skins, the major concern was for a President who was highly regarded on a personal and professional level by his immediate subordinates.

One of the female aides and I were just inside the center door to the East Room, caught in the crowd, but also trying to direct to the front senior people such as the cabinet officers and the top-level staffers.

The plan was to have the junior staffers in the rear, but it was a futile effort. The room was completely full and we just didn't have enough help to control the group. It soon became evident that no one really gave a damn about protocol this morning.

The arrival of the President, Mrs. Nixon, the daughters and their husbands was announced at 9:30 by their Marine Aide, Lieutenant Colonel Jack Brennan. Even if the staff had had seats, there would have been a standing ovation, but they were already on their feet to conserve space. The cheering and applause were thunderous. Without a note to read from and with very few hesitations, Richard Nixon gave one of his finest speeches ever.

I bled a little inside for the man who had been so kind to me. He was perspiring profusely and his voice quavered in several places. It was equally difficult for the family as they struggled with their emotions for the entire time.

Not surprisingly, many of the staff could not contain themselves. There were few dry eyes in the room, and some people cried openly. The Social Aide next to me was beside herself and I had to hold on to her to keep her from collapsing on the floor. I locked my arm under hers and held on tight lest she become a news item herself, but she only responded with a weak grip and periodic sobs of despair. She stayed on the verge of fainting the entire time.

It was an emotionally draining and physically exhausting experience for everyone. When it was finally over, the Nixons and Fords headed out for the South Lawn and a waiting helicopter. The staff followed behind like drugged zombies and stood on the lawn to give them their last good-bye.

Nixon, himself, had scheduled a flight on Air Force One to lift off while he was still President. He may have been playing it safe because of what happened to him in January 1961, when President Kennedy took over from Dwight Eisenhower. As the *former* Vice President, Dick Nixon personally had to go and find his own car to get home from the inauguration.

When the Marine helicopter lifted off, Rose Mary Woods, the President's secretary, who had endured all the humiliation of her beloved boss that she could handle, collapsed on the lawn.

Richard Milhous Nixon would still be President for another hour and a half or so, but few in that crowd would see him again. It was now time for the Vice President to assume new responsibility—that of thirty-eighth President of the United States.

Part Three

F Is for Ford...and Also for Fun

14

The Changing of the Guard

*Y*ou would have to be there to see the mixed emotions on the faces—sadness, apprehension, relief, hope and joy. It was high noon, only hours since Nixon had resigned.

August 9, 1974—Swearing-in Ceremony for the President

Virtually the entire Nixon staff was assembled for Gerald Ford's swearing-in. The East Room was arranged with a small stage between the portraits of George and Martha Washington. Cabinet officers, Supreme Court justices, members of the Joint Chiefs of Staff and congressional leaders joined senior and some junior White House aides to make up the audience of 250.

The actual ceremony took only a few minutes. Gerald R. Ford became the thirty-eighth President of the United States in one of the rare inaugural events in the history of our country that involved no bands, parades or fancy motorcades.

It would have been in bad taste to be too exuberant. After all, a man for whom many people here had cared deeply had just left in disgrace, and it wasn't the end of the story yet. There might be years of investigation and legal procedures—and maybe even prison. No, it was not a White House event that called for a celebration.

It was a solemn occasion.

We aides tried to carry on as usual even though, in a manner of speaking, we were between bosses. But our work was cut out for us by the Social Office and came to us through channels. We got our assignments and carried them out—just as if this were a strictly social occasion.

Afterward, a receiving line and short reception gave everyone a chance to shake the new President's hand and to wish him and the country well.

My job was to supervise the receiving line of guests waiting to greet the Fords, and I exchanged a word or two with people I knew. Spotting a face with a famous name, General Davy Jones, Chief of Staff of the Air Force, I ventured to ask whether, as an Air Force man, he took a little ribbing over his famous nautical namesake.

With a stern smile, he answered, "Only my *four-star* friends joke about it." As a captain in the Army, I wasn't about to challenge that record.

After everyone had gone through the receiving line and had said a few words to the new President and new First Lady, Betty Ford, I was free to enjoy the reception, too. I circulated, trying to be friendly and make conversation with various guests who stood around in a daze.

I tried to maintain a cheerful look, and of course, I avoided political comment of any sort. We were there to help the guests and make every occasion as pleasant as possible. Accentuate the positive and downplay the negative.

The hushed conversation was mostly about the man who wasn't there and what would become of him. I heard one man say, "He will have to pardon him," to which another retorted, "Not a chance. The country would rise up and lynch Ford if he did." The first man spoke again as he sipped his drink, "You'll see. You'll see. Remember you heard it from me."

Some were quoting Gerald Ford's words, "Our long national nightmare is over." Some assured themselves and each other that of course Ford could run the country—he'd been a leader on the Hill and he knew all about leadership. And some—mostly women—placed their sympathy with Pat Nixon. How she must have suffered. How she didn't deserve to suffer so much. And how she had stood by her man like a saint.

Someone came over to complain to me that there would be no Inaugural Ball. "Every new President deserves an Inaugural Ball." The woman I was talking with answered for me almost angrily, "Jim, you be quiet. It would be like dancing on someone's grave."

No, there would be no hoopla for this Inaugural. As the woman had told her friend Jim, "Wait till he gets *elected* President in a couple of years—then you can have your damn ball."

There was much to talk about concerning the strangeness of the situation. We now had a man who was a President by *appointment*. And he had been a Vice President by *appointment*. In a way, there was nothing to celebrate this day of August 9 except one man's good luck in being in the right place at the right time. No gambler in his right mind would have taken a bet on such a thing ever happening.

Even Ford's name was a change. The middle "R" stood for Rudolph. We'd never had a Rudolph before in the two hundred years of the Republic. Well, we had one now, and bit by bit we would learn how different he was in other ways, as well.

The White House has an almost continuous running party. Nothing stops it for more than a moment in history. And so the new First Lady was surprised and a bit dismayed that her first big responsibility would be a State Dinner that was to take place only one week after her husband was sworn in.

It was hard to shift gears as I prepared to attend the first formal dinner under a new First Lady. Driving to the White House, I determined to give Betty Ford the same loyalty I had Pat Nixon, but I admit I felt surrounded by ghosts of parties past.

Charlton Heston came to mind. Still looking a little like the Moses character he portrayed, he had looked at me over the heads of the females surrounding him and made a face, as if to say, do I have to put up with all this? I didn't rescue him because he seemed to be perfectly happy to be under siege at the White House. Would I see him again under the new administration?

And would I see Mike Curb again? Curb, the head of MGM Records, was the only guest I met as aide to the Nixons who had actually walked up to me on his second visit to the White House and said, "Hi, Steve, how are you doing?"—the sole guest among thousands to remember my name. I didn't know it then, but he had an interest in politics. He later became lieutenant governor of California.

I remembered the Governors Dinner just months earlier, when Dick Nixon had been really relaxed, playing the piano and kidding around while Pearl Bailey sang. Would I ever see such a scene again? And would I ever see the two governors I had bumped into when I was leaving after the party—the governor of California, Ronald Reagan, and the governor of Georgia, Jimmy Carter?

Had President Nixon been upset that the governor of Massachusetts, Michael Dukakis, had declined and was conspicuous by his absence? If so, he didn't show it.

This year our Christmas photograph had been *really* late. The President and Mrs. Nixon had posed with us before the Governors Dinner began—March 7. This year I'd hit the jackpot as such things go in the game of protocol.

My seniority among the aides had grown considerably by this time. At more than two years, I had already stayed longer than most of the others. Many had been reassigned from the Washington area, some had left to get married, and one or two were invited not to return. As the second most senior aide, I stood next to the First Lady for the first time. It was a thrilling and rewarding experience.

And I was remembering the kindly and warmhearted Pat—how I would miss her. For some reason, the view of her that came to mind was of Mrs. Nixon accepting a bust of Susan B. Anthony from the International Conference on the Role of Women in the Economy.

It had been given in recognition of the large number of women who had received high positions in government under Nixon's leadership. But who would give credit for that when the only thing in everyone's mind seemed to be Watergate?

And Mamie. I would remember Mamie forever. I made a mental note to try to see the table in the Treaty Room, or the Monroe Room, as it was also called, where she had learned a little secret of White House history.

It had been uncovered when First Lady Mamie Eisenhower invited all descendants of Presidents to visit the White House in 1959. One guest—Laurence Gouverneur Hoes, the great, great grandson of President James Monroe—became excited at the sight of a little desk and showed Mamie how to press a spring to reveal a secret compartment.

Hoes told how, as a child fifty-three years earlier, he had broken the desk by playing roughly, and in the repair, it was discovered that some priceless letters were hidden in a little secret compartment—letters written by Jefferson, Lafayette, Madison and John Marshall, who was chief justice of the United States from 1801 to 1835. The little desk was a reproduction of the one on which President Monroe had signed the Monroe Doctrine.

By Betty Ford's own account, her first party did not go well, and that episode started some friction between her and Lucy Winchester. Those of us who worked there did not agree with Mrs. Ford's complaints about the Social Secretary's Office, but no one ever wins a disagreement with the First Lady.

Evidently, to emphasize Betty Ford's growing concerns about social events, she must have leaned on the entire East Wing. Instructions from the Military Office for the Social Aides suddenly got short and curt such as this one:

August 21, 1974

MEMORANDUM FOR THE WHITE HOUSE SOCIAL AIDES
Do not pick up menus and place cards after state dinners. Guests return to retrieve them for souvenirs.

The Naval Aide to the President

In my three years in the White House, I had never observed or heard of an aide going in to retrieve a guest's seating card as a souvenir. What someone saw or thought he saw was probably a onetime occurrence that would likely not have been repeated whether or not some special edict was issued.

The memo knocked us off balance. The Social Aides and staff continued to perform every ceremony and function just as we had in the Nixon administration, but we wondered if we should be more cautious with a new First Family. There had been no time to anticipate the inevitable changes and to react overnight, which is exactly the length of time everyone on the staff had to adjust.

Although they played a part in the Nixon White House during many social activities, the Fords gave no clues while he was Vice President as how they would do things if given the opportunity. Indeed, that would have been not only presumptuous but politically deadly, and they kept an appropriate distance from the Social Staff at all times.

Most of us survived and the Nixon-to-Ford transition was not a big problem, except for Lucy, who became a casualty and very soon would be replaced. It was a great loss to all of us aides. Things did not get better with Lucy Winchester's leaving. In fact, an honest evaluation a year or two later would probably disclose that Betty Ford would come to miss Lucy's know-how.

And maybe she missed Lucy almost immediately. I remember what happened when Ford decided on his Vice President, Nelson Rockefeller, and needed all the good press he could get in those early days.

Two days after President Ford introduced Rockefeller as his choice for Vice President, Happy Rockefeller came to the White House to visit with the wife of her husband's new boss-to-be. It was nearly a disaster as a media pleaser.

Betty Ford had appointed Nancy Howe as her special assistant. Nancy immediately set out to establish her turf by insulating the First Lady from detailed day by day decisions her staff needed to make to function. So when Happy Rockefeller arrived and failed to stop to allow the reporters to take pictures, there was no one to blame but Nancy.

Giving the press a photo opportunity was both routine and necessary, but it wasn't coordinated with either of the ladies. The naturally shy and reserved Mrs. Rockefeller probably did what her instincts told her to do—duck in and don't make yourself news!

Pat Nixon's Press Secretary, Helen Smith, who agreed to stay on and help out until a replacement was found, made as good a recovery as possible. Helen suggested the ladies step out onto the balcony to wave at reporters and photographers and at least given them a chance to see Happy. It fell short of a meaningful session and would contribute to rumors and stories about Nancy Howe's lack of effectiveness for her entire time on the East Wing Staff.

But Lucy Winchester was not the only one to go. For a time, there seemed to be a revolving door marked, "Military Aides." Two lieutenant colonels—Golden from the Army and Brennan from the Marines—departed immediately. Jack Brennan retired and went to serve as an assistant to Nixon. Air Force Brigadier Lawson followed the other two several months later and was promoted to major general.

Coming in through the revolving door as they went out were the two men who had worked as Military Assistants to Ford when he was Vice President—an Army major named Barrett and a Marine lieutenant colonel named Sardo. These new Military Aides quickly became protective of their exalted positions and preferred that other military people not encroach on their territory.

One of their first actions was to separate themselves from the other uniforms around. The Social Aides having regular access to the Mansion were the handiest and most frequent targets of their attention and their annoyance. It did no good to try to explain why something was done a certain way or was traditional around the White House.

Now that Barrett and Sardo had moved up with the President to the first team, they could run the office as they pleased with the stock comment, "The President would want it that way."

And maybe he did. And maybe he didn't. All I know is that Sardo lasted not even a year. He appeared to be getting along well with the First Lady and may have had a good relationship with the President as well, but he had somehow rubbed Chief of Staff Don Rumsfeld the wrong way. As was the custom at the White House, his reassignment was quiet and orderly.

Barrett stayed on as long as Ford was there and finally was promoted to lieutenant colonel at the end of the Ford administration. But it did him little good since he resigned his commission to follow Jerry Ford into civilian life and continue serving him.

The importance of the Military Aides can not be overstated. The full-time Military Aides perform a valuable and very necessary function for the President. They are the link between the Commander in Chief and the Department of Defense. This simple sounding statement covers substantial territory. The military provides virtually all communication and transportation services to the White House as well as some culinary delights.

Whenever the President or one of the senior staffers want to go on a trip, they call for a Marine Corps helicopter and/or an Air Force jet from the special fleets designated for White House support. The Military Office makes the arrangements.

And then there is the matter of communications. The White House Communications Agency, run by the Army is at the staff's disposal with the most sophisticated equipment in the world available. The operators running the switchboard are famed for being able to track down anyone anywhere, and they do it quite often with the aid of this hi-tech equipment. The Army also runs the motor pool which contains not jeeps but a fleet of black sedans.

Finally, the Navy runs the White House mess, another one of those symbols of power for those who are permitted to eat there. The Navy also operates any presidential yacht.

But then comes the greatest responsibility of all. True, the Military Aides are responsible for pulling all these functions together and making them support the White House in an efficient manner, but above all, they carry the "football."

Designed for instantaneous communications between the President and the military command structure, the football contains coding devices which can be used by the President to activate instant retaliation if a war starts and he isn't in the White House. The aides never bring the football to social functions but it goes everywhere the President goes outside the White House. The codes are changed often to insure absolute security.

How well did these superstar officers do their jobs? By all accounts as well as could be expected. But they weren't perfect. Bill Gulley, who ran the Military Office from Johnson to Carter, reports in his book, *Breaking Cover*, that on one occasion he found the current codes for the football in the office safe.

This meant that the *football*, which dutifully went everywhere the President went, contained outdated codes on the current presidential trip. So, for a brief time, the United States did not possess a retaliatory capability insofar as the Commander in Chief's input was required.

Gulley did not divulge the names of the aides involved, and I dare not speculate about who was dumb enough to let that happen.

My calendar shows a date highlighted that would go down in history:

September 8, 1974—President Ford pardons former President Nixon "for any and all crimes he may have committed"

There was a great hue and cry throughout the land. Some applauded Ford but the noisier ones screamed that this was an outrage and that the "fix" must have been in before Nixon left the White House.

Ford kept insisting that he had thought the matter through and decided that the important thing now was "to heal the nation's wounds"—and that had been his only motivation. The tension in the White House was high. Although Nixon had many friends and admirers in the White House, the pardon and the public reaction to it would create a defensive atmosphere that would temporarily permeate even the social functions.

You could feel its effects at the next White House party:

September 12—State Dinner—Prime Minister and Mrs. Itzhak Rabin of Israel

The President was tired and everyone picked up on that fact quickly. He had worked hard to defend the Nixon pardon and was very sincere in his efforts, but apparently the people wanted blood. They wouldn't get it from Gerald Ford.

The party was quiet by White House standards. Guests always take their cue from the actions and moods of the host and hostess, and the Fords just weren't up to par this evening.

Henry Kissinger tried to lighten the atmosphere a bit by kidding about his wife—a favorite subject with him in the first year of his marriage. Nancy was indeed a commanding figure—good looking and fashionable and also several inches taller than he. Guests were clustered around her, and Henry was wailing, "Hasn't anyone got a good word for me? You know I'm insecure and everyone just pays attention to Nancy." But you could see the pride in his face, too.

Another couple also had an odd request—one I'd never received before.

Steve Allen and Jayne Meadows were guests, and as I met them in the East Room they asked who would be at their table for dinner that they might know. It should have been flattering that they just assumed that every aide knew every obscure detail of the evening like who was sitting at each table. But it quickly became obvious that they were simply nervous about being there, just like any ordinary visitor would be, so I volunteered to find out.

I returned with the news they didn't want to hear, that there were no Hollywood names there. They then asked who would be sitting to their right and left. Once more I went back to retrieve some names that I'm sure they forgot as quickly as I did. It was an odd exchange and the question remained a first and last.

Violinist Eugene Fodor's music lifted a lot of spirits after dinner but it made me sleepy. The President didn't seem to fare any better, as he bid goodnight to the Rabins early. He took Betty's hand and they headed upstairs. In a rare departure from their routine, they skipped the evening dancing.

I see by my records that later in the month a huge White House party made history of a different sort.

September 27—Reception for Participants in the Economic Summit

One thousand of the top movers and shakers gathered to try and reach a consensus on the appropriate direction of national economic policy. They all came to the White House for what was probably the largest cocktail party of the year. As the guests arrived, Betty was secretly checking into the hospital. A nodule was found and she would undergo surgery the next day for cancer of the breast.

The announcement of Betty's hospitalization was made to the news media by the President's Press Secretary while the reception was in progress. This evening was a politically and socially important event and President Ford didn't want to let his personal problems distract the participants. After they had listened carefully to what he had to say, then they would learn about Betty's problems.

President Ford had only been in office seven weeks. Newly-elected Presidents had much longer than that just to think about what they would do upon arriving in their new job. He had to start running the government almost the same day he knew he would be President. By his action this night, Ford demonstrated a remarkable ability to balance conflicting priorities.

But, even the athletic Ford was showing signs of physical fatigue from the constant pressure. Now, faced with a serious threat to Betty's health and perhaps even her life, it would be understandable if the boss were a little distracted from his work.

It is a tribute to Gerald Ford's character and stamina that under all this enormous pressure he was cool and calm on the surface. He never gave a hint in public that the job or Betty's health had rattled him. Later discussions and writings would reveal a man who cared profoundly but in equal measures for his job, his wife and his family.

With his wife slowly recovering from her surgery, it was seventeen-year-old Susan Ford—Jerry's youngest child and only daughter—who took her place as his hostess for the most glamorous White House party of the social season.

October 5—Diplomatic Corps Reception

As far as appearances go, this was the most dazzling evening of my six years in the White House. It was a white-tie affair which for an Army officer meant mother-of-pearl cuff links, wing tip collared shirt, a dickey and a clip-on white tie, all accompanying a winter dress uniform of a black coat and blue trousers. Except for the medals, badges and dress aiguillette, I could not have looked more like a cavalry officer of a nineteenth-century Indian frontier Army fort.

While the Social Aides always looked pretty sharp in their finest military dress uniforms, let me assure you we were by no means the most spectacularly dressed this evening. Almost every ambassador in Washington arrived in full regalia.

Probably nowhere in the world outside the movies have there been so many ornately dressed people assembled in one place. Many ambassadors sported a wide body sash (like beauty contest winners wear) of a color designed to attract the most attention.

Nearly all of them had one or more medals that were variously shaped like stars, sunbursts, or multi-pointed objects that looked as though they could be used for weapons. The distinguished guests gleamed and glistened in bright yellows, royal blues, rich golds and hot reds that fairly shouted, "Status!"

President Ford looked rather plain in comparison to his aides and guests as he had on a simple black tuxedo with white shirt, tie and dickey. His hostess, Susan, however, gave the couple a lot of flair by wearing a stunning red dress she had bought only the day before.

Susan was not at all shy about telling how her Dad had given her a blank check to go shopping—"But I only cost him $50." The money was certainly well spent by this teenager, and in her relatively inexpensive gown, she got even more attention than the best-dressed ambassador.

President Ford began the dancing by taking the Soviet ambassador's wife out on the floor. Later, he also danced with Susan, several of the other wives and even a few of the female reporters.

After awhile, the President seemed to run out of dance partners. He danced again with Susan and one of the staff suggested that they needed to be rescued from each other and the now reluctant guests. Marine Captain Lori Lyons and I were walking over to cut in on them to liven things up a bit when they suddenly decided it was time to retire. We retreated the few steps we had taken and cleared a path through the door.

But before he left, President Ford walked over to chat with me for a minute about how the evening was going. It was true that he was interested in knowing how the guests were enjoying themselves and Social Aides were the best source of information. Equally evident was his interest in bridging the gap between his administration and the old staff people still around from the last one.

And another sign of his role as healer was that Dorothy McCardle of the *Washington Post* was back in good standing at the White House parties with Jerry Ford going out of his way to kid around with her.

But then, both Fords were unique in their warmth toward the press. When Betty had her cancer operation, one of the female reporters covering her was Marjorie Hunter of *The New York Times* and they became quite friendly. When Marjorie suddenly underwent the same operation, the First Lady wrote to her and both Betty and Jerry went to see her at the hospital. In the annals of the presidency, that was a one-time-only incident.

15

Betty Ford and Her Problem...Make That Problems

After Betty Ford got over the shock of suddenly being First Lady, she proved herself to be a great hostess.

Looking back, I would say that of the First Ladies I knew, Betty Ford seemed to enjoy entertaining the most. Both she and the President were naturally gregarious and it clearly showed in the way they interacted with their guests.

The Fords were just natural hosts. The Nixons always had a certain correctness about them that lent an extra air of formality to even a simple tea. There was nothing unfriendly about the Nixon parties, but no one ever let their hair down.

I remember when Jerry Ford suddenly started dancing the Charleston with Pearl Bailey. Everyone else stopped in shocked delight to watch and cleared the floor. It was such a change from the Nixons' White House. And I remember when the comic Marty Allen did a sensational dance with Betty Ford. Again, all others—including the President—got off the floor as the great duo showed everyone how it should be done.

Typical of the Ford parties, many guests—and the Social Aides—

didn't get home till the wee hours of the morning. It wasn't like the old days when aides sometimes conspired to get the guests out early.

Dancing made the difference. The athletic Fords realized that dancing is the life blood of a good White House party. And music. The Marine Band music is perfect for it and so was Betty Ford, who once had been a Martha Graham dancer. Her graceful movements also came from having actually earned a living as a John Robert Powers fashion model.

The Nixons had left the dancing to the guests, but when Betty and Jerry took the floor, everyone became exuberant and followed suit. The Fords made a handsome couple both on and off the floor.

Betty was proud of her position at Jerry's side and did not suffer challenges for her husband's attention from other women—even for a moment. There was one evening which brought this home when Vikki Carr, a vivacious singer of Mexican descent, was the entertainer at a formal affair.

Later, Jerry Ford carried on an animated conversation with her, during which she asked, "What is your favorite Mexican dish?"

Wife Betty, who was standing by, heard her husband reply with enthusiasm, "You are!"

Betty Ford turned to someone and murmured, "That woman will never get into the White House again."

Another time, Betty Ford became upset when *The New York Times* published a photo of Kissinger, Ron Nessen, President Valéry Giscard d'Estaing of France, Jerry Ford, and a beautiful women named Nicole on the beach in Martinique. Betty wanted to know who Nicole was and why she was there. The First Lady was nothing, if not outspoken.

Betty Ford did not hold back on speaking her mind on any subject. A nation was shocked and then proud of the gutsiness of a First Lady who would talk openly about her daughter's sex life—that she would not be surprised if Susan were having an affair before marriage.

But discussion of Susan's possible sex life as a teenager was not Betty Ford's only breakthrough. She also talked candidly about her own breast cancer operation. She could have hidden the fact that the surgery she was having was to remove her breast, but she chose to use herself as a role model to encourage other women to be more open and to seek medical help to save their lives from this silent killer.

Though Betty was called a jealous wife by some, she was also Jerry Ford's greatest booster. When newspapers kept insisting that Ford was merely "acting presidential," or "trying to look presidential," she retorted that her husband didn't just look or act presidential, "he *is* presidential."

Betty was basically a homemaker and a lover of family. She had given up her New York career to return to Grand Rapids, Michigan, and be with her family. But so much did she love dancing that she organized a local dance group. Her public spiritedness also started long before the White House, when she devoted much time to teaching handicapped children to dance.

She had made a great dancer of Jerry, and female guests would tell me how they yearned to dance with the President, hoping perhaps that I could arrange it. Once I got involved in one of the Fords' little dance games. It was at the State Dinner for West German President Walter Scheel in June of 1975 when so many invitees had RSVPed yes that Henry Kissinger had to act as a surrogate host for fifty guests at tables set up in the Blue Room.

With assistance from guests such as Angela Lansbury, Dick Cavett and football's old pro, George Blanda, this special group dining separate from the others hardly missed the Fords for the hour and twenty minutes it took for dinner and toasts.

Everyone was in a good mood when it came time to dance and few people needed encouragement from the Social Aides. That's why I was a little puzzled when one of the President's Military Aides came to me and explained that Elke Sommer was angry at her husband and I was needed to entertain her for an hour. It was a very unusual request but whatever the reason, I was most happy to comply. After all, aides are there to help in any way.

Elke and I danced for half an hour. Her husband was nowhere to be seen and she never mentioned him or the disagreement so it seemed reasonable that she didn't want to be around him for a while. What I didn't understand was how she could be so happy and vivacious while at the same time having a tiff with her spouse.

But I stopped thinking about it. One must dance with Elke Sommer only once to see how concentrating on anything else is virtually impossible.

More than a half dozen dances passed and neither of us paid

attention or talked to anyone else. Finally, with a most impressive hug and a toss of her head, she said we should go meet Tennessee Ernie Ford.

Tennessee Ernie and his "Opryland U.S.A." singers had put on a rousing show that had the sophisticated White House audience clapping hands and tapping toes for most of the performance.

Elke had made it sound as if *she* was the one who would like to be introduced to the folksy Ernie but when we went over, it was obvious that Ernie and she already knew each other and that she just wanted me to get to know him, too.

I found that charming and unusual. Not only was she beautiful, a good dancer and a champion hugger, but she was also thoughtful. I had to remind myself that there was a husband around, even if he was in the dog house.

We found Tennessee Ernie chatting with a fellow from Merrill Lynch named Don Regan. Beyond normal social etiquette, Don didn't rate any special attention in those days so it was no problem when Elke interrupted him to introduce me to the star. It was a bit awkward shaking hands as Elke was holding very tightly to my right arm but we managed. After a few minutes, we migrated over to meet bandleader Harry James and singer Helen O'Connell.

For once it was difficult to make small talk and we shifted our attention rather quickly back to the dance floor. President Scheel departed and that was the signal for everyone to break loose.

Harry James took over the band for a while and even borrowed a trumpet from one of the Marines. Helen O'Connell sang as Elke and I and several others continued to dance. Finally, Ernie joined Helen in singing, "Hey, Good Looking," and the dancers suddenly became an audience.

I didn't appreciate the pause in dancing, and the interruption turned out to be an ill omen for me. When the dancing started again, my Commander in Chief was at my elbow cutting in on me and I lost Elke for the remainder of the evening.

For years I believed that I took care of Elke that night to make the best of a social predicament resulting from a marital squabble. The White House wanted her occupied to prevent a public airing of the problem.

Although marriage therapy is not specifically spelled out in our job description, the need for corrective action certainly fit within the general concept of our duties. Then I read Ron Nessen's book, *It Sure Looks Different From the Inside*. Nessen tells what really happened that evening. Betty Ford noticed that Elke Sommer appeared to be too interested in the President and decided to nip that interest in the bud. She ordered that "a handsome military aide" be assigned to keep Elke busy for the evening. Though not particularly handsome, as it turned out, I was the aide who was dispatched to do the job anyway— and my thanks go to Mrs. Ford for the compliment and the opportunity.

A word to those friends who were misled by an erroneous story about Elke's marital problems. I apologize because it is now obvious that the tale was only a smoke screen sent up by one of the White House aides to protect the First Lady's motives. And to Elke, thanks for the memory.

Some wondered why the beautiful and talented Betty needed to feel so protective and possessive of the man who so obviously loved her—why she was jealous of women who were no prettier than she. Was it because of the atmosphere on Capitol Hill where congressmen are surrounded by eager young secretaries? Or was she insecure because of a previous bad marriage?

Betty was a young divorcee of twenty-nine when she started dating Jerry Ford, a University of Michigan football hero and lawyer who was running for Congress. Jerry won both the girl and the election in 1948. Their four children—Michael, Jack, Steven and Susan—were eagerly welcomed by Betty who loved motherhood even though her husband was too busy campaigning every two years to be a hands-on father. And even too busy with daily and nightly Capitol Hill duties to do much fathering.

Though Betty loved raising children, she had mixed feelings about cooking. At a reception for the National Federation of Republican Women, the month after she moved into the White House, someone asked her opinion of the food there.

Betty said, "It's excellent. That's partly because *I* don't help to prepare it."

To show her caring attitude toward Jerry, even when she was uncomfortable from her operation, Betty decided to surprise Jerry by redecorating the Oval Office and his sitting room. She knew they did not reflect Jerry's taste but rather Richard Nixon's. So in November, after she had returned from the hospital and while the President was away at a SALT II meeting in Vladivostok, she supervised the job.

One of the final touches Betty added to the Oval Office was a huge variegated Swedish ivy she placed on the mantle across the room from Jerry's desk.

I'm so glad she did for a personal reason. The next year, while dating a staffer in the West Wing, I had an opportunity to visit the President's office several times while he was out. On one of these impromptu tours of the area, I was admiring the beautiful greenery and happened to mention that the ivy was one of my favorite house plants.

My staffer friend suggested that I help myself to a few cuttings since it regularly overgrew its pot and they often had to prune it. Before she could change her mind, I had reached around in back and snipped several pieces that would never be missed. The date was cut short that evening just to get the plants home and into water as rapidly as possible.

The friendship did not survive but the ivy did—and so well that it had to be repotted several times. Since the election was coming up soon and all active duty military personnel are prohibited by law from campaigning, I thought there might be a way for the ivy to help out.

Everywhere I went where a house plant grew, I made a point to give the owner a cutting from my Swedish ivy. Carefully pointing out that it had come directly from Gerald Ford's own plant in the Oval Office, I hoped they would think fondly of him when they cared for it.

I didn't say it aloud, being strictly non-political, but the thought did cross my mind that a big part of campaigning was personal association—and so how could anyone not vote for the original owner of their house plant? Unfortunately, we didn't start the ivy campaign soon enough. History shows that we didn't win that election but those variegated Swedish ivies are still spreading good will today.

One of the most memorable evenings with the Fords involved West German Chancellor Helmut Schmidt in early December. The guest of honor, like Ford, lucked into his job when his predecessor had resigned. Despite the lack of an electoral mandate in the unique route to power that they shared, each was self-confident and not only looked but also acted like a world leader.

Betty Ford had essentially recovered (at least physically) from her operation and looked better than ever. She was warm and friendly to everyone and seemed to relish the opportunity to get out and do something. A good State Dinner would perk up anyone's spirits.

Reflecting President Ford's background, the guest list this evening included a dozen members of Congress. Perhaps as a demonstration of the international nature of American business, he also invited the heads of IBM, the *Washington Post*, Union Bank and Trust Company, Braniff Airways, Morgan Guarantee Trust, Volkswagen of America, Lehman Brothers, TRW Inc., and the Boeing Company. Others included were several media people from *Time* magazine, the *Chicago Daily News*, *Reader's Digest*, and *The New Republic*. And for the pleasure of all the local football fans in attendance, there was Larry Brown, the star running back of the Washington Redskins.

When Larry walked in, several of us went over to say hello, but instead of a conventional greeting, we got a black power handshake. It was unorthodox and a complete surprise but Larry can do just about anything he wants, even in the President's home.

Brent Scowcroft, having risen one more star to the rank of lieutenant general, was no less cordial or approachable than before. Both he and his wife never assumed the aloof, self-important attitude displayed by so many longtime participants in Washington's power circles.

Unquestionably, the star of the night was Joel Grey who was a hit both on and off stage—despite the press. The entertainment had been announced in advance and some of the German reporters questioned why Grey would be scheduled to sing numbers from *Cabaret*. They were up in arms because the songs would remind people of the period when the Nazi party rose to power in Germany—and might offend the Chancellor.

The concern was misplaced. After pulling his stage costume of long tails over his dinner tuxedo, the five-foot-five entertainer sang songs from *George M.* Then he launched into two of the most powerful and best known tunes from *Cabaret*, "Wilkommen" and "Money."

As he finished the number, he threw fistfuls of phony $50 bills into the air and they fluttered down over the first two rows of guests including Chancellor Schmidt. The chancellor was so delighted that he jumped up on the stage with President Ford to congratulate Joel. Nothing further was heard from the German reporters.

In helping to seat the afterdinner guests, I noticed a very

attractive lady whom I immediately escorted to a seat near the front. There was no time for pleasantries so I did not discover till some minutes later that she was Deborah Kerr. Continuing back and forth, escorting other guests to their seats, it was difficult to keep my eyes off the famous star. She caught me more than once paying too much attention to her but the encounter ended there.

Incidentally, this evening was the first big function for the new Social Secretary, Nancy Lammerding. It went well enough, but the Social Aides sorely missed the wit of Lucy Winchester, who could make us laugh while making us work.

It was not until January of the following year—1975—that Vice President Rockefeller attended his first formal social function since being sworn in. He immediately joined Henry Kissinger in the hard-to-keep-track-of category as a second *Peck's Bad Boy.* Or, as one of the other aides said, "They're acting like kids at a high school reunion the way they run around socializing."

It was true. Instead of talking to the people around them in Sector I as they waited for the arrival of the President and the start of the receiving line, they invariably roamed through Sector II and III pressing the flesh, as President Johnson used to call it.

Henry was the leader in this minor transgression and Nelson gladly followed suit. I was told that Kissinger had developed this trick in the Nixon Administration for a personal reason—he did not always get along with then Secretary of State William Rogers and had frequently wandered from that area to find someone else to talk to. The other cabinet officers, congressmen, senators and even the Speaker of the House seldom strayed from their proper place in the receiving line but Kissinger and Rockefeller could always be counted on to be missing.

An aide would be sent to find them and try to retrieve each one before the President and the honored guest arrived but they would seldom budge until the last moment.

Rockefeller and Kissinger would smile at the aide and even take a step in the right direction but these were delaying tactics and no sincere movement was ever made until absolutely necessary.

Then, like darting deer, each managed to return to the correct spot as if guided by instinct. Without fail, when these two stepped into position in the receiving line, the President appeared at the entrance

Colonel Stephen M. Bauer (then Captain Bauer) in full dress as a White House Social Aide.

President and Mrs. Richard M. Nixon, surrounded by White House Social Aides. The author is second from right in the first row.

President Nixon and his brother Donald greet unidentified guest. The author is at the right.

The Nixons welcome Israel's Prime Minister Golda Meir to the White House.

The Nixons attend a Christmas party at the White House.

President and Mrs. Gerald Ford greet actress Candice Bergen. With them are Prime Minister and Mrs. Ali Bhutto of Pakistan.

President Ford greets columnist Art Buchwald while author George Plimpton waits his turn.

From left to right: Prime Minister Malcolm Fraser of Australia, the author, President Ford, Ambassador Shirley Temple Black (partially hidden) and Australian tennis star John Newcombe.

The author between President Jimmy Carter and the Rev. Dr. Martin Luther King, Sr. (Wide World)

President Carter greets unidentified guest, while the author stands by.

President and Mrs. Ronald Reagan at one of their many White House functions.

Pearl Bailey is interviewed by members of the Washington women's press corps in the Green Room. The author is at the right.

President Reagan holds a press conference.

To Steve Bauer
With appreciation
and best wishes, *G. Bush*

President George Bush.

to the East Room with the honored guest. It gave the impression of reversing the cause and effect as if the President were cuing on them rather than vice versa.

Kissinger and Rockefeller were not going to steal the show this night which was in honor of British Prime Minister Harold Wilson. Nor would the guest of honor. The real show stoppers were such celebrities as Kirk Douglas, Danny Kaye, Van Cliburn, Cary Grant and a mystery couple who arrived at the last moment. Musicians and Hollywood stars turned everyone's head all evening.

It was amusing that Kirk Douglas couldn't remember how often he had been a guest at the White House. He told one person it was his first visit. A few minutes later, he told someone else he had always enjoyed his visits and this was his eighth time there. He hadn't been there during the past few years but someone recalled that Douglas had been around during the Kennedy and Johnson years.

In passing through the crowd after the entertainment, I found no one who looked bored or in need of company. Most guests were standing around or in an informal line to talk to one of the celebrities. Stopping for a moment to say hello to NBC News anchorman John Chancellor, I got drawn into a rather long and interesting conversation. He was curious about my job and how the Ford parties compared to the Nixons'. We talked at length about the glittering atmosphere which now emanated from the Ford administration. When I asked how all the newsmen felt about Barbara Walters' new million-dollar contract, he grabbed my arm and warned me in a stage whisper that she was right behind me.

She could not have helped but overhear us so we moved off to the side while John complimented her ability, style and professionalism which he said he felt raised the standards of all news people.

The mystery guests were a late addition and the names of the couple had to be added to the typed list only an hour before the first visitors arrived—Warren Beatty and Michelle Phillips, who was one of the singers with The Mamas and the Papas. Word of the new arrivals caused a stir among the aides. The female aides were dying to see Beatty and the males wanted to meet his lovely date.

Spotting them in line inching their way up the Lower Grand Staircase from the ground floor like all the other guests, I quickly conspired with one of the girls so that the two of us would arrive at the top of the stairs at the same time they did. Our efforts paid off and we proceeded to break the house rules by having two aides escort one couple.

As we stepped in front of the press, there was an explosion of flashbulbs. No photographer on the White House beat could possibly face his boss the next morning without a shot of these celebrities entering the party together.

Continuing on to the East Room entrance, I walked as slowly as I dared, just for the chance to chat with the beautiful star. There seemed to be no pressure to move along from the aide behind me with Warren. Sadly we parted a few moments later as we had to leave our superstar visitors with the Sector Aides.

Olympic skier Billy Kidd was a very pleasant fellow and didn't seem to mind at all that several Social Aides wanted to say hello to his date. Nancy Moses was a gorgeous young Wilhelmina model from Dallas, Texas. Since she and I attended rival Southwest Conference schools, we had a lot in common to discuss.

Although aides were generally available for new friendships and Billy Kidd and she seemed to be just friends, I decided not to try to date her. Nancy told me she lived in New York City and I wasn't inclined to commuter dating.

The dean of Hollywood actors and somewhat of a regular guest at White House functions, Cary Grant arrived and was one of the most photographed guests of the evening (after Michelle and Warren). His brilliantly white and carefully groomed hair atop his trim frame caused him to stand out in the crowd even more than his debonair personality. Other guests clustered around to say hello to him.

Van Cliburn for once was not waiting to go on stage. Ordinarily he would be invited because he was performing but tonight he got to sit back and enjoy the beautiful voice of Beverly Sills, whom many called "Bubbles." President Ford remarked that Miss Sills was someone from Brooklyn who had made it in the world. The audience of 120 dinner and 130 afterdinner guests apparently agreed as they gave her a standing ovation when she concluded several operatic arias.

Usually, I was exhausted by the time I got home, but this night with the Fords and their fascinating guests had been so exhilarating that when I arrived at my quarters I felt wide awake.

The Fords definitely set a happier tone for their parties. As everyone saw how that Betty and Jerry were enjoying themselves, the guests, too, let loose. Even we aides, seeing the Fords having such a good time, assumed a more relaxed posture than under the Nixons.

The whole nation did not applaud or go along with Betty Ford on all her opinions. Though she was in the news continually for a time trying to find political support around the country for the Equal Rights Amendment, it was a lost cause—or as Mrs. Ford put it, "a cause before its time."

Nor did Jerry Ford find smooth sailing as he embarked on every party. The State Dinner for President Kenneth Kaunda of Zambia would have tried the patience of a saint, let alone a chief executive.

During the traditional afterdinner toasts, the Zambian leader took advantage of the opportunity to sternly lecture President Ford on the racial unrest of South Africa and to reaffirm his request that the United States stop supporting the black people's oppressors.

Some were stunned. Others chuckled a little—with discomfort. Well, it wasn't a lot of fun, but if you consider an embarrassing public insult to the President as stimulating, it sure was exciting.

President Kaunda was certainly breaking with protocol. What made this unique was that these dinner toasts have always offered a chance for any two leaders to exchange pleasantries in public and Ford did just that.

But this time, in response, he got a hard-hitting emotional speech that startled everyone. The President sat quietly throughout the ordeal, but when dinner was over, the two of them huddled in the Blue Room for what was obviously a very lively discussion. This time our President took the lead. Few people know what was actually said, but their body language made it clear that Ford gave a lot more than he got.

What made this episode even more unusual was the fact that this wasn't an official state visit. That situation may have been the cause for the undiplomatic outburst. Normally, formal state visits provide a number of public forums for such remarks and this visitor had only the afterdinner toasts which he used to the fullest advantage.

Even if he didn't score any social points, he sure got his political ones across to the President and the news media which always listened to these hitherto friendly exchanges on a speaker system.

After the toasts, the guests were reluctant to discuss the outburst with reporters. Secretary Kissinger said little while Roy Wilkins, the executive director of the NAACP, said nothing. Even the unstoppable mouth of Howard Cosell was silent. What everyone needed was some good entertainment to dispel the somber mood before the party turned into a disaster.

I have nothing against piano playing, but ordinarily it almost puts me to sleep, even at the White House. But tonight was different. Perhaps it was the inspired playing of James Tocco and his Iranian wife, Gilan Akbar, that kept all on the edge of their seats this evening. Or maybe it was that the guests were still mulling over the episode they had just witnessed.

What I do know is that President Ford touched everyone's heart in what he did next. In a conciliatory gesture, Ford invited Kaunda up on stage to play his guitar after the piano recital, and he accepted. Kaunda even took his wife and his entire entourage up with him as they performed songs that he had written himself. It was a rare, almost bizarre, experience to have a head of state first lecture the President, then thirty minutes later sing to him from the East Room stage. I long since had learned to expect just about anything at a White House party.

I just never thought I'd have to adjust to a President who turns the other cheek.

16

A Strange Kind of President

In a way, Gerald Ford was a strange President—one of a kind. But then, aren't they all? In Ford's case, it was his very lack of pretension that made him unique. As he once said of himself, "I'm disgustingly sane."

Some thought it slightly insane that he acted so sane and without ego. The perfect example was how Ford reacted—or rather failed to react—to what others considered liberties being taken by an employee. This one was David Kennerly, the President's photographer.

He came and went at will, and once, while photographing the President and his advisers debating action on the *Mayaguez* crisis, he interjected some personal comments and thoughts that startled everyone except Mr. Ford. The others were surprised, not by the content of the remarks, but that they were made at all by a White House subordinate, of all people, and to top it off, that the President listened.

On another occasion, Mr. Ford was sending an Army four-star general to South Vietnam to personally assess the strength of the still struggling South Vietnamese Army when David piped up and asked if he could go as well. The President let him go. That turned out to be a pretty good idea, as the general gave a discouraging oral report, and David brought back graphic pictures to back it up.

Jerry Ford was certainly not like Lyndon Johnson. LBJ was always exploding in anger, without worrying about his language, in front of intimates. Ford, on the other hand, almost never showed anger or spoke an angry word, and the only way you would know he was annoyed was by his tense face and clenched jaw.

I remember a party at which LBJ was the topic of conversation for me and one of the guests. I was an Escort Aide that night, and one of the men who arrived at the top of the stairs from the lower entrance level introduced himself as Peter Benchley. The name did not register. While I walked him to the reception, he told me he had recently written a successful book about sharks and was very excited that a movie also had been made. He said he hadn't seen the final version of *Jaws* yet, but he had helped film many parts and was one of the extras walking down the beach when the shark attacks a second time.

He also told me he had been a former White House speech writer for LBJ, and we talked a while about Lyndon and his disposition. It dawned on me that it was perfectly natural that Mr. Benchley should go on to fame and fortune with such a related subject. In fact, Jaws would have been a marvelous nickname for LBJ had the book come out in time.

I don't remember whether I told Benchley the dog story that was told to me about LBJ and a Social Aide. The former aide who told me the anecdote had become an Army captain by the time I met him but the scene was etched in his mind—as was Johnson's salty language.

The aide had accidentally let one of LBJ's dogs slip out of the Diplomatic Room door to the outside. The President screamed at him in the most vile and unprintable language what he was going to do to that aide if he didn't get his rear out there and catch the dog pronto.

In his dress uniform, the aide went out to chase the dog. Fortunately it was caught—but by a White House policeman. The dog was brought back to LBJ, who said nothing—no apology, no thank-you. The way the aide looked at it, he was lucky he still had a job.

But there was one thing LBJ and Ford were alike in—generosity. Lyndon, I heard, had a penchant for giving gifts to people on impulse. So did Ford. I think I'd have to bet on Ford for the grandest show of impulse giving.

It happened when he was in Vladivostok, and the SALT talks had concluded on a hopeful note that, as Ford put it, the world was a step further advanced in preventing a nuclear holocaust.

The Russian leader, Leonid Brezhnev, had agreed with him wholeheartedly and was giving him a warm and smiling send-off at the airport. Ford had noticed that Brezhnev kept looking at his coat wistfully—an Alaskan wolf fur coat Ford had worn to fend off the severe Russian weather. President Ford simply took off his coat and presented it to Brezhnev as a farewell gift.

Jerry Ford had a fine sense of humor. And he needed it to handle the barrage of jokes about his so-called clumsiness. Of course, he could have growled at people and used punitive measures against those he found spreading the stories of his latest pratfalls, but that wouldn't have been Jerry.

He actually went along with the gag and sought out opportunities to poke fun at himself. We at the White House sometimes wished he wouldn't. For example, at a Radio-Television Correspondents dinner, when Ford got up to speak, he managed to push dishes to the floor, get himself caught in the tablecloth and drop a bunch of pages of his speech on the floor, all at about the same time. It took a full minute for some correspondents to realize it wasn't what it looked like and that only a well-coordinated man could put on an act of such clumsiness—and that he was putting them on.

Of course, some of the mishaps really did happen, and they were things that could have befallen anyone. Unfortunately, Ford just had more than his share. And sometimes all in one day. In Austria in May of 1975, first he caught his shoe on a bad place on the ramp of his plane and came tumbling down the steps. Then, not once but twice he slipped on the stairway of the Residenz Palace.

There was a reason. The stairs were slippery from rain but nobody cared about that—he was the President of the United States and the mishaps made a good story.

But even before he came to the White House, the stories were there about Ford being awkward and uncoordinated. The cards had been stacked against him years before by Lyndon Johnson. Johnson had started the cruel jokes out of his anger that the Republican Minority Leader was managing to thwart some of Democratic President Johnson's best plans for his "Great Society."

LBJ fought back with sarcasm. He was the one who said that Jerry Ford was so dumb he couldn't walk and chew gum at the same time. Only that is the cleaned up version.

And it was Johnson who first said that Jerry Ford had "played football too long without a helmet." When Ford became President, every school kid learned the phrase and was suddenly accusing some playmate of the same thing when a ball was fumbled.

And again, the President did not respond with anger but rather with his low-key humor. It was nothing new. Even earlier, when his tormentor, Lyndon Johnson, was still President, Congressman Ford was asked to speak at the prestigious media Gridiron Club. Ford brought along the football helmet he wore in 1935, at the All-Star game in Chicago.

When he got up to speak, the first thing he did was put on his old helmet, to the roar of laughter. He was having trouble because it was a little tight. Not a bit perturbed, Ford explained, "Heads tend to swell in Washington."

You would only have to be at one of Jerry Ford's White House parties to see that his head had not really swelled at all. Some of the parties were almost like a family affair. One in particular was the State Dinner for Prime Minister Zulfikar Ali Bhutto of Pakistan. One of the best looking attractions to appear in our receiving line for some time was Candice Bergen.

It might be assumed that as a Hollywood star, either her name or her turn simply had come up and she was invited, but that simplistic interpretation didn't explain why she was being escorted by President Ford's personal photographer, David Kennerly. Naturally, the tongues in Washington were flapping faster than Old Glory in a windstorm and came up with a better explanation.

Candice Bergen was an aspiring photographer as well as an accomplished actress, and she latched on to David as an entrée into the Ford's private world (so a popular version of the story goes).

In fact she was so friendly with David that he managed to get her into the White House for a series of photo sessions with the Fords that gave her a great advantage over all the others wishing to capture the First Family on film.

The many unkind suggestions as to what Candice did to deserve this special privilege are neither printable, provable nor probably even true.

She didn't have to maneuver. If she wanted anything from most anyone on the social staff, she would only have had to ask and smile. In fact, she probably did just that with the President. He had a reputation for being attracted to beautiful women.

However it happened, somewhere in the bargain she also got an invitation to this party, which meant David came as a guest, too, and not as a working staff member.

David Kennerly was treated by Ford as almost an adopted son, and it seemed as though many staff members resented him for it. He was so much a part of the family that it was reported that Susan Ford often went to him for brotherly advice when her real brothers weren't at home—which was often.

As if to add fuel to the fires, David frequently took liberties with the family that few other staff members would even dream of. He somehow always knew the proper limits and continually amazed everyone.

I noticed there was often a bit of jealousy when someone would describe Kennerly's latest antics. Unfortunately, when revealed, these stories suggested the President could be swayed or maneuvered by a single individual with questionable credentials for giving such advice. This did not reflect well on the President, even though we all knew he was capable of making his own decisions.

There were a few other stellar attractions at the Bhutto party of a different kind:

Art Buchwald came for the first time and danced again and again. He had written a widely-publicized book titled, *I Never Danced at the White House*, so they finally got around to inviting him after he had advertised his complaint to the world. It was a big joke with the staff and everyone really enjoyed the laugh.

A few days later came a present from columnist Buchwald that did not need to go through the X-ray machine. He had obtained a promotional poster with the book title on it and he crossed out the word "never," signed it and sent it to Betty Ford. She loved it. Buchwald didn't stop making occasional fun of the President in his column, but when he did, even the loyal staff could laugh a little at our perfectly human Commander in Chief.

Dorothy McCardle, the *Washington Post* reporter barred by the Nixon White House from several functions, was invited this evening, not to work but to be a guest. Apparently, Jerry Ford wanted to make sure whatever animosity she harbored was directed only at the previous administration.

More than a dozen members of Congress, General Brent Scowcroft, George Plimpton, Polly Bergen, several corporate and publishing leaders, and the senior staffers from the naval facility where Betty was operated on, all joined together to completely distract everyone's attention from the prime minister of Pakistan.

The afterdinner guests who joined them to listen to Billy Taylor's inspired jazz included L. Bruce Laingen. I would think of this night later when he surfaced on the political scene as senior embassy official held captive in Iran for 444 days of the Carter administration.

Another party at which I became involved with the guests and Ford family in a more personal way was the January 27, 1976, State Dinner for Prime Minister Itzhak Rabin of Israel. Betty Ford and daughter Susan had become interested in a certain sculptor.

Every State Dinner is planned with a theme and this central issue determines what is placed on the dinner tables for decoration. Tonight's display consisted of an individual bronze piece on each table by master sculptor Malcom Moran from Carmel, California. Moran certainly was in good hands. His beautiful daughter Kathy and a female friend were like exquisite bookends that evening and left his side only to dance. The following night they invited me to accompany Kathy to a special dinner in honor of the artist at an exclusive Georgetown Club.

I vividly remember Malcom telling us how Clint Eastwood used the Moran home in Carmel to film many scenes for *Play Misty for Me*. The evening stayed special for me until I discovered that the sculptures on the table at the club were for sale. There were no bargain prices.

The irrepressible David Kennerly was only making mental pictures this evening of his date Suzy Chaffee, the Olympic skiing champion. David would have done the First Family a big favor if he had spent the evening giving First Son Jack Ford some pointers on the opposite sex. Jack's date, Chris Evert, was clearly not enjoying herself.

Come to think of it, it's rather amusing that at a White House party—the Rabin State Dinner—during wallflower patrol, it wasn't a little old lady who needed my help but a young, vibrant and famous female—a very crestfallen Chris Evert.

In the line of duty, I spent some time trying to cheer her up and discovered that she and Jack had been going out all week. Surprisingly, she had not seen any of the popular night spots in town even though Jack's under-drinking-age sister Susan visited them herself and could have given him some pointers.

Chris had thought a President's son would be taking her to the *in* spots. But she was wrong. Either Jack didn't know where to go, or he just wasn't interested.

Quite depressed about the tedious pace Jack set, she wasn't reluctant to say so to me. What made it all the more painful was that she had personally instigated their meeting through a friend at the Virginia Slims tennis tournament only days earlier.

Her friend got Jack Ford to call her for a date. Now she was stuck at a fabulous party with a guy she didn't care for at all. When the press asked about their friendship, however, she was quite evasive and noncommittal, giving the mistaken impression that something serious might be going on.

I knew the truth, which was that Chris didn't want to embarrass Jack or the First Family and had to let the press draw what appeared to be an obvious conclusion.

Eventually, the story died. Chris soon left town, and she and Jack were no longer seen together.

At the Rabin State Dinner, heads were turning easily and often with guests like Calvin Klein, Herman Wouk and Danny Kaye wandering through the crowd. Those and many other superstar distractions made my job as Introducing Aide just that much more difficult. The real test came when I had to introduce two couples: The Walds and the Hamiltons. With advance coordination from the social staff, they were presented as Mr. Jeff Wald and his wife, Helen Reddy, and Mr. Joseph Hamilton and his wife, Carol Burnett.

That covered all bases.

Carol and Helen delighted everyone by singing a number of 1960 hits. Most impressive was their duet, "I Am Woman," done for the two First Ladies, Mrs. Ford and Mrs. Rabin. It was an unusually warm and friendly evening and was one of the best parties of the administration.

Whatever a President does, he will be criticized by some. There were those who thought Ford should have invited more black guests—especially those from Capitol Hill—when, close to presidential election day, a State Dinner was held for the black president of Liberia and Mrs. Tolbert. The speculation was that Ford just didn't want to have too many Democrats clouding up his Republican spirits at the party.

Conspicuous by his absence was Walter Washington, the black Democratic mayor of D.C. He was frequently in the news but seldom in the White House. Representing Capitol Hill, only three black members of Congress were present—Louis Stokes, Barbara Jordan and Charles Rangel, while one member of the Supreme Court, Thurgood Marshall—the only black—also made the list.

But whether it leaned toward the Republicans or the Democrats, it was another example of a great Ford party.

The then relatively unknown author of *Roots*, Alex Haley, was also invited. His inclusion seems in retrospect an understated prediction of his future success. I would also be amazed this night at how a former child movie star had turned into a charismatic and competent government official.

The administration's new Chief of Protocol at the State Department, Shirley Temple Black, performed her primary duty for the evening by introducing the guests to the President in the receiving line. The attention she received might have stopped there, but no one could figure out whether to treat her like a Hollywood star or a Washington bigwig.

As a result, they did both, and she was definitely the center of attention wherever she stopped to speak to guests. Other guests included Olympic gold medalist Bruce Jenner and football commissioner Pete Rozelle. Actor Ernest Borgnine and I had a short conversation because I wanted to tell him how much I used to enjoyed the *McHale's Navy* series.

Though he appreciated the comments, Borgnine soon got very somber over the recent death of his pal, Joe Flynn, who played the part of Captain Wallace Binghamton in the series. Borgnine had almost declined the White House invitation but in the true spirit of his profession he said that the show must go on because Joe would have wanted it that way.

It was clear the famous actor really cared a lot for the man who had been his on-screen nemesis. He missed him greatly.

If Jerry Ford had done nothing else for me, I would still be eternally grateful for the opportunity he gave me to enjoy the presence of two of the most famous women of the world—both royal and both named Elizabeth. The reason I was able to meet them both was that America was celebrating its bicentennial.

Almost two hundred years to the day since the upstart colonies declared their independence from the crown, the reigning monarch of England arrived to a twenty-one gun salute and a full honor guard on the South Lawn of the White House. Crowds, normally permitted to attend such events by the issuance of free tickets to selected people, were much larger than usual and several hundred without tickets stood outside the White House's wrought iron fence hoping for a glimpse of the Queen and Prince Philip. Everywhere she went, a swirl of excitement ensued which kept everyone talking nervously long after her departure.

It was an incredible night.

July 7, 1976—State Dinner for Her Majesty Queen Elizabeth II

Even if one attends more than a single party at the White House, it is always hard to imagine how it would be possible to improve upon a traditional State Dinner. This night would represent a quantum leap above the standards of any previous social function there and would establish a level of excellence almost impossible to surpass.

Guests were directed to arrive on the East Side of the mansion, an entrance normally used by tourists or people with appointments. After a very short walk through the East Wing halls, they were escorted back outside to be grouped in small crowds by Social Aides in the Jacqueline Kennedy Garden and along the circular drive leading to the entrance under the South Portico. The Strolling Strings entertained them there while everyone waited for the dignitaries to arrive.

As if all of us weren't nervous enough about protocol, threatening storm clouds had given us more reason to worry. We had had some very serious rain earlier, and the staff reported that lightning had struck trees on the South Grounds shortly before our arrival. For a while, the thunder sounded like the Fourth of July, but then the weather changed dramatically, just in time for possibly the grandest Washington social function in the nation's history.

When the guests of honor appeared with the Fords, the receiving line was held outside on the driveway. The asphalt was covered by a red carpet which had been vacuumed once every five minutes for a full hour before their arrival. Despite the very dark clouds, not a drop of rain fell this whole time. The evening was magic.

And the Queen was properly regal. She wore a spectacular diamond necklace, diamond earrings and a fabulous diamond tiera.

The duties of Set-Up and Introducing Aides, normally functions of the most experienced and capable officers in our group, were performed this evening by the full-time Military Aides to the President.

This, again, was a most unusual departure from any previous State Dinner. The Military Aides never performed such lowly functions as those assigned to Social Aides, but for the Queen, no sacrifice was too great. The temptation to be near her was just completely irresistible for everyone.

As the number two Social Aide in seniority, I shared what was left of the plum assignments with Major Dave Van Poznak, the senior guy. He picked Pull-Off Aide and I got the temporarily created post of Pre-Set-Up Aide. The irony in it all was that when papers across the country printed pictures of the evening, Dave and I were right there and the Military Aides who had commandeered our positions in the limelight were hidden by some guests. You can bet we had a good laugh over that turn of royal events.

Following the receiving line, guests passed into the Rose Garden and another world. Completely unrecognizable from its normal setting as a backdrop for presidential ceremonies, it was covered by a massive tent under which two dozen tables for eight were decorated with elaborate settings. A sharp eye would have discovered that tonight's guest list represented about one hundred more than ordinarily attend State Dinners. That also meant there would be no afterdinner guests arriving, since there was no room for them.

The afterdinner entertainment was a doubleheader. Just as it began, I slipped over to the far side to stand behind some seated guests and still see the principals. It was an interesting view. The Captain and Tennille sang some of their current hits, which everyone recognized and enjoyed.

But following this innocent beginning was a shocker that brought a stern expression to the Queen's face. The Captain and Tennille had launched into a new number called "Muskrat Love," the story of two animals and how they courted and made out in a swamp.

Though most modern music is hard to understand and takes a good ear to get the storyline, the Queen's face unfortunately showed she caught every syllable all too clearly.

Then there was the matter of Bob Hope's choice of material.

Hope in his monologue chose to poke a little fun at the British monarchy, to the delight of the guests, but it may have been in questionable taste. Referring to the tiara on her head, Hope said, "In this country, when we see a crown, we think of margarine." I would have judged the remark as slightly disrespectful, but the Queen, proving to be a good sport, gave a royal chuckle.

As if this wasn't pushing the good humor of the Queen too far, the worst was yet to come.

Following the entertainment, everyone went to the State Dining Room to dance. Repeat guests would have found this to be a unique experience, for no one on the staff could remember when dancing was held in the room normally reserved for formal dinners.

The President led off the dancing by taking Queen Elizabeth out on the floor. Other guests stood around the room and dutifully watched as the two moved gracefully to the music. Suddenly someone giggled, others frowned and several people laughed out loud. It took only a few moments till everyone realized that the President of the United States and the Queen of England were dancing to the tune "The Lady Is a Tramp."

Of course it was an honest mistake in programming—one of those little details that occasionally slip through without sufficient scrutiny. But three in a night? The entire program for a formal dinner passes through the Social Secretary's office.

Maria Downs had been the Social Secretary for about eight months and was doing measurably better than her predecessor—but no one is perfect. I overheard someone say, "Poor Ford is so accident prone, it's even lousing up this royal party."

But there was no real harm done and the Queen seemed to enjoy herself—who said the British had no sense of humor? Elizabeth II had so electrified the room with her presence that she didn't even have to speak a word. Lynda Day George, Cary Grant, Willie Mays and Barbara Walters could rest easy because the crowds of people who would ordinarily pursue them were focused on the visiting royalty, and so were they.

After everyone had joined in the dancing, I gave Charles Nelson Reilly and Julie Harris an informal guided tour of the State Floor.

They were just like any excited tourists or history buffs. No haughty airs, condescending remarks, or oversized Hollywood egos here, just pure and simple curiosity. We had a great time for half an hour till I finally deposited them with Telly Savalas.

Governor John Connally was there and I tried once again to get him to take a bet on Texas University for its Thanksgiving Day game with A&M. Either his fortunes were already in decline or he sensed that his university just wasn't the football powerhouse that it used to be, as he wouldn't bite. Nothing would have pleased me more than to have the big man pay off on a loss to the Aggies, but he laughingly refused to cooperate.

The honored guests left early but the Fords stayed very late, dancing and visiting with friends. The evening ended well past midnight and to no one's surprise, we did not have to go on wallflower patrol all night.

My second royal Elizabeth came to the White House later in the same month. This Elizabeth was also born in Britain but she had achieved her royal status in Hollywood—Elizabeth Taylor.

The two Elizabeths were treated quite differently at the White House even though the occasion that had brought them there was the same historic celebration:

July 10—A Bicentennial Evening of Entertainment at the White House

I had waited a long time to see up close the legendary beauty of Liz Taylor, and she was everything people had said—and more. When I looked into her large violet eyes, the thought passed my mind that she could drive a man to drink or soberness—whichever.

But the party had not been designed around her and only her own shining beauty and fame caused it to revolve around her anyway.

President Ford invited Washington's diplomatic corps in to enjoy a presentation of American music. More than four hundred guests squeezed into the tents in the Rose Garden to hear Ella Fitzgerald, Roger Miller and Tammy Wynette sing jazz and country and western tunes.

Because John Warner was now administrator of the American Revolution Bicentennial Commission, he was among the invited guests.

The former Secretary of the Navy had a goodly crowd around him all evening, but his achievements in Washington did not yet justify such lavish attention by the diplomatic corps. The real attraction was his date, Elizabeth Taylor.

Everyone came for a closer look at the international superstar and stayed and stayed and stayed. An excuse for remaining was to find out why Elizabeth had a large bandage on her right foot near her ankle. And to commiserate with her.

All this talking and giving of sympathy took time. Much time. The President and First Lady were making no special fuss over her or sending someone to move her to the head of the line, if they indeed even knew of her distress.

When John and Liz finally brought up the tail end of the receiving line, she was in considerable distress from having stood so long. She had spent the day at the country home of her escort, and apparently the last bit of fun she had was going for a ride on his son's motorcycle. Unaccustomed to such activities, she had accidentally touched her bare calf to the motorcycle exhaust pipe and received a very nasty burn. Just standing up caused her considerable pain.

I asked if I could help, and her smile of gratitude was thanks enough. I thought of bringing her a chair, but that was not done around the White House. Nor would the offer to lean on me have been proper. If she wanted to meet the President, she'd have to get there on her own two feet.

So she hung in there, inching along the receiving line while complaining quietly but bitterly about her discomfort. Fortunately— or I should say, unfortunately for us aides—John Warner was able to comfort her, saving us aides from a touchy situation.

Liz came out a winner. She married the handsome Warner and soon found herself the wife of a United States Senator.

I came out a winner, too. At least I can tell my grandchildren some day, "Yes, I met the royal Elizabeth—both of them."

17

Good Guys Finish Last

*T*here was nothing to warn me that an international movie star would flatter me with her attention at the White House. I had occasionally dated guests or staffers, but none was a public personality.

This evening had started like so many of the Ford dinner parties—so happy and relaxed. It was listed on my calendar of February 20, 1976, as "Dinner for the Governors" and coincided with the National Governor's Conference in Washington.

Only forty-three of our nation's governors were there, but they were in high spirits as Pearl Bailey strode on stage—though she was not the entertainer of the evening, but merely a guest—and amazed them by knowing and belting out many of their state songs.

The only sad note of the evening was that Susan Ford had come without a date. To digress for a moment, when her father was Vice President, she dated a fellow named Gardner Britt, living in Blacksburg, Virginia. When Dad assumed the presidency, Gardner came along as part of her personal entourage. However, she wanted to date other fellows as well as Gardner.

Not long afterward, while Susan was suffering over the breakup which she had initiated, I was amused to see Betty Ford's assistant, Sheila Weidenfeld, and another staff woman trying to cheer up

Susan. They were sitting around a table in the Grand Foyer of the White House singing a parody of, "Bye, Bye Blackbird."

Only they were singing, "Bye, Bye Blacksburg," and Susan finally laughed and joined in. I guess it made Susan feel better to have some "girls" to share her sorrow with.

As a consequence of this freedom initiative, and the fact that she often stood in for her ailing mother as hostess, Susan rarely had a date again at an official function. Social Aides watched out for her to make sure she had a dance partner when necessary, but it never went beyond the formalities of duty.

Susan frequented several popular night spots in Georgetown that I often visited, such as Winston's and Pall Mall. We had spoken in passing on a number of occasions, and this evening when she was alone on the sidelines watching the dancers at the White House, I asked Susan for the next number. As fate would have it, the tune was a popular one that apparently only Susan and I recognized as ideal for a new dance called "The Bump." For each heavy beat of the rhythm, the participants were to literally bump hips, lightly.

To get a little variety, a good dancer could bump alternating hips, shoulders, elbows, calves, the back of the hands or even the side of the knees while at the same time switching left and right sides in the process. This was a step beyond the contact normally found in ballroom dancing, although it was in no way provocative or suggestive. But it definitely was different and new, and we were the only ones doing it in the rather large crowd of dancers in the East Room.

Halfway through, we became aware that our dance style had attracted considerable notice. Anyone doing the bump in the White House would surely be noticed, but the President's daughter was noticed no matter what she did. Now we had inadvertently attracted more attention than desired, but it would have been cowardly to stop.

I figured that as the First Daughter, Susan knew, better than I, what she could get away with. If she was comfortable, it wasn't my place to ruin her fun since I was having a good time too.

Dancing takes energy but the bump requires genuine stamina. Running four or five miles almost every day, I was able to handle this exercise without too much effort and for some reason Susan seemed to be doing fairly well too, even though she wasn't a runner. We finished the dance slightly winded but decide to sit out the next one.

As we walked off the dance floor, the Naval Aide to the President appeared beside me and, only half smiling, said, "We don't dance like that at the White House."

I smiled back and asked, "Would you like to tell the President's daughter or should I?" He mumbled something about taking care of it himself as he walked away.

I stepped around behind the people watching the dancers to try to regain some degree of anonymity. It didn't work. A beautiful lady with a distinctly familiar British accent walked up and said, "I like the way you dance." Remarking on how much energy it took, I asked if she would like to try something slower. Unfortunately, it was late and she was already on her way out with a friend and they disappeared.

Asking around, I learned from my friends that the mystery woman was the popular British actress, Diana Rigg. She had starred in the television spy show *The Avengers* as the karate expert, Emma Peale, and had done a number of movies including one of the early James Bond series.

At the moment, she was starring in *The Misanthrope* at the Kennedy Center with Alec McCowen, who had been her escort at the party. I had seen the TV show more than once as well as a couple of her movies but not the play. Still, I didn't recognize her with her hair cut shorter and piled on top of her head.

After considering our brief encounter the night before, I decided to throw caution to the wind and called Diana backstage at the Kennedy Center. A message left for her produced a return call about forty-five minutes later. After identifying myself, I volunteered to escort her around Washington and show her some of the nightlife.

She readily accepted my invitation, but immediately we had a problem. The curtain went up at 8:00 P.M. and she couldn't go to dinner before a performance because her acting would be affected. We settled on a very late dinner after the next show.

The staff at the Watergate Hotel was very accommodating the following evening and actively helped us locate each other in their expansive lobby. Dinner at the Port of Georgetown restaurant was an unusual affair.

Her company was very pleasant, but intruders weren't. People recognized her and stopped by one at a time throughout the meal to get her autograph on a menu or card. Some studied me for a moment, trying to figure out if they should know me and ask for my autograph as well.

We danced there for a while and then went to a disco. She was a superb dancer and a delight to be with, but again it was like dancing in a goldfish bowl. Eventually, we escaped the unwanted attention by going back to the Watergate where celebrities were common enough to be ignored.

We got some privacy at last in the coffee shop. Diana told me a lot about her career adventures, her first marriage to an Israeli, and her vacation home on the island of Ibiza in the Mediterranean. She asked a lot about Vietnam and the White House. The manager left a pot of coffee before retiring. We found ourselves now laughing, now seriously discussing countless topics for hours on end.

We said goodnight as dawn was breaking. This threw her entire schedule off, as she needed plenty of sleep to be her best for the next night's performance—but somehow we just couldn't stop talking and sharing our very different experiences.

The strength of her personality was like a huge magnet. I made time for her in spite of her unique schedule. By now I was calling her Di. Much later I discovered it was a popular nickname for any British girl named Diana.

Attention from a national star would affect anyone. I was somewhere in the clouds until her troupe abruptly moved on to Broadway. I landed back on earth with quite a thud.

For a while, it was only phone calls. Then she called to ask if we could meet in Philadelphia, where she was going to appear on the Merv Griffin show.

Naturally, I agreed and picked her up at the train station. It was as if there had been no time lapse. And as usual, when dealing with a public personality, we started having little adventures immediately. For example, when we stopped at her hotel, we ran into Victoria Federova, the much-in-the-news love child of an American general, who had been on duty in Moscow in the 1950s, and a famous Russian actress. Victoria had just arrived in the States and was on her way to meet her father in Florida. Even without an interpreter, Di hit it off with her like a couple of sisters and communicated very well.

On another occasion, we found ourselves having dinner in the townhouse of a very wealthy man, where Di was the only female among five males. Though I was the one who had brought her, I felt uneasy because it would not have surprised me if these other fellows had made an effort to take Di home. What a mistake that was. All four of these men were gay, and they were certainly interested in Di's career, but as the evening grew late, it was I whom they had their eyes on. We beat a hasty retreat after dinner and had a great laugh over the whole evening.

Backstage at the Merv Griffin show, we met Rita Moreno and George Carlin. They were putting makeup on while laughing uproariously and gossiping about a well-known Hollywood star's sexual escapades during the past week. It would have been nothing out of the ordinary for Hollywood—except that the fellow had just announced his engagement and impending marriage.

I had been thinking a lot about Di and me and our odd friendship, but this conversation made me realize more than ever how different our worlds were. More importantly, it didn't seem like they could or should converge. After the Griffin show, I dropped her at the train station, and a couple of weeks later she returned to England. In the end, I decided to pass up Di's tempting invitation to use her vacation home in the Mediterranean. No, the girl for me would not be found living that life-style. Our paths never crossed again, though I was reminded of her often.

Meanwhile, back at the White House, the First Lady was beset with problems involving her staff. First was the tragedy of April 10, 1975. Retired Army Major James Howe, the husband of Betty Ford's special assistant, Nancy Howe, committed suicide. There had been some speculation about the couple's ties to the Korean businessman, Tongsun Park, who lavished expensive attention on his friends around the Washington area. It was later revealed that the *Washington Post* had been asking questions about their vacations and who had paid for them, and apparently the pressure was just too much for him.

As a result, Nancy Howe disappeared from the East Wing staff, and as time went on, Betty Ford admitted how much she still missed Nancy and the comfort of having a friend in the White House. Now, Sheila Weidenfeld and Nancy Lammerding Ruwe—she had recently married—were in closer contact with the First Lady, but somehow they did not appear to fill the void.

Filling it, in a way, was Pearl Bailey, who became so close to the

First lady that Betty referred to her as a "sister." Everyone responded to Pearl Bailey's marvelously disarming personality. Her down-to-earth attitude about life put everyone instantly at ease.

Once, when Pearl was surrounded by newspaper reporters, I went over to rescue her, only to find myself unneeded but, nevertheless, drawn into her conversation with them long enough for a photographer to come by and record the event.

I remember kidding Pearl that she and Bob Hope were coming to the White House so often, they ought to start limousine pooling together.

This Spirit of Brotherly Love did not run throughout the White House corridors. Sheila Weidenfeld, who was responsible for looking after Mrs. Ford's public image, was having a hard time. The word got around that she was feuding with both East Wing and West Wing staffers. Not getting along with the head honcho of the Military Office was understandable because he came down hard on people.

But there seemed to be a number of people with whom Sheila had running disagreements, and the word was that she spent a lot of time and energy jousting with the President's Press Secretary, Ron Nessen. Understaffed herself, and distracted by petty annoyances, Sheila Weidenfeld appeared to be outflanked at every turn in this male-dominated area.

The Social Aides were not faring much better—and possibly worse. For some unexplained reason, we were called in for a complete review and discussion of all current policy and procedures concerning our duties. Reading between the lines, one might conclude that we had a lot of new and inexperienced people. In fact we had a few, but no more than the normal turnover would generate.

The real problem seemed to be in the Social Secretary's Office. All the parties were going well, and everyone, primarily the guests, enjoyed themselves immensely. When guests were happy, the aides were happy as well and it apparently showed. The rehash of basic "don'ts" and an occasional "do" appeared to be an unspoken effort to put us back in our places.

The truth of the matter was that for weeks, rumors had circulated that we as a group were too relaxed, and a general opinion developed that we enjoyed ourselves too much. But no specific criticism was leveled, and we were often commended for doing an excellent job. The pointed reminders, however, of what was acceptable conduct and what was not were just to heavy to be directed at the few new faces among the aides.

A new high—or low—was reached when the Military Office spoke up.

In a continuation of their effort to put a damper on the Social Aides, the Military Office took this opportunity to insist on some changes in procedures. Like any group of officers, we had a cup and flower fund that took care of incidental gifts and cards, etc., and also provided each aide with an engraved sterling silver ice or champagne bucket when he or she departed the program.

These funds were in a proper checking account in the name of the White House Social Aides. The Military Office had suddenly taken a great interest in our removing the words "White House" from the name of the account to insure that no financial problem would appear "that could embarrass the President." As always, we did what the office wanted, but it cost them a measure of respect from the aides.

Things could get worse—and did. There was growing discontent among the Social Aides, first because of the pettiness of the Military Office, but even more because of the offhand way the Social Secretary's office was handling things as compared to how carefully Lucy Winchester had issued instructions and shown helpfulness.

For just one example, we had been left to our own devices in finding out the pronunciation of a foreign dignitary's name, when we had to introduce him on the loudspeaker and, later, to the President. Lucy had always checked out these things with the State Department. On occasion, I had had to call the State Department myself to get the phonetic spelling of a tongue twister.

Aides were not in a position to complain aloud about anything, but somehow the accumulation of internal discontent from a number of sources finally got the message across to the person that mattered. Betty Ford decided that her second Social Secretary, Nancy Lammerding Ruwe, had to go, but before she could exit gracefully, someone published a story in the newspaper that she was being fired.

Publicly leaking privileged information was and is a popular sport in Washington, as well as a way of forcing a change. The problem is that it often circumvents official prerogatives of senior officials to do things their own way. In this case, Nancy was let go in a very unceremonious manner that even her detractors deplored.

Her replacement, Maria Downs, arrived, and we could only hope that she would be a bit more helpful to the aides, effective in her party planning—and of course, it wouldn't hurt if she was also likable.

More and more, we aides were becoming aware that Gerald Ford was thinking of that election down the trail ahead. And more and more, the guest list was influenced by it.

Though Ford was no stranger to campaigning, having hit the trail every two years to keep his Michigan congressional seat, he decided to start his presidential quest early since he'd never won a *national* campaign.

The kickoff, so to speak, was a White House luncheon on June 11, 1975, for the American Newspaper Publishers Association, which was meeting in Washington.

This event departed from custom in several respects. Henry Kissinger showed up for a *social* lunch. That happened very rarely. Other senior administration officials also were present. The word was that they were supposed to critique the event and tell Ford what they thought about how each publisher felt about him and the comments he made to them. He wanted an analysis.

Cocktails were served before and liqueurs after lunch. President Ford told stories and was a charming luncheon companion, and afterward, he made a few remarks and invited questions from the group. He answered candidly and off the cuff.

When it was over, the President's staff realized that Ford had a lot of work ahead in learning how to give the answers that would be true to himself and his program without antagonizing publishers whose editorials influence the nation's readers.

I recall one White House party that should have been billed as a political party rather than a State Dinner to honor Prime Minister Malcolm Fraser of Australia.

No one paid an excessive amount of attention to the guest of honor. Nearly all of the numerous congressional and uncommitted delegate guests were engrossed in the upcoming Republican National Convention. Governor Ronald Reagan had just announced liberal Senator Richard Schweiker as his vice presidential running mate.

Most guests on July 27, 1976, were jubilant because they supported Ford and felt this extraordinary move by conservative candidate Reagan would simply give the nomination to President Ford. A few guests who supported Reagan were clearly unhappy over the situation, which further boosted the morale of the Ford people and reinforced their feelings of victory. The director of the CIA, George Bush, stayed firmly but politely in President Ford's corner without making too many enemies on the other side.

History would show that loyalty paid off. Bush's skill as the consummate politician would eventually be rewarded as he climbed the ladder to the Oval Office itself with the support of both Ford and Reagan.

The few guests not overly engrossed in politics were Gregory Peck, Rod Steiger, Malcolm Forbes and John Newcombe. Most of the Social Aides and many of the guests were politely watching tennis star Jimmy Conners' date, Marjorie Wallace. It was abundantly clear why she was an international beauty queen.

Jimmy was drinking a glass of wine even though he was playing on the tennis circuit, so I asked him about his physical training regimen to stay in shape. He explained that it would take him two weeks of exercise to get the one glass out of his system, but it was worth it because this was a very special night to him. We noted that at two weeks per glass, some of the other guests had years of hard work ahead of them.

Getting the nomination was the easier part. The rest was uphill and it was as if the ghost of Richard Nixon was riding on Gerald Ford's shoulders. It didn't help that the accident prone Ford continued to stumble or slip, hit people with golf balls, and bump his head. And it didn't help that the wrong word would pop out or that he had sudden lapses of memory in his campaign travels. He couldn't remember how to pronounce Mesa College and got it wrong twice. Speaking at Iowa State, he thought he was at Ohio State.

When a guest kiddingly repeated some of the "dumb" jokes about Ford, I quickly pointed out that the President could not be too lacking in intelligence since he had graduated in the top third of his class at Yale Law School and, before that, in the top third of his class at the University of Michigan.

I don't know if it convinced anyone, but we tried. It didn't help that Johnny Carson and others kept their comedy writers busy dreaming up new gags about imagined Ford stumbles, tumbles or mumbles. Or repeated some of his real slips of tongue.

Other gaffes paled into insignificance compared with the simply unbelievable mistake he made during his TV debate with Democratic candidate Jimmy Carter.

White House Aides, including myself, cringed as Jerry Ford said:

"There is no Soviet domination of Eastern Europe and there never will be under the Ford administration."

Challenged by a *New York Times* reporter, Ford made it worse when he replied that he didn't believe the Romanians considered themselves "dominated by the Soviet Union." He went on to say:

"I don't believe that the Poles consider themselves dominated by the Soviet Union. Each of these countries is independent, autonomous. It has its own territorial integrity and the United States does not concede that those countries are under the domination of the Soviet Union."

Ethnic Americans were up in arms and well-read Americans were aghast as Ford tried to make things better in the days that followed by issuing clarifying statements. In the end, he had to invite ethnic Eastern European groups to the White House to apologize and admit that he had not expressed himself well.

Greater ethnic support at the polls might have helped, but in the end, it probably was his pardoning of Richard Nixon that buried Ford's chance to be elected for his own term in the White House. As one aide put it, "He threw a monkey wrench into the wheels of justice and it exploded in his face election day."

Everyone liked Jerry Ford being a nice guy but he had carried niceness one step too far and the public could not forgive him. In attempting to "heal the nation's wounds," by pardoning Nixon, he had succeeded in wounding himself. And all the staffers.

November 4, 1976

Ford lost the election. Unlike the last transition, nearly every member of the staff would be gone in January and they all knew it. Those that were certain to remain included the Social Aides, the maids, butlers, ushers, kitchen staff, doormen, the White House Police and the Secret Service. For almost everyone else, it would be wholesale housecleaning because the Democrats were coming to town for the first time since LBJ.

December 13—Christmas Party for the United States Secret Service

Billed as a party, it wasn't really a social event as they normally occur. This was one of the annual thank-you parties honoring key support groups at the Mansion. While literally thousands are assigned to the Secret Service organization around the world, and in spite of the fact that the headquarters were next door in the Treasury Department, only two hundred members and their guests attended this function.

One guest's date was the girl who had helped me clip Gerald Ford's Swedish ivy and who told the story about Brezhnev's stewardesses coming face to face with Pat Nixon at six in the morning in San Clemente. The agent who brought her clearly didn't want to talk about his experiences with the Russian leader, and he wasn't too pleased with her that she had obviously told me. Such is Washington where there are few, if any, real secrets.

Then the Social Aides were given a Christmas party. We got personal invitations, hors d'oeuvres and the works, but the President never showed. Seeing Betty and Jerry at parties every week lessened the importance of this nonevent for us, but his nonappearance was a little hard to explain to our dates. They were supposed to be impressed by meeting the President.

January 10, 1977—Ceremony for the Presentation of the Presidential Medals of Freedom

It was hardly a coincidence that just about a week before the Ford administration departed, there were a number of presidential awards approved. There was no discernible pattern beyond the obvious fact that every recipient was a figure of world renown. Lady Bird Johnson, I. W. Able, James A. Michener, Nelson Rockefeller, Lowell Thomas, Arthur Fiedler and several others were each easily capable of drawing a substantial crowd anywhere.

Aside from the moments facing the news media to receive accolades, they really didn't look or act too excited about this event. After years in the public spotlight, dropping by the White House to pick up an award evidently felt routine.

An interesting thing happened when General of the Army (five star) Omar Bradley arrived. His military aide-de-camp turned out to be an old "friend" of mine. Before he departed our last station at Fort Benning, Georgia, seven years earlier for the Far East, I had given him money to buy me a new watch. When it didn't arrive several weeks later, I started making inquiries but never got a response. After several letters to his military and home addresses went unanswered, I gave it and our friendship up as a loss.

And here he was now. He stammered a weak hello and immediately took his boss to position him for the ceremony. When he returned, and before I could say a word, he reached into his pocket and pulled out the money he had owed me for seven years. After five years in the mansion, there had been many thanks from First Family and staff members as well as plenty of food, drink and excitement, but this was the only time I received money for being there. This good fortune was only due to my perceived status as a potentially powerful aide in the White House and nothing else. Who said that ninety percent of life is just showing up?

There was an aura of sadness at the next party—the last one.

January 14, 1977—Reception for the National Republican Committee

In a final ritual for the Republicans, the party leadership gathered at the White House for one last celebration before turning the reins of government and control of the mansion over to the Democrats. They had all worked hard to overcome the taint of Watergate on their party and to elect Gerald Ford. Although the team placed a close second, Ford was still very gracious in thanking them for their efforts. They all vowed to work hard again to recover the presidency and the White House, but for now they could only plan for the immediate future of their party.

As the President was departing the event, we met in front of the elevator for the last time. I offered the sincere appreciation of all the Social Aides for every kindness the First Family had shown us over the past two years. President Ford was truly pleased and thanked me with great emotion. He repeated emphatically the often-heard remark that the parties couldn't go on without the Social Aides. We shook hands and parted, not to meet again for two and a half years. Following his request, I passed his thanks to the other aides.

President-elect Carter's new Military Aides had been selected and were standing around watching us do our jobs for the past month. Some of the issues and concerns they addressed and the tough line of questions they were asking suggested that a new broom was indeed sweeping down on us. I hoped the bristles wouldn't be too rough.

Part Four

Carter—The Impossible Dream

18

Cultural Shock Around the White House

*I*t wasn't as artless as it looked. Everyone thought it was a spontaneous move when Jimmy Carter jumped out of the car and walked the mile and a half down Pennsylvania Avenue—all the way to the White House—after the swearing in ceremony at the Capitol.

The truth was something else—known only to a few people at the White House. Actually President-elect Jimmy Carter had decided weeks before the ceremony to take the dramatic walk but shared the information with only a few people for security reasons. Even the local police were unprepared but quickly recovered since they had expected Carter at least to leap out and shake hands here and there.

These early maneuvers suggest a man operating from a programmed script and not just a typical peanut farmer who happened to be elected President of the United States.

Starting with that strenuous walk, which was really more than a mile and a half when you count the zigzagging back and forth to shake hands with the crowd, the new President in every way strove to present a picture of vigor and youth. And also to proclaim that the nation's new leader was a regular guy. He hiked. He rejected limos. He scorned the morning suits previous Presidents had worn for their swearing-in ceremonies and decreed that at his ceremony everyone would wear business suits.

Carter's would be the last inaugural to have so little emphasis on safety and was marked by a notable lack of federal and district security personnel. Much of the credit for this upbeat and optimistic mood went to Gerald Ford for healing the nation's wounds and for restoring confidence in the honor of the presidency.

I was pleased to hear Carter, a Democrat, praise a Republican in his inaugural address—"I want to thank my predecessor for all he has done to heal our land." Major war protests now appeared to be a thing of the past and everyone could look forward to a new beginning with a different kind of leader who was definitely not part of the establishment—nor did he want to be.

I attended the Carter swearing-in, but having special tickets to a standing room area a bit closer than the general public stood was not a big help. My friends and I could barely see what was happening in any detail.

The ceremony at the Capitol was attended by more people than attended the previous three Republican events. But there were nowhere near the crowds that flocked twelve years earlier to see the last Democrat, Lyndon Baines Johnson, take office.

The changes came fast and furious. Even at the Inaugural parties. Jimmy Carter was not going to subject people to the traditional fanfare that arriving Presidents had always received.

Gone was "Ruffles and Flourishes" and the band did not play "Hail to the Chief." Carter was determined to set a less imperial tone for his administration, and this would be another way to symbolically show the public he was simply a grass-roots American. Eliminating the pomp and circumstance that everyone had grown accustomed to was the quickest route to this objective.

To reinforce the point that this President was as unremarkable as the average citizen, the Carters elected not to use a limousine to go to the People's Inauguration Parties but instead rode in a modest Lincoln—a tan town car.

Carter continued to use this relatively humble vehicle for his transportation for some time. In doing so he seemed to feel that he was staying close to the people or at least setting a good example for the rest of the government. This point was reinforced a few days later when the President decided that all senior members of his staff would have to get themselves to work on their own, rather than depend on the fleet of White House limousines.

There would be much wailing and wringing of hands. One of the more significant perks provided to high-level officials of previous administrations, limousine service not only was a great convenience but also was a very visible demonstration of enormous power in a city that thrived on it.

But the Inaugural Week was the Carter honeymoon—he could do no wrong. People applauded the new President's style not realizing that it had been well thought out. A good example was the handling of the traditional Inaugural Balls.

To begin with, Jimmy Carter decreed that they were not Inaugural Balls but were only to be called "People's Inauguration Parties." However, everything about the *humble*, de-escalated balls was programmed. So was Jimmy. So was his wife.

Fully aware that her every movement at the parties would be closely watched by the press and all others in sight, Rosalynn Carter wore a dress that she had used before at Jimmy's gubernatorial inaugural function back in Georgia. It was a blue chiffon with gold braid trim and matching sleeveless coat. The Carters said it was sentiment, but they gave every indication that they meant to say they were thrifty, just like most of the people facing them.

Each time the Carters stopped at one of the seven party sites to visit with the crowds, the President would get up on stage and ask, "What do you think of my wife's old dress?" or sometimes, "Does everyone like my wife's old dress?"

The applause was a resounding yes! The inside story was that Rosalynn, whose mother had been a seamstress, had made the gown for her husband's swearing-in as governor of Georgia in 1970. The outfit seemed so right among that crowd where very few female guests were wearing clothes that one would classify as designer made or opulent.

Not lost in all this symbolism was the fact that the cost of admission for each of these inaugural parties was only $25 per person. Even so, some complained that it was too much. (In later years, $25 would be much closer to the parking fee than the price of admission.) Carter wanted the multitudes to share his joy.

So it was important that it be affordable to all. Over 300,000 invitations were mailed out to Democratic campaign workers all across the nation. Many others were told that if they thought they should have gotten a ticket and hadn't, they should just come anyway because everyone truly was welcome.

At the National Guard Armory, it appeared that too many people had taken them up on the offer. Billed as the official gathering place for the Georgians, some of whom had arrived on the Peanut Special from Plains, this was the place to be to meet the new power people and Carter friends. Washington regulars who showed up to greet the new insiders seemed cautious and hesitant. It was an amusing situation, considering how sophisticated they generally were. Unaccustomed to country music and dancing, they were conspicuous as they stood watching the new arrivals in town jump right in and take over the party. Wallflower patrol would have been a problem here if the Social Aides had been on duty which—thankfully—we were not. Fortunately for all, not only were we off duty but many of the Washington regulars simply stayed home and let the Georgia Brigade take over.

First Brother Billy Carter was not his usual self, all scrubbed up and looking very dapper in a black tuxedo. He compromised this new display of elegance though by drinking beer from a can.

There was one woman—not young—who stole the show. Miss Lillian, the President's mother, was having more fun than just about anyone. So few women had lived long enough to see their sons elected to the highest office in the land that Miss Lillian surely merited the enormous attention, affection and praise showered on her by everyone.

Without question, the President's mother was the warmest, friendliest member of the Carter clan and was amazed at the compliments bestowed on her throughout those first hectic months.

She just couldn't believe her son was presidential material. When Jimmy had first told her he thought he might run for President, she had asked, "Of what?"

Evidently, he couldn't get used to the idea either.

While the Fords and the Nixons had loved all the trappings that went with the White House position, the Carters seemed bent on stamping out every bit of pomp and circumstance. They worked to avoid it to the extent that many in Washington began to look upon their humble, subdued manner as posturing. Whether or not the Carters had gone out of their way to create a down-home image, the

people attending these parties were loving the opportunity to celebrate *any* Democratic victory. It had been a long, dry spell.

Even Hollywood stars whom no one could remember having
campaigned for Jimmy Carter showed up when invited for the
Inaugural. Like many Americans, they were reacting to the office
itself and not necessarily the man.

Most of them ended up at the Kennedy Center Inaugural Ball (a
ball by any other name was still traditionally called a ball no matter
what Jimmy Carter called it). Tickets to such an event are always
considered to be a mark of the importance of the holders, and they
normally go to powerful inside and higher echelon party workers as
well as to the largest contributors.

But then, all tickets are hard to get. Although, in theory, everyone
in the nation was invited to Carter's inaugural parties, you had to be
someone or know someone even to get the right to buy the tickets.

One woman from Ohio had gone to a lot of trouble to get a ticket
but she still almost had her heart broken at an inaugural "party." She
had brought with her a big bag of *organic* peanuts from her health
food store in Youngstown. After all, wasn't Jimmy Carter the man
who would appreciate a good peanut?

She had worked for Jimmy's election in her state and fully
expected to have a moment at the Washington Hilton ball to present
her peanuts to the President when he put in his appearance. But she
hadn't counted on security around the President. She tried but had
to give up. As she put it, "I was afraid I'd be wrestled to the ground
with my peanuts."

Already, Jimmy Carter's vow to be accessible to everyone was just
not working—nor could it for any modern President.

After the swearing-in and the parade and the Inaugural parties
came the second tidal wave of partying—the flood of guests to the
White House. I had never seen so many parties crammed into such a
short period of time there. Until it was over, the Executive Mansion
was a madhouse.

January 21 and 22, 1977—Receptions for the Carter Clan, Old
Friends, Diplomats, and Other Dignitaries

There was only an hour or so break between receptions at the
White House and it took two full days for the new President to

complete his marathon. I never worked harder as an aide or witnessed more breaks with protocol.

The first party was thrown to honor and give thanks to the army of people who had provided various Carter family members with room and board during the long and expensive campaign. More than one thousand guests from all over the United States crowded onto the State Floor to be welcomed personally by their now famous houseguest.

Standing in the formal receiving line in front of the entrance to the Blue Room, Jimmy and Rosalynn—the former guests—now proudly served as host and hostess to their benefactors.

Jubilant would not adequately describe the mood of this crowd. Many had believed deeply in Jimmy Carter before most of the nation had even heard his name. References to moral leadership, deep personal integrity, religious orientation and the simplicity of the Carter life-style were common among the crowd of devoted followers.

It seemed like a class reunion as people who supported the campaign for up to two years were reunited with the grateful Carter clan of Georgia.

A reception in the most famous residence in the world was not the only reward they would receive for opening their homes to the candidate and his relatives. Each family also was given a four-by-six inch bronze plaque with black engraving that read: "A member of the Jimmy Carter family stayed in this house during the 1976 Presidential Campaign."

The aides had a devil of a time trying to memorize faces. According to tradition, the Social Aides are supposed to know important or repeat guests on sight. But now there was an army of new people to contend with and the best we could hope for was to identify the ones who had been in the newspapers more than once. Complicating the problem was that everything was done at the last minute. The Carters had not mailed invitations to the guests.

They felt it would not have looked right to use the mail since the guests would have had to receive the invitation to visit the White House before the Carters were actually in the Executive Mansion. The guests were called individually and asked to come, and their invitations were to be picked up at the door when they arrived.

Guests could also save them as souvenirs.

What a security headache and what a mess!

Standing just behind the staff assistants, we had to wait for each guest to announce his or her name to receive the souvenir invitation and then we made a mental note of their faces. With so many people coming through so fast, even this shortcut became too much to handle and we aides gave up and decided to wait for the next day's society columns to see *who* we had seen.

Washington protocol was sent reeling by the new President. In one of the first really significant departures from the procedure to which the Social Staff was accustomed, the Carters decided to share the glory with the Mondales by giving the Vice President his own receiving line.

It was a riot. No one could remember seeing it done before. Especially this way. The line was endless. Winding around from the main hall through the State Dining Room, the Red Room, Blue Room and into the Green Room, it gave the guests the opportunity to look over as they passed an open door and see what the people way ahead of them in line were up to. It was just like being in a queue at Busch Gardens for the most popular ride. It was the longest receiving line anyone on the staff ever remembered seeing at the White House.

The Carters had their reception out in the Cross Hall at the entrance to the Blue Room—a conspicuous place—while the Mondales took their stations tucked away in the State Dining Room.

The wait was interminable. Some guests hopped around like jumping beans. Others stood like zombies and shuffled along inch by inch when prodded. The line was so long that by the time guests reached the President, shook his hand and staggered away, many had that frozen smile that some people get when they have just gotten off the Loch Ness Monster roller coaster ride.

Soothing their nerves was the fragrance throughout the Mansion. The Garden Club of Georgia had brought in mountains of Georgia greenery and blooms. An aide commented that it wasn't even Christmas and already the Carter Family had done itself proud. Only at the holiday season did the White House look so good, and even then it had never smelled so sweet.

All of these blossoms, buds and flowering plants could be found in the Plains area—Jimmy's hometown. There were snapdragons, white camellias, clivia, southern smilax, yellow roses and goldband holly, all interspersed with peaches and other fruits to form a most colorful feast for the eyes.

The garden clubbers, including the mother of President Ford's former campaign manager, Bo Callaway, had worked around the clock on the elaborate flower arrangements. The hordes of people standing in the receiving line had plenty of time to stop and smell the roses.

Maybe Rosalynn thought she was back in her Georgia garden because suddenly she took off her shoes. Aides looked at each other in disbelief at this shocking parting with protocol. Someone wondered aloud why Rosalynn hadn't sent an assistant to get her a change of shoes.

Evidently, the First Lady felt enough at home after a single day in the White House to take off her shoes and stand in the receiving line in her stocking feet to greet guests. Fortunately, the visitors who would ordinarily take their cues from the First Family did not follow suit.

At each new reception, the Social Aides traded jobs so that no one would get too tired or complacent in doing the same task over and over again during the marathon of White House receptions.

Other groups invited during the two day period included governors, friends from Georgia, political supporters from the Democratic National Committee, labor and business leaders, the diplomatic corps of Washington, including those from the Organization of American States, plus the Pentagon's top brass and the Congress.

Some people wore a gold peanut on their jacket lapels. I had a good laugh remembering Nixon's supporters with their gold R.N. pins, but I wasn't about to confuse these men and women with the current Secret Service detail. They were merely a few devoted supporters of the new regime. The lapel decorations were not even a coordinated effort by the Democrats who probably could have sold thousands of them as souvenirs.

More than seven thousand guests had to be introduced individually to Jimmy and Rosalynn Carter. And also to Fritz and Joan Mondale during the periods when the Vice President and his wife had their own line. My job, at one point, was to be the Set-Up Aide for the Carter receiving line. Everything would proceed smoothly until there would be a delay while someone stayed too long talking to the President. At such times I would be forced to listen to the conversations of those in the line.

Democratic National Committee chairman Robert Strauss happened to be standing in front of me when he chose to give those of us within earshot a short dissertation as to why this change to Jimmy Carter was such a great and beneficial moment in our nation's history—the country needed a *plain*, humble man of the people. This from a man who was known to build himself as a big spender, and anything but a simple man—"Twenty-five grand? Hell, I give twenty-five grand for a good table." And this from a man who later complained when the Carter White House staff tried to book him in tourist class, saying, "I'll quit flying first class when they invent something better."

What was also interesting about this lecture was that Bob Strauss was really no friend of Jimmy Carter's. The two had maintained a love-hate relationship for some time. Strauss had actually opposed Carter in the primary election by backing Senator Scoop Jackson of the state of Washington.

In fact, he was quoted as saying of candidate Carter in those early days, "I like the little guy—but that born again Christian stuff..." His disdain hung in the air. But he conveniently switched his allegiance after Carter won the Democratic nomination.

Despite this early opposition to his candidacy, Jimmy Carter gave Strauss an important post and Strauss gave the President public accolades in return. I wasn't buying Strauss' sales pitch at the party and my mind was saying, *wait and see*

Governor Jerry Brown of California came through the line with his girlfriend, Linda Ronstadt, while I was Introducing Aide. He had been elected to office two years earlier and by now was comfortable with his celebrity status. Linda managed to hold his eye during this whole event along with that of every young-at-heart male in the room. I nearly forgot the governor's name when I bent the rules a bit by talking to her just before their introduction.

The new Vice President got into a lengthy conversation with one visitor in his receiving line. Since Mondale was upstream from us and had temporarily stopped the flow of people, the President and I had a moment to get acquainted. We chatted briefly about a guest who had just passed by, mentalist Yuri Geller. He is the performer who appears to bend metal keys with thought waves. The President was quite impressed with his ability, apparently seen him perform somewhere and was particularly surprised to discover that I already had a key that Yuri had bent in a backstage demonstration for Diana Rigg at the "Merv Griffin Show." Di didn't really accept his act at face value and gave the key to me. Her concern may have been well founded but I kept it anyway, just in case. Even the new President didn't have one of those.

When the line resumed, I continued asking all guests for their names before introducing them to the President. Surprisingly, Jimmy Carter not only knew many of these non-famous people by first name but remembered many things about their homes or their special interests, and they often held up the line while the President discussed these things with them at some length.

It was a constant source of wonder to me, but this President had one of the most incredible minds of any human I have ever met—brilliant and retentive. (Maybe Strauss was right.) Carter did not, however, know all of the people and that was one area where the Social Aides has always been indispensable.

The Introducing Aide saved everyone from possible embarrassment by asking every guest his or her name. Some did not understand the need to give this information when they had already met Mr. Carter before and questioned the request. As one elderly black gentleman approached the President, I asked for his name. He said, "That's not necessary."

"Sir, but I must have your name to properly introduce you to the President," I urged in friendly persuasion.

He replied in a rather loud and somewhat irritated voice, "Oh, don't worry. Jimmy knows me!" I persisted but by this time the previous visitor was gone. President Carter turned and heard us and burst out laughing at me exclaiming, "Of course I know Daddy King!"

Dr. Martin Luther King, Sr., and the President engaged in a vigorous bear hug. The Reverend, known to his close friends as Daddy King, grimaced and laughed so hard that his tongue extended way out of his mouth in one of the most excited guffaws that probably ever graced a presidential receiving line.

The news media chose that moment to take dozens of pictures with me standing between them, and the tip of Dr. King's tongue on his chin.

That picture appeared in major papers all over the country. Friends called for days to find out what had happened. I had to confess, it was just the growing pains of a political party that had been out of the White House too long.

In a characteristic display of support for the office of the President, Shirley Temple Black, who carried the rank of ambassador as the Chief of Protocol at the State Department, performed the introducing function for the last time at the reception for diplomats. She was being replaced, as were virtually all the senior political appointees, but she did not want to let the new President down, even if her loyalty was to the Republicans.

President Ford had asked his staff to cooperate with Carter as much as possible. We would really miss Shirley after she was gone. She was truly fun to be around and every good party requires at least a few bubbling personalities like hers.

One of the most lively Hollywood celebrities to appear at these receptions was Freddie Prinze, the twenty-two-year-old star of TV's *Chico and the Man*.

He was an exuberant extrovert with a great personality—bouncing around, cracking jokes and keeping things interesting for those jaded few who bored easily at parties. Therefore, it was a tremendous shock to hear only seven days later that Freddie—the happy man—had fatally shot himself in the head. If there were any telltale signs of despair, they were not evident a week earlier when he met the President.

Was this tragedy an omen of the bad luck that would stalk the Carter administration? One would have to feel sorry for Jimmy Carter—he meant so well. And kept stubbing his toes.

First there were the things he said. The man did have a way of blurting out the wrong thing. Any experienced politician could have told Jimmy to bite his tongue before he admitted he had ever looked at a woman outside of wedlock with lust. But Jimmy, whose political life had been confined to Georgia, wanted to show he was worldly.

And more than that, that he was not a prudish man even though he was a Baptist fundamentalist. To prove his point, he told a *Playboy* reporter, "I have looked at a lot of women with lust. This is something God recognizes I will do."

As if this wasn't bad enough, he went on to confess that he was no better than the man who "leaves his wife and shacks up with someone out of wedlock." The point had already been made and people did not want to think that someone of presidential stature talked of such things openly.

It's a little late to be coming to his defense, but for the sake of history, let it be known that as far as we aides could see—and we could often see pretty far—Carter had a perfect record as far as women were concerned during his White House years. I never saw or heard of him flirting with anyone or acting the slightest bit romantic except with his own pretty wife.

So if, as he said, he lusted, it never surfaced in his actions. And from the happy look on Rosalynn's face at parties, she did not seem jealous of other women—as was, say, Betty Ford. In fact, some women said they wished they had a Jimmy Carter type to make them feel secure.

Many considered it poor judgment to include little Amy as a guest at sit-down formal dinners for chiefs of state. It was no place for a child. Amy behaved like most any little nine-year-old would and skittered around the rooms before and after the dinner.

One aide said it would be just fine to have her around if only we could nail one of her shoes to the floor to slow her down. But I guess Amy was making history by being the youngest person to sit at the President's table during a formal State Dinner—at least within the memory of the White House Staff.

Nor did the proud father wait long to introduce Amy to the diplomatic world. She attended her first State Dinner in the second month of his administration, February 14, 1977, when the guest of honor was President José Lopez Portillo of Mexico.

We were relieved at the next State Dinner when Amy chose not to come and the guests were spared the effort necessary to carry on a conversation at dinner alternating between adults and a child.

Some guests were not particularly history minded and did not appreciate the fact that Amy Carter was making history. They resented having to sit at a special function next to a child—especially one who also had a book along to keep her from being bored.

After one party, a socialite, who had flown down from New York, complained that she had bought a new designer gown for this party and had hired a limo, only to find herself trying to impress a nine-year-old beside her. But of course she did not tell this to the hosts who continued to invite Amy.

News gets around fast and at the first Governors' Dinner the Carters hosted, Governor James Rhodes of Ohio showed up with two grandchildren. There had been no prior warning and so an aide told the governor there were no places for the children.

The governor and his grandchildren turned around and left.

Rosalynn heard what had just happened and sent a staffer rushing out to find the Rhodeses—but it was too late. They were gone.

Sometimes Amy made the news by *not* attending a party. On June 28, 1977, it was reported that Amy did not attend the State Dinner for Venezualan President Carlos Pérez but did show up for the outdoor entertainment later. Brother Chip reported that Amy preferred to watch TV this night, but since she had once wanted to be a ballet dancer, she had attended the ballet for old times' sake.

The stage was set up on the South Lawn, and the principal dancers from the American Ballet Theater—Ted Kivitt and Cynthia Gregory—performed selections from *Giselle*.

As for Amy, when I knew her, she was out of ballet and dedicated to becoming a violinist. Her parents were springing for lessons. Guests were spared having to listen to her perform, but some staffers were half afraid it would one day happen.

The presence of Amy seemed to give the stamp of approval for children to share in the formal entertainment of the White House. Eventually, the Mondales also brought a youngster to a State Dinner at which the guest of honor was Italian President Giulio Andreotti.

Social Aides were slightly horrified to hear the fifteen-year-old kid referring to the President familiarly as "J.C." but did not feel it was their place to correct him. It did confirm my judgment, though, that these formal functions should be reserved for adults.

Just as interesting to me as the fact that a nine year old was seated at a State Dinner was what Vice President Mondale revealed—that this night was the first in many years that he and Joan had been at the White House. The Nixons and Fords, he said, had not gotten around to inviting them.

More devastating for the guests than the *addition* of a child at the table was the *subtraction* of liquor at White House parties. And then there were some strange alterations in the handling of the receiving line at formal parties.

The force behind implementing and perhaps suggesting some of the changes of procedures at these functions was the new Social Secretary, Gretchen Poston. Unlike many ladies who preceded her, Gretchen was not a close family friend of the Carters but rather a longtime confidante of Joan Mondale. In one of our first meetings with her, Gretchen told us how much she looked forward to the job because she had never even been invited to a White House function.

After the meeting, one aide commented that it was fortunate the airlines are prevented from hiring pilots that way. The eager new Social Secretary made it one of her first orders of business to help the First Lady cope with the receiving line.

In consulting with Rosalynn Carter, Gretchen reestablished one of the most awkward positions for a Social Aide—the Whispering Aide. It made the First Lady co-equal with the President by giving her the same help the President got in the receiving line. It also signaled to us that this First Lady was going to be a power and not just the "helpmate" previous First Ladies had been. A strong hint of things to come.

Traditionally, Presidents always had the help of the Introducing Aide or the State Department's Chief of Protocol standing at the ear of the Chief Executive to give the proper pronunciation of a guest's name. But the First Lady had no such dependable support.

The President introduced each in turn to the honored guest. The First Lady, however, had to rely on the honored guest to pass on the correct pronunciation of each name.

Recent Presidents had felt confident that the First Lady would handle the introductions well. They felt she would be forgiven if she occasionally got a name wrong and gave it no further concern. But Rosalynn Carter was not your average First Lady and she was determined to pronounce every last name correctly. And from what we heard, Jimmy was usually quick to go along with Rosalynn's new ideas. Thus was reborn the Whispering Aide.

The Whispering Aide had the rather delicate assignment of standing behind the President, the First Lady, the honored guest and spouse in the receiving line. As an individual was introduced to the President, the Whispering Aide would note the name, move behind the honored guest and whisper the name to the First Lady as that person arrived.

It was reasoned that while the visiting head of state might have his mind on other things, a Whispering Aide could be relied upon to give this important and delicate task his undivided attention.

This whole process presupposed that either the President or the guest of honor would forget or mispronounce someone's name as he or she went through the line. Anything was possible, of course, but the appearance of giving up and not trusting these two heads of state to get a name right seemed more damaging than the occasional gaffe.

And despite their best intentions, the Whispering Aide's potential for error was extremely high. With the President first and Mrs. Carter third in the line, the Aide had to catch the name being given to President Carter, remember the name of the person talking to the honored guest and give yet another name for the person meeting the First Lady so that only the First Lady could hear.

This cumbersome process was followed for each of the 120 dinner guests. Who knows how often the name whispered in her ear matched the person she was meeting.

But not all the changes in procedures at social and ceremonial events were deliberately planned by the Carters. At the State Dinner honoring British Prime Minister James Callaghan, the routine nineteen-gun salute was eliminated from his arrival ceremony on the South Lawn earlier in the day. It seemed like a pointed insult to the guest of honor and some people assumed it was another of the President's moves to *depomp* everything in sight.

But the truth in this case was simply bad luck. Twelve Hanafi Muslim terrorists were holding 134 hostages within a few blocks of the White House. The nineteen-gun salute had been eliminated to avoid panicking them into some terrible action, which Carter later said he had explained to the Prime Minister.

The hostages were released unharmed during the night but too late to help Carter entertain his dignitary as he would have wanted to. I would like to say that that was the end of the bad luck incidents that befell Jimmy Carter.

A superstitious person would say that the bad luck omen seemed to work overtime in the Carter Administration. Some felt that Carter was even hexed in his choice of staffers—some tanked up on liquor at night clubs, some were said to sniff coke at parties. And one was accused by a beautiful woman of spitting some of his drink— Amaretto and cream—into the cleavage of her dress. Fortunately, that did not happen at the White House but at a bar.

One staffer who had turned out good speeches for Carter was found to have been moonlighting and using a pseudonym to sell articles that were definitely off the beaten track. Titles like, "How Jimmy Carter Can Find Out What Government Is Doing."

There was the revelation by country music star Willie Nelson that he had smoked pot on the roof of the White House. Though the President did not know about it, others did, and one even smoked marijuana with him.

As Willie Nelson told of it several years later, he had been caught with marijuana in the Bahamas and deported and he had flown straight to Washington "to see President Carter. A few hours later I was on the White House roof smoking dope."

It did not help Jimmy Carter's image that Brother Billy seemed to be trading on the family name in putting out his own brand of Billy Beer. And a further smudge on the Carter image resulted when Brother Billy went to work as a consultant for the Libyan government. As one insider put it, "It may not be illegal but it certainly is not good taste—and it does nothing to help Jimmy Carter."

One Presidential son, Chip—James Earl Carter II—also caused a little White House heartache when he became smitten by rock star Linda Ronstadt. He was competing with California Governor Jerry Brown for her attention, leaving his pregnant wife at home, and for a short period of time, some members of the Carter family even feared there might be a divorce.

Nor was it the end of hostage trouble. In 1979, there was an assault on the United States Embassy in Teheran, Iran, and the taking of ninety hostages—sixty-three of them American—by followers of the Ayatollah Khomeini. In an ill-fated effort to rescue them, eight Americans would lose their lives and five would be wounded.

For the rest of his administration, Jimmy Carter would labor unceasingly to free the hostages—not even taking vacations. In fact, it was said that he was as much a hostage as they were. But it was to no avail and the hostages were not released until the very hour the new President was sworn in.

Yes, a superstitious man would say the Carter hex never let up until he left office.

19

Depomping the Presidency

here was a parallel between the lives of Teddy Roosevelt and Jimmy Carter. Roosevelt was a young political genius who, while still in his twenties, became majority leader in the New York state legislature. But then in one day, his life fell apart with the death of both his wife and his mother—his wife died giving birth to the child who would become famous as Alice Roosevelt Longworth.

Teddy Roosevelt gave up everything, moved to North Dakota and became a rancher. The thinking he did there led to the White House.

Jimmy Carter was also a young genius who looked forward to a brilliant career—but in the military. He was well on his way. He was in the top sixty of 820 in his U.S. Naval Academy class of 1946 and was chosen by Admiral Hyman Rickover to be part of the nuclear submarine program. Then his father died.

Carter dropped everything and went back to Plains, Georgia, to take over his father's small peanut business and to farm. And his thinking, as he surveyed the fields, also led to the White House.

Theirs wasn't an overnight trip—they didn't walk out of the fields and into the White House. Both Roosevelt and Carter worked very hard at winning local and state elections. Some were successful efforts and some ended in failure.

But the country experience triggered by death of a loved one had given each man incentive to probe his own mind in solitude, to find a philosophy of life and a dedication to the public good.

But there the parallel ended. Theodore Roosevelt had a bubbly personality that drew everyone to him. Jimmy Carter seemed austere and even righteous and unyielding although, strangely enough, his famous grin was sometimes compared with Teddy Roosevelt's.

An anecdote shows how rigid and unyielding Carter could be. It happened when he was still governor of Georgia and a state commissioner was to meet him at the airport to take off in a small plane. Carter was on time, but the man was a little late.

Carter was in the plane and watched the commissioner running toward him. The engines were running and the plane had begun to taxi. The pilot would have stopped, but Carter ordered him to take off, adding, "If he can't be on time, it's too bad."

It must not have occurred to Carter that the man might have a really good reason. Or if it did, he wasn't patient enough to wait to hear it.

But at least we didn't have to put up with the kind of meanness Lyndon Johnson was said to exhibit around the White House.

The word was that LBJ simply loved to throw his weight around in a battle of wills with those around him. To him it was a sport, but some called it bullying. At any rate, the story was told that President Lyndon Johnson lost his excellent Press Secretary—Pierre Salinger, who had also been John Kennedy's image maker—over just such a battle.

Salinger was one of the guests at a presidential luncheon when LBJ made him the center of attention by hollering down the table that Pierre hadn't eaten his beans.

Pierre replied that he didn't care for beans.

The President did not drop it but ordered him to eat his beans.

There was an uncomfortable silence as Pierre ate his beans and after he left the table, he proceeded to resign, all because of LBJ's hangup—power.

Carter, the man of humility, seemed to have a youth hang-up. His name of choice was the first signal. The legal name of the new President was James Earl Carter, Jr., but he insisted he be addressed only by the informal nickname of Jimmy. He was sworn into office as Jimmy Carter. There was a lot of grumbling around Washington over this decision because many felt that it demeaned the office to be so informal on such an auspicious and historic occasion.

Some pointed out that James Earl Carter was following an illustrious line of Presidents who had used the formal name of James—Madison, Monroe, Garfield, Buchanan, Polk. The first Southern President since the Civil War would not be swayed, however, by the establishment, and so Jimmy it was.

In official Washington, those steeped in tradition wished the new man would switch to the more dignified name, at least for signing historic documents. But no, he chose to sign them, "Jimmy Carter."

At least we were spared his more youthful nickname. When he was a kid, his relatives referred to the future President as Hotshot. They were always giving each other friendly labels to describe their primary attribute or characteristic. Later, as Jimmy grew older and more successful, they shortened it to simply Hot. In the tradition of the rural South, the thirty-ninth President of the United States was also referred to as Cousin Hot in private—especially by his first cousin, Hugh Carter.

Backstairs at the White House, we were told to expect Jimmy and Rosalynn Carter to be a team in pursuing the youthful image. They jogged. They exercised. They dieted. The word was that in preparation for the White House, Rosalynn Carter had gone to a skin clinic and had a chemical face peel to rejuvenate her complexion.

Later, Carter's Press Secretary, Jody Powell, admitted that Rosalynn had had a little plastic surgery around her eyes. As for Jimmy, eventually his dieting and strenuous exercising almost did him in. In a running race, he started out looking quite jaunty in headband and jogging clothes but ended up almost collapsing in a faint. It didn't stop his effort to look young.

One woman said little Amy Carter was the cause of it all. Carter, who was fifty-two when he took office, wanted to look like a suitable father to a nine-year-old child. If he was trying to keep up with his energetic daughter, it was a losing game. None of us could.

One story that made the rounds was that Jimmy Carter had really wanted Senator Ed Muskie as his running mate but his ego could not tolerate standing beside a man so much taller and more authoritative looking than he. Maybe if Carter could have risen above his own feelings, Muskie could have guided him to win reelection.

It's one of those ifs historians love to ponder.

The fact remains, Carter chose a man who looked almost as much like himself to be two peanuts in a shell—and they quickly became known as the team of Fritz and Grits. The first was for Walter Frederick Mondale's nickname and the second for Jimmy's Southern roots.

At the White House, we tried to understand our new President but it was tough going. He seemed to be several people rolled into one. That wouldn't have bothered me if there had been great White House social affairs—that's what I was there for. But the disappointments continued and escalated.

Drab was the color of the Carter parties. Except for the accent. Being from Texas, I was used to guests saying "Mah" and "Ah" for "My" and "I." Gone was the gutteral German accent of Henry Kissinger. I missed the way he could laugh at himself. I had to smile as I remembered being told how Henry had reacted when he was introduced to a beautiful Texan with a heavy Southern drawl. He said, "I love to meet Texas women because they think I got my accent at Harvard."

But none of the aides were much amused by the way the pageantry had been taken away from White House parties or by the sudden increase in the amount of work we had to do—those of us who were left. As one aide put it, "We're doing more and enjoying it less."

The straws had been in the wind even before Jimmy Carter moved in. He wanted an absolute minimum military presence whenever possible.

In one of the first acts, even before taking office, the Carter administration decided that there would be only two full-time Military Aides. Normally there was one from each of the services including the Coast Guard, but only the Air Force and Navy Aides were replaced when the Ford people departed.

A rough road lay ahead of them. These two poor fellows would have to rotate through all the assigned duties normally performed by four or five full-timers. Since the President had to have an aide with him everywhere he went outside the White House to carry the football and handle other coordination with the Department of Defense, the two would be very busy indeed.

If the few Military Aides who had to be around him bothered him, then the formal military ceremonies would make him apoplectic.

Jimmy Carter decided he did not like the military cordons which usually lined the drive as dignitaries approached the Executive Mansion. Such visible display of power did not set well with the country peanut farmer and former governor who felt they performed no practical function and were too imperial. Poof! They were gone. Simply eliminated.

Next, the Herald Trumpets and the traditional band, all of which added flashing color and a very audible presence of military power were axed. Our new Commander in Chief did not enjoy them and they were eliminated, to our disbelief.

At the same formal ceremonies, the troops who usually carried the fifty-six flags of the states and territories were also pointedly left off the program. Jody Powell, the President's Press Secretary, referred to these early moves as Carter's efforts to "depomp the presidency" by making things more informal.

Jody had a lot of clout around the White House and there was a belief among certain staffers that some of these moves to reduce the military presence were a subconscious reflection of the fact that, as a cadet student, Jody Powell had been dismissed from the Air Force Academy. He had been caught cheating on a history test in his senior year.

We Social Aides were having our own problems.

Carter's disdain of the traditional trappings of his new office became well-publicized during his first days in the White House. Specific instructions to us made the issue even more clear. He did not want anyone in the military—even Social Aides—to be around him any more than was necessary.

This meant we were to do our jobs but stay in the background as much as possible. The apparent contradiction left us confused. Without sufficient guidance as to how this could be done, there remained among us aides some question as to what was a tolerable presence of uniforms.

I could not believe the blow our Social Aide group received next in trying to be kind to a member of the Carter family. The President's mother, Miss Lillian, was especially appreciative of the assistance offered by the Senior Social Aide, Dave Van Poznak, who had recently been promoted to lieutenant colonel in the Air Force. There were so many events going on in a house much too big and so many people to get acquainted with on short notice that Dave took it upon himself to make sure that she was properly briefed on the current and upcoming events.

Miz Lillian, as she was called, liked the special attention, as anyone would under the circumstances, and Dave continued to make himself as useful as she deemed necessary. Once she got the hang of it, his help would no longer be needed, but the new Military Aides to the President intervened before she reached this level of familiarity.

Seeing Dave as a threat to their domain as the only full-time uniformed support to the First Family, they made it clear that he was to stay away from her. Apparently there had been some friction over the past several weeks while the transition was in progress and they had already had other disagreements on policies and procedures for Social Aides and the conduct of social functions.

Now settled in, they lost no time making a point and putting all the Social Aides in their places by closely directing the actions of the senior aide. It was an interesting attitude for two captains to take with a lieutenant colonel who had more than five years of experience in the job, but they exercised considerable power from the Military office.

Dave continued to follow his own judgment despite the warnings he had been given by the two junior officers. He performed his own work and continued to look after Miz Lillian, in response to her interest and requests.

When the Military Aides discovered Dave's so-called transgression one day, they directed that he be stationed downstairs—where the junior Social Aides always worked—for the duration of the day's receptions. Colonel Van Poznak did not like the directive or the message behind it. He finished out the day and left, electing on his own never to return.

It is very possible that there were much more powerful forces behind this unfortunate disagreement between the Social Aides and the Carter White House Military Office.

It has been widely reported that Rosalynn Carter and the President's mother were not terribly fond of each other. They were sometimes seen by family members as competing for his attention. When Governor Carter was moving into the Georgia chief executive's mansion, Rosalynn is reported to have pointedly told Miz Lillian, who had brought plenty of baggage for a long stay, that she should plan to return to Plains when they were settled.

Miz Lillian took the hint and left.

Now that her son was moving into the White House, perhaps she saw a Military Social Aide of her own as a way of keeping up with Rosalynn in learning how things worked in Washington. If Rosalynn saw the situation as giving her this advantage, she may well have been the one to order a stop to it.

Whatever the reason, the exile and departure of the senior Social Aide left a bitter taste in our mouths.

The impact of recent changes on the military around the White House became even more significant when the President's Press Secretary announced that the new Commander in Chief had pardoned all the draft dodgers remaining from the Vietnam War. Eerily similar to Ford's pardon of Nixon, it was explained that this step was necessary to heal the nation. My personal reaction was, "Used oats!"

And like his predecessor's experience, there was immediate negative reaction from the general public which Carter correctly predicted and conveniently avoided by not making a public statement himself as Gerald Ford had. This act would not exactly endear the new President to the few military people remaining around the mansion, most of whom had served in Vietnam.

Our first State Dinner under the Carters on February 14, 1977, to honor President Portillo, was a cultural shock for the aides. And I'm sure for some of the seasoned guests.

Until now we had only experienced the major changes made at the White House in small unconnected events. This evening, for the first time, they all came together at once, and the full effect of the new Carter symbolism was evident at this State visit. The cordon on the driveway was missing for the honored guest's arrival at the North Portico, as was the color guard when the principals descended the Grand Staircase. No "Ruffles and Flourishes" or Herald Trumpets were heard. The only music allowed was "Hail to the Chief."

This small concession ceremony signaled a modest change back to more traditional procedures as the press had made several pointed comments about the very significant lack of ceremony in recent White House functions. Only three weeks earlier, the President had sworn in his Cabinet officers but had completely eliminated the appropriate music for his entrance. Jimmy Carter later admitted in his book, *Keeping Faith*, that he had overreacted in the beginning of his presidency to the elaborate ceremony that came with the office.

He said he wanted to set a tone that he felt reflected his own simple life-style and signaled that he was accessible to the press and public. He confessed that once he finally allowed "Hail to the Chief" to be played, it was impressive and he enjoyed it.

To more closely mirror the Carter's life-style, the evening's schedule of events was moved up by about thirty minutes. Dinner formalities were now scheduled to begin at 7:30 P.M. rather than the usual 8:00 P.M. The party would also end much sooner than before because the Carters concluded that it wasn't necessary to stay around and dance after the entertainment as had always been the custom.

This would not have been so unusual if the First Couple had simply skipped this activity, as the Nixons had, and graciously told the guests to enjoy their dancing. But the Carters decreed that if they weren't dancing themselves, nobody else should—and there went the fun part.

At the time, we mistook this schedule change and the dancing ban for another of the Carter's attempts to show how simple they could remain even in the White House, unimpressed by their predecessor's imperial style and aloof from Washington's social pressures.

The truth is, they were just being tight. In fact, the Carters had brought a young cousin, Hugh Carter, Jr., into the White House to run it efficiently and economically. He quickly earned himself the nickname of "Cousin Cheap," which of course, was not said to him directly. Hugh Carter lived up to his nickname and the President got all the credit.

Take the matter of the dancing.

Both Jimmy Carter and Rosalynn took ballroom dancing lessons and easily could have led off every evening with a quick turn around the floor as many of their predecessors had. But that would have meant the guests would stay, and the Carters didn't want them there after midnight. The reason was simple—the staff would have to be paid overtime.

A guest at the Portillo dinner muttered that he was used to dancing, but if he couldn't dance, he could use a drink. This became another sore spot throughout the evening.

One of the first major shifts in social conduct at the Carter White House was the elimination of hard liquor during the normal cocktail hour. What they served instead was a choice of plain orange juice or white wine mixed with black currant liqueur. The kitchen staff called it a Vermouth Cassis.

Someone ruefully said it had probably been invented by Amy, when playing house. One sip convinced me it was something for which one had to acquire a taste. Suddenly, the orange juice seemed the ideal choice.

The prohibition against drinking unfortunately also was extended by the Carters to include the afterdinner brandies and liqueurs that, as far back as I can remember, had always been served to the diners before they viewed the entertainment in the East Room.

The reaction was predictable. The mood of the parties took on a much more somber tone. Guests who were accustomed to having a good time were not pleased with the symbolic message about strong drink and felt uncomfortable with this unusual constraint on their social lives.

The custom of serving liquor during the cocktail hour dated back to the Kennedy administration where parties were among the most elegant in history. As for the afterdinner drinks, the White House maitre d', John Ficklin, had even served them in the Truman White House when Ficklin had started working there as a waiter in the 1940s.

Since there were no libations to help Carter's guests break down barriers, the social staff and aides had to work that much harder to encourage people to relax and mingle with other guests. Wallflowers seemed to be more prevalent and the parties broke up earlier—guests could hardly wait to get out. There would be no need to trot any late-staying turkeys out of these no-dance, no-drink affairs.

I did not see it with my own eyes but later heard that some guests, knowing they were entering Carter's dry belt, took along a little flask in their cars and that a few other White House regulars took to holding pre-White House party cocktail hours in their homes for their friends who were also heading for the mansion.

What they did not know was that Jimmy Carter didn't always live up to the abstemious image he and his staff carefully crafted. The inside story is that when President Carter went to London in the first year of his presidency, he arrived at the U.S. Ambassador's residence and wanted a drink. But there was not a drop of liquor in sight.

Undoubtedly, the ambassador was simply following Carter's lead and was guided by what was served at the White House. As the story went, if Jimmy Carter considered drinking orange juice, he ruled it out in favor of booze and sent his Naval Aide all the way back to the airport to retrieve a bottle from Air Force One.

This incident illustrates once again that our Presidents do not always live in private as they would have us believe with their carefully molded public image.

The greater surprise in this story is not that Jimmy Carter would want a drink instead of wine or orange juice, but that he would keep liquor around on Air Force One where he and his staff friends could drink in private when there was such a fuss made for the benefit of the press about not having it at White House parties. In his heart Jimmy Carter truly lusted for liquor that night.

And did the whole thing really make sense? Some said no!

Carter may have made a wrong decision when he banned hard liquor from his parties. That played well with Baptist church groups and it certainly delighted "Cousin Cheap," who had to manage the budget. It did not play well, though, at the very important social functions where President Carter was supposedly trying to make friends and influence people—and *votes*.

And it caused a big problem for the Social Aides in finding some way to get the guests to move out of the way following a formal dinner.

In the past, in order to separate the afterdinner guests, who were just arriving to go through the receiving line before enjoying the entertainment, from the earlier dinner guests who had already been through the line, we used the promise of a little libation. Liqueurs were served in the Red, Blue and Green Rooms to lure the guests exiting the State Dining Room and keep them out of the way while the President said hello to the new group. Also, this gave us extra time to seat all the guests in the East Room for the night's stage performance.

Since this method was now forbidden and orange juice and coffee were not inducement enough, a desperate innovation was necessary. Much as Jimmy Carter hated the show of uniforms at the White House, there was now a sort of military action.

I have to chuckle as I recall the military cordon that the Social Secretary directed be formed from the door of the State Dining Room to the Blue Room. Like pom-pom girls heralding the arrival of a football team coming out of the stadium tunnel, we gently herded the guests directly to the side rooms regardless of their personal desires. The only ones who escaped this maneuver were those brave enough to ask for directions to the rest rooms.

Unlike our usual toeing of the line on the carpet edge or the outdoor cordon on the drive, in this exercise we stood very near our comrades opposite us, making a very narrow corridor and giving the guests very little room to move anywhere but forward. It was not only a tacky maneuver, but it employed the very ornately dressed Military Social Aides which, as I said, the President specifically wanted kept in the background as much as possible. At least when we were spread out we were not too obvious.

The way we were aggregated here suddenly made it look like inauguration day at a banana republic. If the turkey trot was cute, then this cattle drive was downright offensive. Such is the difference between an incoming President's rhetoric and what really takes place in the operation of the White House.

For outdoor arrivals of chiefs of state, Carter had to swallow hard and continue to give foreign dignitaries at least a modicum of the homage they were accustomed to—but it was precious little.

Carter seemed to feel it was a nuisance that everyone had to look at that sea of military spit and polish on the South Lawn in the form of the sharpest looking soldiers, sailors, airmen and marines the service had to offer. Each ceremony literally required these troops to stand on parade in spiffy dress uniforms in a formation in front of the two heads-of-state. The troops could not be eliminated but the heavy presence of additional uniformed personnel would be measurably reduced.

So gone was the marvelous fanfare of the U.S. Army Herald Trumpets announcing the appearance of dignitaries at outdoor functions, and gone, too, was the military marching band, which also performed whenever a formal arrival ceremony for a head of state was scheduled.

It was still interesting to meet new people at White House parties, although I felt a little uncomfortable having an extended talk in view of the Carter edict that uniforms were to be seen and not heard—and only seen or heard when absolutely necessary.

There was one time, however, that I didn't care how conspicuous I was—I had to satisfy my curiosity.

Through the years, it had been suggested by various people that I resembled certain public figures—namely, film star Ben Gazzara, Chuck Robb and Lt. Rusty Calley. It was amusing that someone thought that I could look like a man convicted of slaughtering twenty-two people in the Mylai massacre as well as like a very upstanding governor of a state or a movie star.

Since anyone who reads the newspapers knows that there is very little resemblance between these three men, I wondered how I could look like all of them. Therefore, I was very grateful to President Carter for giving me the opportunity to let a very knowledgeable person settle at least one comparison once and for all. Looking back, I should have passed up the chance.

Lynda Bird Johnson Robb, who met her husband while she *lived* in and he *worked* in the White House, came to one of the afternoon receptions in the Carter administration. Moving through the crowds we chanced to come face to face and we introduced ourselves.

We talked about our home state of Texas and she commented that it was nice to be back in the Mansion again and to see some of the same people who had worked there under her father.

I wondered aloud if my face looked at all familiar to her—"Did I resemble anyone she knew?" In answer to her negative reaction, I explained that more than one person had suggested that there was a certain resemblance between her husband, Chuck Robb, and me.

The slightly pained expression on her face was answer enough, but for clarity she added, "Well, I'm sure it was a compliment to both of you," and walked off in somewhat of a huff.

Fortunately, I didn't have to tell her about the circumstance of the first misidentification. I had walked into a sauna with only a towel. Two gentlemen interrupted their conversation long enough for one to inquire casually, "Excuse me, but you *are* Chuck Robb, aren't you?" It really made me wonder where they thought they had seen him last.

I had expected Lynda Bird Robb to be gentler than she was and I had expected another guest to be more fierce—Geraldo Rivera of ABC. He exhibited none of the temperament or sensational tendencies that he became famous for in his TV talk show. He was just a quiet, gentle fellow with a great interest in history.

Someone who did get more than his share of attention at a White

House party was George Meany, head of AFL-CIO. Other guests clustered around him one evening as if he were a Hollywood star. I remember that some of us were amused that Meany didn't try to appear humble in the Carter tradition by arriving in a standard car—he came in a limo.

I was saddened when Senator Hubert Humphrey of Minnesota lost his battle with cancer at sixty-six. I would miss seeing him at the White House because he had been always cheerful, always laughing.

Senator Humphrey and I reminisced more than once about the trip he took to the Demilitarized Zone between North and South Korea in 1969. I was the aide to the commanding general of the Second Infantry Division at the time and we had escorted him up to look at the defenses and to peer into the North through high powered binoculars. He had enjoyed himself tremendously and commented several times how great it was to get away from Washington for a while.

When I learned that President Andreotti of Italy would be at a State Dinner, I fully expected that I would see Frank Sinatra again since he was one of the most notable Americans of Italian ancestry. Surely, he would be asked to entertain again.

But I was wrong and he did not appear that night. Of course he had last been at the White House during another administration but there are no secrets about how guests behave. Current, future and former First Ladies have many sources of information. Had he declined to come or had Rosalynn Carter heard about how his belligerent actions off stage had caused nearly as big a stir as had his fine performance on stage?

As it turned out, he wasn't even in the audience and we all had to settle for an opera singer performing Italian arias.

As a frequent Introducing Aide, I now worked closely with the new Chief of Protocol, Ambassador Evan Dobelle. He was a likeable fellow and, at thirty-one, was only about half the age of all his recent predecessors—another sign to me that Carter liked to be surrounded by youthful people who made him feel young, too.

But Dobelle had no formal diplomatic experience at all, which might explain why his office sent out background information on President and Mrs. Perez of Venezuela in which he called Mrs. Perez, "a short, somewhat plump woman..." while describing her husband in glowing terms—as he did other members of the entourage. It was obvious that Dobelle had meant to flatter them—except for his tasteless comment about Venezuela's First Lady.

It was just one more sign that the very important social side of the White House was in the control of too many inexperienced hands when it should have rated the most professional treatment.

Later, Carter switched Kit Dobelle with her husband and *she* became the Chief of Protocol. Still later, when the President decided to call in truly professional help, the White House drafted Albelardo Valdez for the job—taking him away from the Agency for International Development.

Ambassador Valdez had been a captain in the Army and a Military Social Aide, just like me, but back during the LBJ years. And just by coincidence, Albelardo was the first guy I met at Texas A&M when I was a raw freshman in 1961.

Who could have predicted either one of us would end up with a White House connection? Nobody. Well, maybe our mothers...

20

A Time to Stay...A Time to Go

*W*e'd had a President who didn't believe anyone should have to wash his dirty socks—Truman. Now we had a man who not only washed his own socks but also didn't believe anyone should have to sew his buttons or fix a rip in his pants for him—he did his own.

Jimmy Carter even carried on an interview with a reporter one day as he sat, needle and thread in hand—repairing a tear in a jacket. This was especially revealing since his wife was an expert seamstress. Theirs was a marriage of equals.

In their home in Plains, Jimmy had been known for his penchant for sharing cooking duties with his wife. In the White House, Rosalynn seemed to be returning the favor by sitting in on Cabinet meetings and participating in other phases of presidential business. The public and some staffers around the White House disapproved and said Jimmy Carter had been elected President and not his wife.

But this didn't stop the President from drawing his wife further and further into his official life. He admitted her into certain high-level conferences and appointed her to represent him at ceremonies and to serve as his emissary on trips to various Latin American countries—without payment, of course. Except in prestige.

However, Rosalynn was not the first presidential wife to travel for her husband. Pat Nixon flew in a cargo plane carrying food and medicine to Peru after it had been devastated by an earthquake. Eleanor Roosevelt had gone overseas to visit World War II troops and in fact traveled so much that her Secret Service code name was "Rover."

Rosalynn Carter was one of the few First Ladies to show up daily at her office in the East Wing to work on formal parties and problems of protocol. And from what I heard, she was a hard taskmaster. As one disgruntled secretary said, out of Rosalynn's hearing, of course, "Rose thinks she's still in Plains working on the ledgers and helping run the peanut business."

Whether it was Rosalynn's doing or a joint venture with the President, suddenly "economy" was the key word around the White House. And of course, it was always in the name of the President.

The first shock came on the second day of Jimmy Carter's brand new administration when the wide-eyed and rosy-cheeked guests at the first reception were treated to an indoor temperature in the White House that did not exceed sixty-five degrees. The President personally ordered the change as his answer to the continuing energy crisis.

He declared the issue to be the Moral Equivalent of War. His antagonists scorned the program and heaped criticism upon him by assigning the effort the acronym MEOW. Fortunately he left the lights on, unlike President Johnson who regularly went around the White House turning them off. One place he would turn them off was in the ladies room. He wouldn't actually go in but he would open the door, reach in and flip off the light without calling out to find out if anyone was in there.

Female staffers who were trapped in the dark, were furious, according to the reports, but knowing that it could be only one person—the President—on the warpath, bit their tongues and did not shout out what they were thinking.

It was an amusingly ironic touch that Lyndon Johnson had a battery of extra shower heads installed in his private bathroom stall for special effects and presumably wasted more money in hot water than he saved in electricity.

With Carter, obviously, saving energy was just one small part of the drive to save every penny. Congressional leaders, used to a hearty breakfast when they came to the White House for a "working breakfast," suddenly found that all they got was sweet rolls, juice and coffee. Needless to say, this did not make them like Carter more or put them in the best frame of mind.

If Congress wanted food, then let them have hearty food, Jimmy decided. He invited them to another breakfast, served bacon and eggs and billed the attendees $4.75 each. Again they were insulted and they were not going to take it lying down.

The law was that the President could keep whatever was left over from his $50,000 entertainment allowance. They noted exactly how much he was able to pocket and simply changed the law, decreeing that unspent entertainment funds must be returned to the Treasury. But before the law was changed, according to one report, Carter was able to pocket $37,000 in one year.

Gerald Ford had spent about $120 to $150 per person at State Dinners. Carter was able to bring the cost down to about $60 per head. Of course not all the money is spent on food but on flowers, drinks and serving staff.

Guests yearned for the elegant foods they had been served at the White House in administrations past. At one formal dinner, the main dish served was catfish. Most people ate what was put before them, like it or not, but one guest at a Carter party was observed dropping his food into his napkin surreptiously and slipping it into his pocket.

At various times the new cuisine included peanut paté, grits, spoonbread, catfish fritters and a thing called Plains Cheese Ring. The ring was a favorite of Rosalynn's and was made with cream cheese and gelatin.

Reflecting the new food at the White House, which social Washington named *cuisine ordinaire*, restaurants all over town were serving dishes like Carter Chinese chicken with Georgia peanuts and grits souffle.

I was amused to hear that Bob Strauss, whom Carter had made special representative for trade negotiations with the rank of ambassador, attempted to broaden Rosalynn's food likes. He took her to the internationally famous Duke Ziebert's, a posh Washington eating place, to have her try matzoh ball soup.

The report was that she ate it politely though not with enthusiasm, but she loved a peanut concoction and returned for more.

A lot of money was saved by cutting out the serving of hard liquor at the White House parties. A tiny bit of money was saved by no longer mailing Social Aides advance information and instructions that we needed to study prior to an event.

It is difficult to believe that the Carters would be interested in saving on a few stamps. I suspect the Military Office used the Carters' fiscal restraint as a cover to rid themselves of a tedious chore. But skipping this advance information giving us the who, what, and why of an event and all pertinent details—including where to park—was not the way to run a precision operation with such an obvious opportunity for social or diplomatic disaster.

Another new and unusual economy measure hit the Social Aides particularly hard. In the past we were able to go to the staff mess under the Oval Office and enjoy a fine meal while the guests dined upstairs. This was one of the very few tangible rewards for many hours of work performed without any extra pay. To save money, they decided we could get by with a plate of cold cuts from which we made our own sandwiches.

There just wasn't a lot of fun left in the job.

The general level of discontent was rising in many private conversations among the staff. We all remembered the unceremonious departure earlier in the year of Colonel Van Poznak as a good example of how jealously Military Aides guarded their proximity to the First Family. At this point nothing would surprise us.

By now, some staffers were even viewing with a jaundiced eye the stories about how Jimmy Carter carried his own suitcase during the campaign—had he acquired the habit in the old days because he didn't like to tip? Of course, in the White House, the Secret Service carried his luggage and tipping was not an issue.

It made headlines when Carter decided on another economy—the selling of the presidential yacht, the *Sequoia*. Some were horrified and said that the *Sequoia* was part of history and should be kept and simply put in storage if Carter didn't want it.

But Carter would not budge. He wanted it gone and *sold*. He viewed it as not only an expensive luxury but also as an extreme example of the imperial style which his predecessors enjoyed so much and he so little.

Not long after it was gone, the *Sequoia* could have saved the White House some real money. On September 8, 1977, when Rosalynn wanted to take one hundred ladies out to Mount Vernon by boat for lunch, she had to rent a commercial tour ship. After the Social Office was done redecorating the vessel to make it suitable for this type of entertaining, it is anybody's guess as to which would have been cheaper for the taxpayers.

The women were the wives of the principals of the Panama Canal Treaty signing ceremony and they had been guests with their husbands at a White House dinner the night before. On this rare occasion, no effort seemed too great, on the part of Carter, to please the people he needed for backing his plan to turn over the canal to the people of Panama.

Twenty-three of us were sent to Mount Vernon to escort the ladies in viewing the grounds and to make sure each of the actually one hundred plus women eventually got into the correct automobile to get back to Washington. Since they would arrive by water, they would have no idea of which driver was assigned to them.

Beyond the absolutely beautiful weather and the opportunity to tour the grounds while we waited for the Rent-a-Yacht to arrive, there was little exciting about this social gathering. We were counting on Helga Orfila to liven things up, but after the ladies arrived, we discovered she was wearing something far less provocative than we had been treated to the night before.

She had stolen the show. Even the Panama Treaty had to take second place until everyone adjusted to this bombshell in the room that seemed tightly packed and ready to explode.

As she entered, everyone in the room—men *and* women, old and young—turned to gaze upon one of the most stunning beautiful women in the world wearing what was unquestionably the most daring and revealing dress ever seen in the White House.

Alejandro Orfila, the exceedingly popular bachelor Secretary General of the Organization of American States, had been quite a ladies man around Washington for some time, both going to and giving many great parties, and at least once that I recall, squiring Barbara Walters to the White House.

Orfila had recently gotten married and, as the old saying goes, settled down. His new bride, Helga, was anything but settled. The thirty-two-year-old blonde German model and former beauty queen was as unique in her fashions as she was in her incomparable beauty.

She'd worn a clinging white silk dress with a neckline that dipped to within a fraction of an inch of her navel and was at least three inches wide at that narrowest point. There was something left to the imagination, but not much. Many of the men had a strained look on their faces as if they were trying to conjure up the unknown.

There wasn't a conversation within view of her that continued uninterrupted. Whatever attention was being paid to the dozens of distinguished dignitaries was immediately turned on this stunning lady who knew exactly what she was doing.

Compared to Mrs. Orfila, the other ladies couldn't get the attention of a desperate cab driver with an emergency hand flare. Their veiled comments about her attire may have been motivated more by jealousy than strict concern for propriety. Even in the receiving line, her appearance was an unspoken issue. Virtually everyone from Mrs. Carter to former President Gerald Ford took at least one glance.

Everyone, that is, but Carter. After the trouble he got into over his statement about lusting in his heart for other women, he simply couldn't afford to have someone catch him peeking. His eyes stayed riveted on hers while he gave her a cool welcome through a tense smile.

But that had been Helga last night at the White House and this was today at Mount Vernon—and what a letdown!

She overcompensated for the previous night's display. Not only did Helga Orfila have on a high collar but she also wore a scarf around her neck. It was clearly a disappointment to the male aides and no doubt to the press as well.

Upon our departure, we were all given one of the small silver flower baskets that were also provided to the guests as a souvenir of the day. It was a beautiful gift and a big surprise to all the Social Aides because the Carters had done nothing but eliminate perks for us since they took office.

The sudden generosity showed us how important the upcoming Senate vote on the Panama Canal was to the President, if we didn't know it already. And if we didn't know, we certainly should have. We aides had been amazed to find the President bending over backward to be a stickler for protocol for the first time.

I'm amused as I remember how the Carters, the Social Office and all the rest of us worked to make this the protocol-perfect party.

September 7, 1977—President Carter's Panama Treaty Dinner

Earlier in the day the President signed the treaties which would turn over control of the Panama Canal if the U.S. Senate ratified the agreement. It was not gone yet but it was going, despite the fact that the majority of Americans did not approve of the gift. This event was to celebrate the culmination of many years of low-level discussions and very recent high-level negotiations for the giveaway.

What a turnout! Everyone who had played a significant part in the effort was invited, as well as those who might reflect credibility on the act by their presence. The guest list swelled to 140, including fifteen heads of state and eleven representatives from the highest levels of the governments of other countries. Also invited were one quarter of the United States Senators who at this point sat in the drivers seat on the entire issue, having to vote on the treaties by a two-thirds majority before they would be ratified.

With all these world leaders present, security was as tight as a drum.

Whether Mrs. Carter or the Social Office decided the visiting Lady Bird Johnson needed as much help as Rosalynn did, I do not know. Whatever the reason, it was decided to give not one but two Social Aides the oppressive, almost ridiculuous job of Whispering Aide. At that, it could have been worse—there could have been three Social Aides assigned to the job of whispering.

That's because both former President Gerald Ford and former First Lady Lady Bird Johnson had been invited by the Carters to join them in the receiving line and help greet guests. Evidently, it was felt that Ford could handle his hellos without help as he had done throughout his administration.

I'm smiling now, but at the time, it was quite terrifying to watch these fellows dart back and forth behind the principals, passing names as they went. We all crossed our fingers that they wouldn't accidently collide and tumble over one of our distinguished hosts.

In the end, they survived not only this episode but a repeat of this maneuver for the second receiving line when the afterdinner guests arrived.

Ordinarily we might have been shorthanded, assigning two officers to whisper in the principal's ears, but not this evening. With so many heads of state present, the full-time Military Aides to the

President decided either the Social Aides should not be trusted with too much responsibility or they just wanted to get in on the action. They scheduled themselves for the tasks of Set-Up and Pull-Off.

To add a little problem of protocol, one of the guests to go down the receiving line was inebriated—he didn't get that way at the White House—and had to be delicately urged to move along—it wasn't like a home party where the host can say, "You're drunk, George, and you'd better go home."

Tonight's guest list would produce plenty of action for the photographers, aside from Helga Orfila. The head of the Panamanian government, General Omar Torrijos, and his wife were first through the line followed by President Alfredo Stroessner of Paraguay. Others notable for their places in history since then were Presidents Joaquín Balaguer of the Dominican Republic and General Augusto Pinochet of Chile.

Uninvited guests included seven hundred protesters who had to stay in Lafayette Park across the street from the White House due to space limitations, and the fact that they gave every indication that they would gladly exterminate several of the honored guests if given the chance. They didn't this evening, but several of the honored guests subsequently experienced very turbulent passings to the afterlife.

Two distinguished guests wore uniforms that rivaled the Social Aides' in their ornate color and design. The presidents of Ecuador and Peru looked very impressive, festooned with gold braids and numerous medals. If they hadn't been much older and constantly accompanied by their wives, someone might easily have mistaken them for aides and asked them for directions to the ladies powder room.

All these dignitaries greatly complicated the protocol problems. After dinner, as he was accustomed to do for years, Henry Kissinger entered the East Room and automatically went to the front row to watch the entertainment. But he wasn't Secretary of State anymore and this night everything went strictly by protocol.

I had to send him all the way back to the *seventh* row. Even a former President—Ford—and the sitting Vice President—Mondale—only made it to the fourth row, following the strict protocol order for seating.

But the most far-out use of protocol came toward the end of the party and showed the mental state the social staff must have been in.

Much was riding on this milestone in the Carter presidency and the social staff had been working hard to coordinate every possible detail for this event. They were so absolutely petrified someone would feel deliberately slighted for any breach of protocol that we were not even permitted to let the twenty-six distinguished guests go from room to room except in protocol order. And when it came time to leave, they all had to go out the door in the same order. If there was any doubt that the staff could control these movements in the house, there was none concerning the departure.

The rule for leaving was that cars could be summoned only in the proper protocol sequence. This prevented anyone from leaving before those who stood higher on the protocol ladder had left. Needless to say there was much gnashing of teeth as some guests were made to wait.

This extreme of diplomatic politeness seemed a little preposterous in view of the relaxed folksy image the Carters had been cultivating for so long.

When the party was over, Carter went back to being Carter—but even he seemed a little confused over which Carter that was. There had always been fits and starts of innovations from the moment he'd arrived in Washington to show the nation and the White House how he felt things should be done.

I remember a funny story that was making the rounds of social Washington while humble Jimmy was doing away with all the pomp and ceremony at the White House. Someone's little son was being urged to run for the class presidency and the kid was protesting, "But I don't know anything about how to act like a president."

His father—a Democrat—was reported to have told him, "That's okay. Neither does Jimmy Carter, but you don't see that stopping him."

Rather than accepting and appreciating the time-honored traditions that had been practiced at the White House for many, many years, the Carters seemed to view their tenure as an opportunity to change the presidency. Carter did it, he said, to lessen pomposity and bring a more democratic attitude to the presidency, but some of us silently wondered what he was really up to. He seemed to be adding to pomposity when, at the ceremony for Prime Minister Malcolm Fraser of Australia, he did an unheard of thing. He had the band play his campaign song, "Man of the Hour," instead of the traditional "Hail to the Chief," which he had agreed to use at the previous ceremony. Some people viewed this substitution as more of an ego trip than an act of humility. One aide said in dismay, "A President should rise above proclaiming himself 'the man of the hour.'"

That should be left to others. "Hail to the Chief" simply salutes whichever President is in office and is a very dignified part of the formal ceremony of welcome, or of announcing the arrival of the chief executive.

A flip-flop occurred the next month at the State Dinner for President Andreotti of Italy.

Someone got to Carter and convinced him that he had de-emphasized the ceremonial aspects of his office so much that it was affecting the public image. The latest substitution of his campaign song had not played well in Peoria, as the saying goes, and the Marine Band once again was instructed to play "Hail to the Chief" to signal Carter's arrival. We sighed with relief.

Actually, Jimmy Carter preferred a different kind of party. He liked to entertain outdoors and once the Carters even held a casual "backyard barbecue" type party for the prime minister of Japan in May of 1979.

One of their most successful outdoor fêtes on a sunny day in June 1978 was a jazz festival that starred ninety-five-year-old Eubie Blake still banging out his incomparable ragtime on the piano.

On other occasions, Rosalynn chose to emulate Jacqueline Kennedy's lead in upgrading the quality of the entertainment at the White House, inviting world famous ballet dancers, opera stars and musicians to perform for chiefs of state in the East Room—pianist Rudolf Serkin and violinist Itzak Perlman among them.

There was another way in which Rosalynn Carter and Jacqueline Kennedy were similar and that was in their love of flowers of the field. Rosalynn preferred bouquets around the White House that featured daisies among the other casual flowers, as had Jacqueline.

When Jackie came to the White House, her wide array of field flowers in bowls came as a big surprise to a nation used to hearing of Mamie Eisenhower's stiff, formal vases of fern and long stem pink roses. Rosalynn's field flowers were also a significant change from predecessor Betty Ford's choice of formal long-stemmed lilies.

Rosalynn also had a link with Jacqueline Kennedy in caring greatly about the historic significance of the White House rooms. One case that points it up is what she did to the Presidential Dining Room, which had had a wallpaper mural with scenes of the American Revolution. This historic wallpaper, based on early nineteenth century engravings, had been chosen by Jackie in 1961 when the private Presidential Dining Room had come into being, and it had survived the Johnsons and Nixons.

But Betty Ford had thought the blue cast of the paper was not cheerful enough and had bright yellow paper put up instead. Fortunately, the historic paper which Jackie put up had been carefully removed and stored away, and when Mrs. Carter discovered it, she immediately had it replaced.

Though formal entertaining went with the job of being President, the Carters were determined to have a private life not unlike what they were accustomed to in Georgia. Simple and without airs.

Right after the Carters moved in, Rosalynn picked up the phone and told the operator she wished to be connected with Jimmy. "Jimmy who?" asked the operator. It was Mrs. Carter's first indication that Plains, Georgia, folksiness wasn't going to work around the White House.

But she tried. In fact, the whole family shied away from using the formidable goldfish type, servant-filled living rooms on the first and second floors which were used by other First Families.

Rosalynn looked around and found a room that piqued her imagination. It was on the third floor, which once had been called the attic at the White House. Lincoln had fixed up an area for his children to play up there and Teddy Roosevelt's children had followed suit. First Lady Grace Coolidge had fallen in love with it and had sat sewing up there.

Grace called it her "Sky Parlor," but it actually had become a solarium which other First Ladies used for its great view of the grounds and monuments down to the Potomac River, and for a place to relax. Jacqueline Kennedy had even used the room for little Caroline's kindergarten, inviting other children to join.

Rosalynn saw the room as a place for the whole family to escape people and just be by themselves. And here they sat to talk, watch television, read and listen to Amy's school adventures of the day. Mrs. Carter made the solarium into a cozy family living room.

Like children before her, Amy Carter had a pet at the White House—a Siamese cat named Misty Malarky Ying Yang. Caroline Kennedy, I was told, had also had a cat until her father's allergy to cats drove Jacqueline to give it to her secretary, Mary Barelli Gallagher. Presidents have had pets, too—Coolidge with his raccoon, Rebecca, and FDR with his world famous dog, Fala.

Jimmy Carter was not completely frugal when it came to his family. When Amy wanted a birthday party on turning ten on October 19, 1977, he footed the bill himself. The cost did not break the bank. Amy and her fourteen guests from the Thaddeus Stevens School she attended had a simple party fare of hamburgers, cake, and ice cream.

The entertainment, however, was a little more special and in keeping with the Halloween theme—the showing of the original *Frankenstein* movie in the White House projection room.

Part of Jimmy Carter's daily routine was to read the Bible. And every Sunday that he was in Washington found him teaching Sunday school at a Baptist church near the White House. In his interest in the Bible, he was not unlike an earlier occupant of the White House, John Quincy Adams, who recorded in his diary that he rose at five and started the day with the Bible. Adams especially concerned himself with the work of a contemporary scholar, Thomas Scott, and his book *The Holy Bible Containing the Old and New Testaments . . . with Explanatory Notes, Practical Observations and Copious Marginal References.*

It was ironic that Jimmy Carter, of all people, became the first President in history to entertain a pontiff. They may have been far apart in their religious beliefs, but Southern Baptist Jimmy Carter and Pope John Paul II found they had much in common in their interest in solving the problem of poverty when they met at the White House in 1979.

There was living proof at the White House that Jimmy Carter was sincere in trying to live the tenets of his religion. While governor, Carter had gone to the Georgia corrections system to find a babysitter for his daughter. The woman selected, Mary Fitzpatrick, had been serving a sentence for murder when the new governor gave her a new chance in life. Amy became so attached to her that she convinced her father to bring Mary to the White House when they moved north.

There was a period of time in Washington when everyone was incredulous over this revelation. Doubters soon came to accept the fact that the woman was being rehabilitated and showed every indication that she would be absorbed back into society. Many even began to admire the Carters for the complete confidence they had placed in her. Few of us would take such a leap of faith.

Carter, though puritanical in his own thinking, understood that God had made man with imperfections, and he did not fire anyone for living in sin. But he was concerned with the private lives of the people on his team.

One of the favorite Carter stories around the White House showed Jimmy's reaction when he learned that an appointee, fairly high in his administration, was living with a woman.

As the story goes, Carter caught the man in a moment when they could be alone and asked, "Do you two have plans for getting married?"

"Oh, certainly," the fellow replied.

"When?" Jimmy pursued.

"Well, we were thinking of getting married when the azaleas were in bloom," the man hedged.

Jimmy looked him in the eye and said, "Where *I* come from, the azaleas are in bloom right now."

The story ends happily with a wedding soon after.

But things were not too happy at the White House parties.

No doubt remarks about the dullness of recent evenings prompted the major decoration of the Grand Foyer and Cross Hall with huge hanging pots of plants from the Botanic Gardens. This did not make up for he lack of drink or dance. How long could one stand around admiring the greenery?

Some of the Social Aides were becoming increasingly discouraged by the fits and starts and constant changes made in the party plans. Those we could adjust to but we could not adjust to the humiliation of being served cold cuts and bread while a full meal was being eaten by the guests in the State Dining Room. What was delivered to us for making sandwiches was so bad and so unappetizing that I actually saw Social Aides bring their own "brown bag" meal into the White House so they could have something decent to eat.

We were strictly volunteers, proud to serve our President. But we were not proud of the way we were being treated in return.

Frugality had been carried to the outer limit. Hugh Carter, Jr.—Cousin Cheap—had finally gone too far. Or had he? Was *he* the one who had come up with this brainstorm to save money on food? Or was it the full-time Military Aides?

Did Jimmy and Rosalyn know how the Social Aides were being rewarded for the hours of sleep lost to make each of their parties flow smoothly? Didn't they have to approve changes?

No longer could the aides have a little party of our own with a few drinks and good food while the President and his guests were feasting in the State Dining Room. So just what *was* our reward? It was hard to know—especially since we were also supposed to be all but invisible.

I was starting to wonder what I was doing there. The sheer enjoyment and glamour and prestige of attending White House parties in themselves were no longer enough. But they had been enough until the Carters had made us feel like second class citizens. In fact, by the end of Ford's term of office, my life had revolved around the friendly First Family, their parties and the general White House social life.

When Ford lost his presidential campaign, everything began going downhill for the Social Aides. Maybe it was time to move along—six years as a volunteer White House Social Aide is considered a very long stint and few stay longer than one or two years. And besides, I had fallen into the tender trap of love and was having more fun the nights I wasn't at the White House than the nights I was.

Her name was Linda Haner and she was not, as my mother had predicted, a debutante. Nor did I meet her at the White House. But she was everything I had been looking for right along. Actually, a couple of buddies—George and Dan—had gone with me to a Sunday brunch at a singles-oriented apartment complex across the street from the condo where I lived in Alexandria, Virginia. And there she was! It suddenly gave credence to that old song that you'll find happiness there, "right in your own back yard."

It wasn't hard to spot Linda that day. She was the one with the cluster of men around her, laughing a lot—all of them. And she was the tallest girl there, standing a good inch higher than me, in her high heels. And to my taste, the most beautiful.

There was a contest for her attention. Several of the other guys wanted her phone number but I was the one who ended up calling and getting a date with her for that Tuesday night. It was love at first date for me. It was lucky that she didn't go out with my friend first because it might have posed a problem between him and me.

Later, I discovered that the reason she had said yes so quickly when I called for a date was that some fellow had been standing at her door and she was using me to get rid of him.

From that hilarious beginning, we kept on laughing. Linda had a delightful sense of humor and there was almost no subject she couldn't joke about. And she had a streak of kindness a mile wide—at least once a week she went over and read books to a blind woman whom Linda had not even known when she had moved to Washington.

Maybe her intuition told her this chance meeting of ours was something different—that we were meant to be together. We even shared the same hardworking Germanic background and our ancestors had helped make the great American Midwest what it is today.

Like me, Linda had lived abroad. She had been a student teacher in Bogota, Colombia. She knew Capitol Hill and had been an intern for Congresswoman Elizabeth Holtzman, working on constituent problems.

As we grew closer together, we began to draw away from the traditional singles scene of endless parties. We went water- and snow-skiing and even powerboating with friends but often wound up talking to each other rather than everyone else. Often, we would do something old-fashioned like ride bicycles, picnic in the park, or go for a hike.

My parents lived in San Luis Obispo, California, and had not been to D.C. since Linda and I met, so Linda did not get to know them till the wedding. I had the advantage of meeting her parents one afternoon, well before we were engaged.

They drove down from Warren, Ohio, for a weekend and I was invited over for dinner. They were already there when I arrived at her apartment and she wasn't ready yet so I immediately stepped in and acted as host, just like at the White House. I had been at ease in

Linda's house long enough to know where everything was in the kitchen and I offered them a drink. As a Social Aide, I was accustomed to taking charge of any social situation.

Years later, Mrs. Haner confessed to being downright shocked at what seemed like my boldness in her daughter's home.

Linda and I were engaged for several weeks before she actually got a ring. We shopped to find the style and then asked a jeweler friend to make it. When the ring was ready, I didn't tell Linda but invited her to an early dinner for two at a fancy restaurant in downtown Washington, bringing along my camera to take some shots of the Ellipse and the South Grounds of the White House.

We walked out to the stone milepost marker at the top of the Ellipse and I asked her to hold my lens cover while I took pictures. Giving her the ring box, I rushed to my position.

The distraction worked just long enough. The lens cover was in a very small and curiously square box which required examination. Linda shrieked with delight as she discovered her diamond ring—my camera rolled.

We were married in the chapel at Fort Myer, and took a horse and buggy ride to the Officer's Club for a reception.

The honeymoon was at Fort A.P. Hill (the same place where we got engaged) in a lovely lodge meant to house twenty-four people. But we had it all to ourselves. Complete solitude. It was like something out of a Hollywood movie—a Gothic movie—complete with strange night noises that had to be investigated, creaking rafters and creaking boards, creaking doors. The works.

The experience just added to Linda's joke file. Marriage did not change her puckish humor. One fine day after we had moved to Columbus, Ohio, I picked up the phone and it was a TV station telling me I had won a contest fulfilling my dream. I would be news anchor for a day.

"Who the hell is this?" I demanded. "And what's the joke?"

It was no joke. Linda had proceeded to enter me in the contest after she heard me sound off one time that I could do as good a job as the one we were listening to—maybe better.

I went along with the gag and found myself with a TV cameraman interviewing Arnold Schwarzenegger exercising in a gym.

Arriving early I met Arnold, then sat down to wait for the crew with a senior reporter from a rival station who almost fell off her bench when I told her why I was there. We worked all afternoon for one minute and twenty-five seconds of air time. I developed a new admiration for the White House press corps.

I also developed new admiration for Linda, who set about starting a career as a writer. Her compassionate side hadn't changed, though. She donated the advance of her first book, *The American Sampler Cookbook*, to the American Red Cross Famine Relief Fund. The book contained the favorite recipes of famous political figures from the President and Vice President to the elected representatives of all the states and territories.

For a number of weeks, while the publisher was having the manuscript proofread, and Linda was calling congressmen and other high government officials concerning missing ingredients and the like, I was almost afraid to answer the phone. More often than not, it was some senator or his wife launching into a discussion of a recipe.

Linda is now working on a sequel to her cookbook and this one will benefit World Vision. Looking back I realize I married one of the thousand points of light long before the phrase became popular.

Getting married caused me to lose my White House Social Aide status and I happily left to start my new life. President Carter also lost his White House status but he was not so happy. He departed Washington in humiliating defeat, having received only forty-nine electoral votes to Ronald Reagan's landslide of 489

Carter had tried very hard, but his success rate was not high. The area in which he did succeed was as a peacemaker. One of his initiatives resulted in the Camp David Accords, which I consider his greatest triumph. Convinced that there could be lasting peace between Egypt and Israel in spite of the 1973 Yom Kippur War and a long history of hostility, Carter appointed himself mediator.

Acting as host in September 1978, he brought together the two great antagonists, President Anwar Sadat of Egypt and Prime Minister Menachem Begin of Israel, in the peaceful atmosphere of Camp David, where they could have absolute privacy.

All three men put their cards on the table and discussed the Israeli-Egyptian problem until a solution was arrived at. The sad note was that Sadat was assassinated in his homeland several years later by an angry dissident. The happy note is that the Accords endured and remained in force under Sadat's successor.

There was another field in which Carter might have changed the course of history if he had only had more time. The truth was, according to a former high official of the Department of Energy, that Carter had a program underway for the development of substitute fuels.

Naturally, oil men were not thrilled about the program which would cut into gasoline profits but Carter was determined to free the United States from its dependence on Mideast oil. Then Carter lost the election and under the new administration of Ronald Reagan, the substitute energy program was scuttled.

Why had Carter so antagonized the American people—and the voters? There were various explanations.

He had engineered the giving away of the Panama Canal and many conservatives bitterly resented it.

He was tricked by Castro into accepting the dregs from Cuba's prisons.

He tried to change the Presidency and it hadn't worked. He had tried to improve the life of the common man and he had ended up with double-digit inflation. He had been cursed with the Iranian hostage crisis and the Ayatollah deliberately delayed release of the hostages until the very hour Reagan was sworn into office.

I thought of all this later, looking back at Washington with a surprising amount of nostalgia.

After many years in the Washington area, it became apparent to me that, in spite of my disenchantment with the Carter social scene, by becoming at ease in the White House, I had acquired a common ailment known in the area as Potomac Fever.

It was not the driving passion others contracted that would make them do anything to get to Washington again. Rather, when I discovered in 1987 that my Army career would take me back to the nation's capital anyway, getting a job at the White House became my first priority. My chance would come under the Reagan administration.

This time, I would actually receive money for my White House job, and this time I was the proud father of two little boys—Michael and Christopher.

Part Five

In the Catbird Seat With the Reagans and the Bushes

21

The Regal Reagans

*W*ith the second outsider to hit Washington—Reagan—the White House exploded in the greatest show of pomp and ceremony that old hands had ever seen. It was as if the White House had sat in darkness during the Carter administration and Ronald Reagan had materialized and said, "Let there be light!"

Every aspect of the diplomatic, ceremonial and social White House which had been eliminated, reduced or otherwise diminished by the Carter administration was immediately reinstated to its original glory when the Reagans moved into 1600 Pennsylvania Avenue. Some of the old glorious ways were even improved upon while other new layers of glitter were added.

The Reagans seemed inclined toward majestic pageantry and Ronnie's stunning victory became a mandate not only for political change but also ceremonial change.

Herald Trumpets were back. "Ruffles and Flourishes" and "Hail to the Chief" would ring out whenever Ronald Reagan made a formal entrance.

When I returned to the White House eventually, I was exhilarated to watch the formal military arrival ceremonies on the South Lawn for visiting heads of state. I had seldom been able to see many before because whenever I was at the White House, I was busy with guests.

Listening to the cannons roar, I felt that I was reliving the historic days of Washington and Adams and even earlier, when cannons were used to hail a ship as it entered a harbor. Today's honored guest arrived by limousine but he still got his gun salute.

But what especially impressed me was the ceremony, which included an ancient weapon called a pike.

A part of history is relived in this ceremony when the Fife and Drum Corps from the Old Guard performs in their authentically reproduced Revolutionary War musicians' uniforms. The leader of this group carries a pike in his right hand. (It is a long wooden shaft with a metal spearhead with which soldiers of an earlier era sought to impale their enemies.) As they pass in review, the leader lowers the pike and salutes with his left hand. He is the only person in the United States Army permanently authorized to do so.

The grandeur of every occasion where Reagan performed his ceremonial role as the head of state and host was further underscored by the sheer glamour of everyone's appearance. Under Carter, business suits had been good enough on many formal occasions. And women had worn understated gowns, remembering Rosalynn's home-made blue Inaugural outfit.

Now, while men were still limited to variations of the black tuxedo, female guests suddenly exploded in a great range of designer gowns, furs, jewelry and accessories to project themselves and to make their statement in the new administration.

It was a time-consuming job for Washington wives who had to go far beyond their normal effort, just to keep up with the new First Lady, but Nancy's out-of-town guests were used to it. They had the money *and* the time. As one insider put it, "Nancy has no *poor* women friends."

Nancy quickly became legendary in her ability to organize and execute very elaborate and splendid social functions and to dress the part of a glamorous First Lady. Even though many of her clothes were wildly expensive and some she wore were borrowed from top designers, she was able to make women who read about her feel that she represented *all* of them—even those with moderate means.

Nancy Reagan's confidence and success in running the social side of the White House was so outstanding that she contributed very substantially to the notion that things would be done well by her husband in running the country. An aura of success permeated the

White House. The Reagans were perfect hosts. White House parties were IN. Dancing was back.

Alcoholic beverages were quietly reinstated to all aspects of social functions including the afterdinner waiting period for the entertainment. Guests were allowed to control their own behavior rather than have the host do it for them.

The foods served were pricey, the menus elegant. More times than not, the most expensive meat—veal—was the entree of choice. After dinner and entertainment came dancing—and so did wallflower patrol.

But with an important difference.

First Lady Nancy was determined that only the most elegant manners would do. Therefore she decreed that female Social Aides no longer could take the initiative in asking lonely looking male guests to dance. That would be *unladylike*.

Under the Reagan manual for Social Aides, a female aide could chat with a male wallflower, but could dance only if *he* asked *her*.

But women fared better in another White House situation. After years of taking a back seat to the men, women were now gallantly allowed to precede their escorts in any receiving line for an informal function. The logic associated with everyday courtesy of men toward women had finally prevailed over the antiquated procedure of many previous administrations.

Nancy could be thanked for this step forward. But this new chivalry did not hold true for formal events. The more prominent guests continued to go first *regardless of gender*. In this manner, the guest of honor and the President would *first* greet the person who was the primary reason for the couple's presence at the formal affair. With increasing frequency in Washington—the direct result of President Reagan appointing women to high office—the more prominent person, among the couples invited to the White House, was apt to be a woman rather than a man.

Some of the most obvious examples of the new changes would be reflected in the way the Social Secretary, the Military Office and the Social Aides conducted the parties. Many differences were subtle and may not have been noticed by even the regular Republican guests who, in the main, did not attend the previous Democratic administration's events.

For one thing, the Reagans instituted a new practice, seeing to it that their guests received souvenir photographs showing them at the White House. It could be called "the Hollywood touch."

During the majority of social events, one or more official White House photographers were on duty. Their primary responsibility was to snap the First Couple with each guest coming through the receiving line. It was a real rat race for the busy lensmen to catch every single handshake.

To keep things straight so that each guest would get the proper glossy photo souvenir, a new aide category was designated—the Recording Aide. His job was to record the names of people as they had their picture taken with the Reagans. It is hard to imagine a less exciting task for a military officer than being a photographer's assistant, even in the White House. There is little doubt that this job fell to the newest, greenest, and most junior aide in the group.

Ronald Reagan would be credited with bringing the office of the presidency into the golden age of visual and verbal communication and his wife tried to do the same with the social side of the White House, attempting to make each party a masterpiece.

In the past we had used eighteen to twenty Social Aides for each important large social event. The Reagans in their drive for excellence used as many as thirty or more Social Aides. And instructions were carefully prepared.

It's hard to eliminate a practice once it is started. And so the dreaded Whispering Aide job was still there and was used occasionally. It was a small price for the social staff to continue to pay to be part of what was suddenly transformed into a glamorous and exciting environment.

Unfortunately, it was no longer an exclusive and clubby thing to become a Social Aide at the White House. Now, perhaps reflecting Nancy's early days in show business when she went to auditions to try out for a role, so did Social Aide hopefuls.

Potential aides were no longer invited on an individual basis. Instead, a cattle call was used, just as on Broadway. Once a year a notice went out to all military organizations in the area asking for volunteers to meet and apply for entrance.

When selected, aides were now told up front they could only remain in the program for four years and then had to leave. The Military Office apparently did not want anyone to feel too at ease in the White House.

Three or four of us must have given their predecessors some concern when our experience levels passed five years and we had been around much longer than other Military Aides and longer than the presidents.

Though I wasn't at the White House in the early Reagan years, I was happy to discover some of the changes that lightened the burden of the Social Aides.

The Social Aide in charge of a major event was now asked to appear the day before to walk through the scenario. Rather than trying to cram everything in the thirty minutes he used to have before the other aides arrived, he would have plenty of time to plan and to solve potential problems.

Guest lists were also secured a day ahead so that the aides in key announcing or introducing positions could study them to prevent slipups in the pronunciation of names and titles.

The aide in charge of a function was now briefed by the Social Secretary rather than by the Duty Military Aide. There had always been some confusion as to whom we Military Social Aides worked for, with the result being that we worked for both the Social Secretary and the Military Office.

On the rare occasions when they gave what appeared to be conflicting guidance, the Social Secretary's instructions would prevail until the discrepancy could be resolved. Fortunately, actual contradictions in instructions were very infrequent because regard less of who briefed us, we always made a courtesy call on the other office for any special instructions or information. At that time a quick rundown of the plan identified problem areas that required a decision.

In the past, when our briefings had come from the Duty Military Aide first, there was a higher incidence of corrected or changed procedure by the social office. Putting the Social Secretary in clear control served to highlight the point that the Social Office really ran things and even though we were in uniform, we more often than not followed civilian rather than military direction.

The life of a Social Aide became more pleasant with some of the Reagan changes. After countless homemade sandwiches and "brown bag" snacks during State Dinners, full meals were again being served to the aides in the staff mess. Cold cuts, which had been viewed as a deliberate slight to us by the Carter White House, were out.

Another improvement was in the matter of the parking passes issued which allowed aides to use special reserved spaces just outside the gate when space was limited on the grounds. This had been a sore point for us more than once under the Carters. They occasionally asked us to work afternoon hours during peak tourist season but because of ceremonial or other parking restrictions, we could not park on the grounds.

It became a safety concern for the female aides who might have to return to their cars after dark. This new parking arrangement not only would be a convenience to the aides but also would help insure our timely arrival at the White House as well as a safer return home.

Some of the changes were not for the better. We often had been permitted to remove our gloves and enjoy refreshments with the guests after the President and First Lady had departed a function. Now the gloves had to stay on until the very last guest had finally left. In contrast, the Nixons and Fords had made us feel welcome to enjoy the feast.

This included not only afterdinner champagne but more importantly, excellent hors d'oeuvres at late afternoon receptions. It was a privilege for us and, as a practical matter, it also made it easier for us to blend in and function more efficiently. But under the Reagans, the aides were prohibited from touching anything until all the guests had gone.

The theory was that this would keep aides more alert and available when some task had to be performed, but it also would insure that many aides would go home at least a little hungry. Those not fast on their feet when the last guest was out the door had to go without, as certain delicacies disappeared almost as in a shark feeding frenzy.

Something quite unusual and theatrical was instituted to please the press. For years, the news media had been complaining that they could not figure out by sight alone who some of the visitors were.

Announcing Aides were designated to proclaim the guests' arrivals for the media stationed downstairs at both the South and East entrances. This calling out of names gave the impression that one was entering an event not unlike the Academy Awards—which certainly did not dampen the arrivals' spirits. Or like "Showtime at the Apollo" and the guests were making a stage "entrance."

Suddenly there was great emphasis on price tags, and price was no object. Nancy's Inaugural outfit had cost about $23,000 and her

Second Inaugural outfit had doubled that, topping $46,000 with her Galanos Inaugural Ball gown alone valued at $22,500.

And then there was Nancy's expensive taste in redecorating the family quarters of the White House. The government supplies $50,000 to each new family moving into the White House so that the Family Rooms on the Second Floor can be fixed to fit in with each President's style. That did not begin to do the redecorating job Nancy had in mind and friends rushed to bridge the gap. There was a $50,000 private contribution for the makeover and a $70,000 gift for the makeover and on and on until the total reached $800,000.

Enough was enough. Suddenly things had gotten a little too regal, too expensive and, perhaps, even wasteful. As I looked back with nostalgia, Carter was starting to look a lot better. I remembered that Mrs. Carter had not used all of their $50,000 decorating allowance and the rest had gone back to the Treasury. And I remembered Jimmy—how he wore sweaters all the time because he had turned the thermostat down to sixty-five degrees.

It was known at the White House that Rosalynn had pleaded with him to turn it up to a more reasonable sixty-eight degrees but he had refused, as a matter of principle. The man really stuck to his principles. As a plebe at Annapolis, young Jimmy had been hazed unmercifully because he refused to sing "Marching Through Georgia" when ordered to by an upper classmate. And no matter what they did to him throughout that year, he still refused to sing a Yankee song which told of Northern soldiers laying waste his state.

As a result, he had to answer to the nickname of Johnny Reb.

Even when Jimmy Carter was running for President, he did not want to hear *that* song, and he once took a high school band to task when they thought they were pleasing him by playing it on his arrival in Phoenix, Arizona.

It was no wonder that when he called for turning thermostats down to save heat, he was not asking more of the public than he was willing to do himself.

I remember meeting a girl who told me that when her parents had seen Jimmy Carter on TV giving his fireside chat in a sweater, they had also immediately turned down their thermostats to sixty-five to help the President save energy in the gas crisis. She said that her parents had been proud of Jimmy Carter and the sweater became the badge of honor in their home just as in the White House.

As sentiment against Nancy Reagan's extravagant life-style rose, some women found ways to express their disapproval. There were letters to the editor and articles written. And when Nancy let it be known that she did not approve of the wearing of slacks by female White House staffers and some agencies seemed ready to go along, other women throughout government offices took their cue. They gleefully started coming to work in slacks—even if they never before had worn them.

Incidentally, so many clothes did Nancy Reagan have and acquire, that she turned several rooms into huge closets—the two rooms that had been Amy Carter's.

The message now was spend, spend, not conserve, conserve. *Frugality* had a bad name and conspicuous consumption was IN.

And Hollywood guests were very IN. And so were MOVIES. The Reagans added a new social event that was pure Hollywood—movie screenings. The screening was a celebration of Hollywood's newest motion pictures with the stars as honored guests. Nancy served an informal dinner and then everyone, including the aides on duty, would go down to the White House theater in the East Wing to watch the film. Having stars appear at large dinners was always exciting but this event would condense everything to just a few fascinating people with the majority of them celebrities. There would never be a problem finding volunteers willing to work this function.

Hollywood stars became a staple in the makeup of the more than four dozen State Dinners held during the Reagan years. Presidents have always relied on a few movie stars to keep guests entertained but the Reagans took the concept to new heights.

Congressional and diplomatic guests were of course flattered to be chatting with Hollywood's finest in such a casual way. Of course some might say Reagan was using his movie star connections to his own ends, such as getting votes for certain bills—and some did make snide remarks. But didn't a man have the right to invite old friends and neighbors who just happened also to be the most sought-after Hollywood stars? Ronnie and Nancy thought so.

When I returned to Washington in the spring of 1988, it was like coming home again. I once more was connected with the White House. I was assigned to the Executive Office of the President not as a Social Aide but rather as an active duty Army colonel on loan from the Department of Defense to work on procurement policy issues in the New Executive Office Building. I answered inquiries to the White House on how to do business with the federal government, and I led the administration's efforts to establish a single nationwide comprehensive list of all potential bidders for defense contracts. The fact that I had previously coordinated the government's defense of the purchase of the $618.20 toilet shroud was a big plus.

My title was long and impressive—Deputy Associate Administrator of the Office of Federal Procurement Policy—but though my military career had most certainly moved up, my freedom around the White House had taken a decided downward turn.

Staffers from my office did not go over to the Executive Mansion except when invited to certain informal functions.

Getting a badge just to enter the Old Executive Office Building next to the White House took several months of additional background investigation to update my existing security clearance.

I was amazed at how much the security around the White House had been beefed up since the Carter days. Of course, as far back as I can remember, there has always been a good deal of security and most people walking by the White House do not realize what they say can be picked up surreptitiously and listened to by security men. Next time you are in Washington, check it out.

Careful scrutiny of the area inside the Mansion's decorative high security fence will reveal a series of microphones, lights and speakers. I've had occasion to visit the White House security center. It's interesting as well as necessary for the security staff to know what people are doing out by the fence as there have been numerous attempted and actual penetrations of the White House grounds. Usually, someone climbing the fence is apprehended immediately.

Occasionally, some nut will get near the mansion itself. Some have even crashed automobiles through the gates and gotten as far as the main door. Fortunately this is no longer possible as the use of car bombs in the Middle East necessitated the placing of heavy impenetrable barriers at each entrance to foil such attempts. Even a casual glance at the imposing steel and concrete posts should convince the craziest of people to write a nasty letter instead of trying to go through the protective barricade.

One of the unique breaches of security occurred when an Army enlisted man stole a Huey helicopter in the state of Maryland and led the highway patrol on a very wild chase into Washington. He was not a trained pilot but, as a helicopter mechanic, he had been around the craft enough to have a fundamental knowledge of how things worked.

Fortunately, the amateur pilot handled the helicopter well enough so that when he decided to land on the South Lawn in the middle of the night, he was able to do it without flying into the President's bedroom by accident. Needless to say, that was a hell of a shock to the security forces, and classified plans were developed to prevent a recurrence.

Now, when I came to work each day at the Executive Office Building located very close to the White House and considered a part of it, I could hardly believe how different things looked.

The safety barriers for the White House complex had become by all outward appearances, virtually impregnable and clearly reflected the terrorist mood throughout the world. Even the roads around the complex had changed. The East Executive Avenue which runs between the Treasury Building and the East Wing has been closed to vehicle traffic and turned into a park with a well-traveled public sidewalk.

The visitors' entrance is still there, but a new security check point has been built just inside the gate to permit careful screening of every person who enters the compound.

The street in front of the town houses on Jackson Place next to Blair House is also closed to through traffic. But you can't stay in the protection of the White House complex. In at least one off-duty incident, a female aide friend was probably saved from certain harm by a Military Aide.

While in civilian clothes one evening, the two were walking down a desolate street where muggers frequently took advantage of innocents. One jumped out of the dark at this apparently naive couple and demanded her purse and his money, probably thinking the guy would not risk her safety by contesting the robbery. He judged wrong.

The Military Aide to the President pulled out a hidden knife and fought the attacker off until he ran away. My friend told me the two went on their way after the Military Aide casually returned the blade to its secret place. No one on the street bothered them again.

Because space is very tight in the Executive Office Building, several of the overflow offices have been located next to Blair House. They require protection similar to the remainder of the White House complex, but the real concern has to be the distinguished visitors who stay there as guests of the President. It is a prerequisite for public events and certainly contrary to good security measures, but the presence of a VIP is always announced through a barrage of news stories.

Security increases accordingly. Whenever a dignitary is in town, not only are the appropriate flags of the visitor's country and the host flown on all the poles along Pennsylvania Avenue, but police barricades are put up so that all pedestrian traffic is restricted from passing in front of Blair House and routed safely across the street. No risks are taken that can be avoided.

Some of the first State Dinners held by the Reagans went so far as to include very tall white screens placed around the North Portico entrance of the White House itself. Concern was very high at that time that some unfriendly organization might try to use these events to make a statement.

Screens allowed the President and First Lady free access of movement outside the doorway when their honored guests arrived. They could easily step out and greet the guests without fear of being in a sniper's cross hairs. Eventually this measure was eliminated, once again giving the moment a renewed feeling of relaxed openness.

July 4, 1988

Each year, the President and First Lady invite the entire White House staff—with the exception of part-time help such as the Social Aides—to sit on the South Lawn to view the nation's great fireworks display with them. It is an ideal site since the lawn slopes gently down towards the Washington Monument, where all the fireworks action takes place—actually they are shot off in a safe area between the Monument and the Lincoln Memorial.

This year, invitations had been sent to some two thousand staffers of the Executive Office of the President. And guests were invited to bring members of their immediate families.

Because aides were not included in the past, this was my first opportunity to attend as a staff member. Also, this being our first year back in Washington after several Army moves, Linda and I wanted our two boys who loved Fourth of July celebrations to see this very special one. We even called the in-laws who drove down from Ohio for this unique opportunity.

Getting into Washington on the Fourth of July is a challenge—a test of driving skill and endurance. Some avoid the traffic snarls by coming early and having a picnic on the mall till darkness arrives.

Many look forward to the military bands that entertain the crowds in advance of the fireworks and the numerous other events scheduled throughout the day for the half million visitors expected. We left home in time to fight the traffic, invent a parking space, and arrive at the White House about an hour and a half before the show.

Ushered through portable metal detectors at the Southwest Gate just like all visitors, we joined the rather large crowd that had already arrived. Many of the staff members had been coming for years and quite a few skipped this evening. They knew that those like us who brought their extended families would manage to fill the entire South Lawn rather quickly. About fifteen hundred adults and an equal number of children had settled down to await the grand show.

In the meantime, stages were set up for live entertainment and plenty of soft drinks and popcorn were available for the price of a short wait in line. A children's petting zoo and a number of clowns— no, they weren't staff members picked at random—kept the little ones' attention till dark.

I was surprised to find that the Reagans had even provided portable toilets, the quality of which greatly surpassed those found at construction sites or fly-by-night town fairs. This gesture was partially in self-defense to avoid having crowds of people coming into the White House to use the powder room.

A few minutes before the show started, the President and Nancy appeared from inside the Mansion with several of their special guests, including columnist George Will and composer Marvin Hamlisch. We got a pep talk and a thank you from the boss and then the show began. It lasted almost a full hour and was truly spectacular. In all my previous years in Washington, I had never been up that close, having observed the event often but from the Virginia side of the Potomac River.

Even the Bicentennial celebration, in 1976, which we witnessed from a private boat on the river, could not match the excitement of being on the South Lawn so near to ground zero. Each major burst felt like it was pressing directly on us as the rainbow of lights cascading down toward earth seemed to be nearly over our heads.

Some smaller children greatly protested the noise but none of the grown-up children made a move to take them home. The magnificent finish seemed more spectacular than any fireworks show ever held in Washington. Multiple bursts of red, white and blue streaked downward, disappearing just before they struck earth while the booms of exploding shells echoed across the mall.

In addition to the very plentiful reminders of our national colors, the sky virtually lit up with every other conceivable hue of light. As the end neared, the roar of the explosions was like combat and so intense that the protesting youngsters could only be seen and not heard. This glorious conclusion to the fireworks foretold of an equally grand departure from Washington for the Reagans and their administration.

October 6—State Arrival—President Traore of Mali

In all my years as a Social Aide, I had only seen a couple of arrival ceremonies because no more than one or two aides were ever used for this type event. Now, as a staff member, I could simply stroll over from the office, watch briefly, and be back behind my desk in no time.

Suddenly, knowing that the ceremonial troops would be led by soldiers from my former unit, the Old Guard at Fort Myer, I was even more anxious to see a Reagan-style full honor arrival ceremony and compare it to the adulterated variation used by President Carter. Once again, staffers were invited to bring family members, and many of us gathered on the South Lawn on a beautiful, crisp, sunny morning.

We excused our oldest son, Michael, from school knowing he would benefit more from this unique experience than from a day in third grade. He was most agreeable. Our four-year-old, Christopher, reacted less enthusiastically. He carefully explained to us that we had all gone to the White House for the Fourth of July celebration and they hadn't even let us inside. We said, "Well, come along anyway, Chris." We were kidding of course—there was no way we would leave him behind—but he took it very seriously and decided to humor us by gracing us with his company.

It was a dazzlingly clear day and the cold morning air quickly turned warm as the South Lawn soaked up the bright sun. Men and women from every branch of the services were in place when the two Presidents made their dramatic appearance with split-second timing.

The visiting dignitary arrived at the South Portico entrance and President Reagan stepped out the door to greet him just as Traoré's limousine pulled up to the red carpet, which had been rolled out for the occasion.

Then it began and it was a feast for the eye and the ear. The Herald Trumpets sounded a fanfare, the band played "Hail to the Chief," and the substantial crowd of partisan staffers and special guests applauded.

Both the visitor's anthem and the national anthem were played, followed by short speeches exchanging greetings of the two men. For this exchange of official remarks, a platform had been set up at the top of the South Lawn, beside the White House. Television crews and other media people filled a large temporary stand erected to overlook the podium.

When the honored guest reviewed the troops stationed in a long line below the platform, he saw not only the soldiers and musicians but also the vivid ceremonial display of fifty-seven state and territorial flags—a display Reagan's predecessor had banished.

It was clear to see that even President Traoré's very colorful and flowing robes could not compete with the majestic demonstration of military pomp and circumstance in his honor. Jimmy Carter would probably have been repelled if he had seen this magnificent ceremony.

But Carter wasn't there this day and only little Christopher was present to show how unimpressed he was with all this hoopla. And even worse, he again did not get to go into the White House and he was sorely disappointed. He sat on his coat on the grass and didn't even want to get up when both Presidents walked right in front of him. Some day I'll tell him about it.

December 17—Christmas Open House for Executive Office of the President's Staff

The most beautiful time of the year at the White House is during the holiday season. It takes three full days of work to get all the decorations in place and all public tours are halted for this effort.

Once the magical transformation is completed, the public is

invited to enjoy the winter wonderland during regular daily tours as well as the special Candlelight Tours held in the evenings between Christmas and New Year's Eve. Each major segment of support for the mansion, such as the Secret Service and White House police, Military Office and Executive Office Building staff, was also invited to attend its own special open house hosted by the Reagans. Families were included again but our children weren't excited about this new adventure. We had difficulty convincing Christopher that he would actually get to go inside the White House this time.

The Christmas party had something for everyone. After arriving through the regular visitors' entrance and undergoing normal security checks, we were ushered in through the East Portico to the strains of harps and violins. Many children stood by patiently while all the adults wandered through the various rooms on the ground floor, looking at china, vermeil and library books. Upstairs, everyone passed very slowly through the Grand Foyer and Cross Hall which were festooned with Christmas garlands. A short detour by the cookie and punch table entertained the boys till we got to the East Room.

The entertainment normally provided would have been different had the Melody Bells from Indiana not refused the First Lady's request to perform. They apparently were told that there would only be room for about half their normal complement. They responded that the entire group of the children's hand bell choir had come on previous occasions and if there was not room for them all then none of them would be available to take part. It was a reasonable explanation, but after many years of being associated with White House functions, I found the refusal to participate absolutely unprecedented.

Many occupants had worked hard to make the White House beautiful at past Christmases but no one had done it as well as Nancy this year. Eight gorgeous trees covered with decorator snow were beautifully lit by the dimmed chandelier lights of the East Room as though one were walking through a mountain meadow at night under a full moon.

It was a breathtaking sight to see and the joy of every visitor from our little Chris to the oldest adult was apparent in everyone's awed expression. Moving through the various parlor rooms on the State Floor, we were brought up short by our children in the Blue Room.

As in many years past, the chandelier had been removed for the season to make way for the Christmas tree which took up nearly the entire twenty-foot distance to the ceiling. Their young eyes were fixed, however, on the electric train circling round the base, just far enough inside the velvet rope to keep little hands at a safe distance.

It was amusing that like every mode of Presidential transportation, Railroad One even had a press car behind it with Santa Claus riding in the caboose. Disappointed that they were not permitted to play with the toys, Michael and Chris could only stand and look.

With some encouragement, the boys agreed to come to the State Dining Room to see the gingerbread house. There was no Marine guard this time so each Mom and Dad performed that task. More cookies, cake and punch kept the kids busy while their father joined most of the other adults for a spiked egg nog.

Then it was back to the choochoo train. When asked where they wanted to go next, the boys both quickly exclaimed, "Home." It was late and these normally very active children were tired of just looking. They weren't even willing to wait for the President to appear.

Someday, I will tell them about this, too.

Everything was winding down in January as the nation prepared to welcome Ronald Reagan's successor to its bosom. Reagan was so popular that if he wanted George Bush, *they* wanted George Bush.

I, for one, was proud of Reagan and the job he had done. We had two terms of economic growth under his leadership. Millions of jobs had been created. Interest rates had been reduced. Our nation's defenses had been modernized and strengthened.

If I had a complaint, it was that he had not stepped forward to accept responsibility for the Iran-Contra affair as he did for the bombing of the Marine barracks in Lebanon. But I was not walking in his shoes...

And suddenly Reagan was gone into the history books—the man they called "The Teflon President," because he could do no wrong.

It was over and the nation took stock. Reagan had wanted government regulators to get off everyone's back, and now suddenly it seemed that lack of regulation had brought about the biggest financial scandal in history. The general public will have to make up the multibillion-dollar losses of people who had put their money in savings and loan banks—a $2,000 share for every American.

Reagan had promised to cut the high cost of government and balance the budget, and when he left his watch, the national debt had tripled to an unprecedented figure approaching $3 trillion.

I felt sympathy for George Bush—he would have a lot of work to do.

22

The Insider's President—Bush

I knew George Bush from the Nixon and Ford administrations. As a senior government official, he was at most of the really important parties—State Dinners and such—and sometimes I engaged in little exchanges with him.

He had a friendly way about him, and when he asked where I'd gone to school, we discovered that we shared something special—a Texas background. I had gone to Texas A&M and told him I actually enjoyed a good Aggie joke.

In the southwest, Texas A&M has been the most common target of humor. I didn't mind the jokes any more—I always enjoyed hearing a new one, as did Bush. Whenever I could, I boned up on Aggie jokes in case I got a chance to banter with him:

"Did you hear that the Aggie school library burned down? Both books were lost, but only one was colored in."

"How many Aggies does it take to pop popcorn? Five. One to hold the pan and four to shake the stove."

"What do they call one hundred Aggies in parachutes? Air pollution."

"What do they call an Aggie four years after he graduates? Boss!"

President Nixon had made George Bush head of the CIA but for a supersleuth, he was always very mild mannered and friendly to a fault. If ever a man had been training all his life to be President, George Bush was that man. He knew everyone in Washington and had worked with everyone in one way or another.

Starting with business experience—oil company executive—he had become, in turn, a Texas congressman, a diplomat—U.S. Ambassador to the U.N.—chairman of the Republican National Committee, Director of the CIA, and even a former presidential candidate—defeated by Ronald Reagan.

I was sorry I could not routinely attend Bush presidential functions, but I had several opportunities to be present when he was performing his ceremonial role as head of state. There was no more time for small talk and no time for Aggie jokes. He wasn't just a guest anymore.

Ronald Reagan had been a popular man—a charismatic figure whom people had to like when they met him, in spite of themselves. Now we had a man who did not have that kind of movie star charisma, but who had such warmth that you could feel the glow.

George Bush was the kind of man who could and did take a shower with his dog, Millie, every now and then without feeling apologetic about it. He was the kind of man who, when he heard an Associated Press White House reporter—Rita Beamish—was getting married, sent a bottle of champagne. It did not bother him that Beamish was marrying into the enemy camp—fiancé Paul Costello had been Kitty Dukakis' press secretary during the presidential campaign.

I went to the Bush inauguration ceremonies and it was certainly an exciting and exhausting week. The variety of public and invitation-only events was staggering. One could go all week to rallies, receptions, dinners and ball after ball if one only had the right connections, plenty of stamina and unlimited funds.

The prices—like the variety—were staggering. One of the pre-inaugural dinners alone was $1,500 a plate. All the other functions were below that pricey atmosphere but still almost out of sight for average people. Tickets for the Inaugural Balls cost $175 per person—$350 a couple—a big change from the Carter "People's Parties" twelve years earlier, which were $25 per person.

The swearing-in was free to everyone. So was the parade—if you didn't mind standing. Some people paid $75 each just for one ticket in the viewing stands in front of the White House.

I smile as I remember one couple later complaining that they purchased these expensive tickets and barely got to see the new President because they were seated a half block past the White House. The Bushes, on impulse, got out of the parade and entered the presidential enclosure directly in front of the Executive Mansion when they reached it, never actually completing the full parade route.

We chose to stand where we could make a quick exit and beat the crowds out of the area. We were much further back on the route, standing in the shrubs on a retaining wall near the Archives Building. That evening at the party, when anyone asked if we went to the ceremony or parade, we could honestly say we spent the entire afternoon with the bushes.

But to return to the swearing-in on the Capitol grounds, when the gates were opened, we won the two-hundred-yard dash to the front of the standing-room-only area. Not only could we see everything at the podium but we got to watch the rich and famous walk by to the reserved seating area.

It was a very cold morning and almost everyone wore his or her best winter coat to this auspicious occasion. There were so many gorgeous animal pelts it was difficult to tell the merely rich from the truly rich and famous personalities.

Wayne Newton, one of the first celebrities to pass us, had on a full-length fur overcoat and really looked like a superstar, but Cheryl Ladd's attire was noticeably subdued and she wore sunglasses as if she were hiding from the public. Sitting directly in front of us, Cheryl couldn't make it forty-five minutes without smoking at least two cigarettes.

Fred Travolina sat in front of her and kept his video camera trained on the podium most of the time when he wasn't chasing after his active kids. It was a real joy to see him without a nanny and functioning like any normal parent.

Donald Trump came by, but we almost didn't recognize him. We noticed Ivana arriving in her full-length off-white fur coat because the sun was still low on the horizon and it made both her hair and fur look almost orange. Watching this conspicuous but still almost unknown lady go by, someone said the guy with her was Trump himself, and the crowd reacted like a bunch of news media cameramen. While we watched him weave his way through the crowd to his seat up front, someone announced that we had just missed seeing Michael J. Fox.

One gentleman kept walking back out alone and coming in with someone new. It took us a while to figure out that he was carrying out his group's tickets everyone kept for souvenirs and bringing in others he knew who had no tickets at all. He would have probably passed unnoticed except for the dramatic long fur coat he wore and the fourteen-inch cigar he had stuck unlit in his face. Could this have been one of the party's "high rollers"?

Invitations to the ball—or rather, invitations to buy tickets for the ball—were hard to come by, and I failed. When I asked around the office, it quickly became evident that no one in my section of the White House complex had the necessary connections in the new Bush administration to get me an invitation. My disappointment quickly turned to chagrin when my wife received two complete and separate sets of the coveted invitations to purchase a pair of tickets for any or all events. I was once again reminded that the pen is mightier than the sword. Even a sword in the Commander in Chief's own camp.

Linda and I chose to attend the ball at the Washington Hilton, since it included the Ohio contingent. We had come from there in my last military assignment and we were planning to move back there again in the near future. Before the evening was over, more than ten thousand people had gathered in this one location to celebrate and wait for the arrival of George Bush.

We were lucky. By getting there early, we managed to have our own table. The $350 entitled us to a so-so band, an incredible crush of people, and all the pretzels we could eat. Still, it was an exciting experience.

It was interesting to compare this event with the Asian-American Inaugural Ball which we attended earlier in the week. That one had been held in a single ballroom and only cost $50 a ticket. But that included plenty of great food, a good dance band and no security problems.

In defense of the Hilton affair, I should say that the Bushes and Quayles did show up and we actually managed to run into a couple of old acquaintances. I got to chat for a few minutes with Richard Nixon's brother Ed, who stood out in the crowd primarily because he looks almost exactly like the former President. He was on his way to

Upper Saddle River, New Jersey, to visit and promised to pass on my best regards to both the former President and Pat.

I asked him about Mrs. Nixon's health and was told that Pat was not feeling very well as she suffered from emphysema. But she was otherwise enjoying the privacy of being out of the international spotlight and away from Washington.

Actually, we went to three Inaugural Balls and the greatest one was the third, which took place the night after the official one.

January 21—Texas State Society Inaugural Ball

Many would consider this event anticlimactic since it was not an official function and most of the celebrating for the new Commander in Chief was already over. But like the Asian-American Ball and a number of other major events, it was "sanctioned" by the Inaugural Committee, and more importantly, the new President was sure to show up as he had for all of the Texas State Society's recent major parties.

Soon after the election of the Pride of Texas to the highest office in the land and well before Christmas arrived, all the five thousand tickets were spoken for and a waiting list of more than three thousand names was developed in case anyone was foolish enough to turn tickets back.

The Society was so besieged with requests that for a month it had a recorded phone message about the unavailability of the $50 tickets. Once again, the cost was not the issue as some tickets reportedly changed hands for up to $1,000 each.

A day late or not, the Texas Ball turned out to be the most fun of all. Great Tex-Mex food was available at several serving tables around the main ballroom of the Hilton as were drinks and plenty of long neck Lone Star and Mexican brand beers. Despite the overwhelming public interest in this party, the crowd was not nearly as awesome as the official ball held the evening before in the same room.

Texas ladies wore extravagant gowns, of course, but the men wore black-tie tuxedos and cowboy boots with the styles and colors about as varied as any rodeo. In the typical manner of Texas, strangers were friendly and everyone said "howdy" whether or not they knew the other person.

President Bush did not disappoint his Lone Star State supporters or the television camera crews that came from Texas to film the event for their local news audiences. When he appeared, he first greeted the University of Texas alumni with the longhorns hand-sign and then saluted the former Texas A&M students with the "Gig 'em Aggies" thumbs up.

The crowd loved his salute and cheered to indicate approval. They also approved and hailed his dressing in a tux plus a pair of cowboy boots that had been handmade by a bootmaker in the audience. Although tired and going hoarse from the week's events, he and Barbara stayed longer than they had at the official balls the night before.

My favorite Bush Inauguration story involves one of my wife's friends who was hired to bake a cake for one of the Inaugural parties. It was to have a thousand points of light as well as a considerable amount of colorful decoration. She was doing the trim with frosting bags that had various sized tips to produce different shapes, designs, and colors. She and her helpers were working furiously as the Secret Service advance team had already arrived and checked out the surrounding area President-elect Bush was about to walk in to inspect their handiwork.

As one pastry bag ran out, she required another immediately to maintain the continuity of this massive effort on a cake so large. In her haste, she loudly instructed a chef, "Hand me that loaded twenty-two!" Instantly the Secret Service detail of a half dozen agents descended on her, then learned she referred to a bag of frosting with a special sized decorator tip. For her, the President's appearance a few moments later was totally anticlimactic.

The Inaugural was not the only thing on my mind in January of 1989. I was also concerned about my mother who was in the hospital. I wanted to do something very special for her.

January 27, 1989

One of the privileges the staff in the Executive Office of the President has is to get the boss to sign a letter to someone for a special occasion. This may range from a birthday, wedding, anniversary, graduation or retirement for an individual or group to a letter of condolence. The first time I tried this, my mother was in Letterman

Army Hospital in San Francisco for major surgery, and President Reagan sent her a note wishing her a speedy recovery.

Not only did it greatly improve her spirits but it increased the fine attention she was already receiving from the doctors and nurses there. Following her second such operation in three months, I made an effort to get the new President to send another message of support.

Returning to the White House Correspondence unit each day following the inauguration, I always was informed that it had to await approval from the new administration to continue the policy as well as the format of the request form. No letters could go out until then.

Finally one morning I was told that only a few minutes earlier approval had been given for the practice and my mother was sent one of the first such presidential greetings of the new Bush administration.

Policies change from time to time but the public can also make similar requests for senior citizens and very unusual events. The Greetings Office in the Old Executive Office Building has a staff of three dozen or more unpaid volunteers who fill all manner of public requests for presidential recognition. Responses come in several categories: weddings, retirement, graduation, illness, condolence, anniversary, or general joyous occasion.

The most popular request is for a presidential birthday card but one will only be sent if the person is over eighty. A special category exists for those over one hundred. The card is notably bigger and displays a gold embossed seal of the President of the United States over a red, white and blue ribbon. Bearing the signature of both the President and the First Lady, it proudly proclaims that the White House sends birthday greetings on a very memorable occasion.

These letters and cards do not always have the personal touch everyone would desire. Although his signature appears on many pieces of mail leaving the White House each day, the President does not actually sign them all. Many are inscribed by an Auto Pen which reproduces the individual's signature exactly. Others have the signatures already printed on them although it is an authentic reproduction.

A select few on the White House staff use this Auto Pen service as well, primarily because of the volume of paper they handle. The

Special Assistant for Legislative Affairs is a good example. This special office for Presidential signatures handles as many as eleven hundred of these automatic signatures each day while the Greetings Office staff sends out over sixty thousand cards for various occasions each month. At Easter, the Auto Pen worked overtime, egged on, as it were, by the crowds.

March 17–18, 1989

First Dog Millie gave birth to six puppies. Despite advance public announcements that the offspring were already spoken for within the Bush family, many people wrote and offered to provide homes for them. Little did anyone realize just how privileged these canines were.

People came by to pay their respects to the little princes and princesses of dogdom. Unfortunately, none of them would have won any prize in a beauty contest since they took after their mother, who had been singled out in *Washington* magazine as "the ugliest dog" in America.

Though the President huffed and puffed and defended the beauty of Millie, the inside story was that when Barbara Bush first set eyes on Millie, the First Lady had whispered in Millie's ear that she loved her in spite of her bow legs, her piggy nose and her other less than perfect features.

She would. That's the kind of person this First Lady is—and not just when it comes to animals.

Barbara Bush is a hands-on hostess, grabbing and hugging and putting her arm around shy female guests when their pictures are being taken with her. It was a tragedy in her life that made her decide to show warmth whenever possible. Few people know that when her first little daughter, Robin, was three, she died of leukemia.

It was a devastating experience and brought the successful, carefree young couple up short, harshly reminding them of the pain that is part of the human condition. It changed their attitude toward everyone around them. Barbara Bush has commented on that point, saying, "Because of Robin, George and I love every human being more."

To be in the presence of Barbara Bush is to feel her warmth

reaching out—and her warmth reaches out to many groups whom she helps, usually without hoopla. The homeless, the elderly, the victims of AIDS. The one field in which the First Lady welcomed all the hoopla she could cause—and continues to do so—was literacy, a subject she became interested in when one of her sons—Neil—had a reading problem in school.

Thinking of all the children and adults who share Neil's reading problem or any reading problem, Mrs. Bush became chairman of a very energetic and ambitious group, the Barbara Bush Foundation for Family Literacy.

To make money for the foundation, even First Dog Millie pitched in, dictating her life story to a willing Barbara Bush, who helped collect the photos for it. *Millie's Book*, a dog's-eye-view of life in the White House, ended up in the number one spot of *The New York Times* best-seller list. But proving that everyone—even a dog—is without honor in his own land, the book was only number six in Washington.

To show the power of one dog, the Family Literacy Foundation had already received $75,000 at this writing, with undoubtedly much more on the way.

The love story of Barbara Pierce and George Bush is like something out of a romance novel. She was only sixteen. She spied him at a Christmas vacation dance and it was all over for her. He was tall, dark and handsome and a senior at Phillips Academy at Andover, Massachusetts.

A year and a half later, when George was scheduled to go off to fight in World War II as a Navy pilot, they became engaged and Barbara happily dropped out of Smith College to marry him when George came home on a leave in January of 1945.

But marriage did not mean they would spend their time together and the advancement of George's career in and out of government meant that much of the time he traveled alone. But each time his career took them to a new locale, Barbara Bush sprang into action—sometimes doing all the work. The White House was the twenty-ninth time Barbara—and George, when available—moved the family.

Some wives might have been lonely, but not Barbara, who filled her hours with old friends, with needlepoint projects, with children and grandchildren, with causes and volunteerism, with long walks and tennis and swimming. With making new friends and living by her slogan, DO SOME GOOD EVERY DAY, if only to further some piece of needlework or do a favor.

A marvelous example of how her slogan influences her daily life came to my attention one day when Gordon Smith, who was chairman of the National Press Club committee on speakers and entertainment, was reminiscing about Barbara. It had happened at the annual Congressional Club luncheon in 1987 when Barbara Bush, as wife of the Vice President, was one of the two honored guests—the other being Nancy Reagan.

Gordon was invited to the reception preceding the annual luncheon of the Congressional wives and with him were the president of FTD, who had arranged for the contribution of flowers, and several other friends.

As Gordon told the story, "Mrs. Bush arrived ahead of Nancy Reagan—without fanfare and in fact, quite unobtrusively—and she walked around greeting guests in a low key. I had my camera along and on impulse, I asked her to pose with my FTD client-friend which she graciously did.

"Then she said, just spontaneously, 'Here, let me have your camera and I'll take a memento picture of your group.' Then, laughing and chatting about her picture experiences with her family, she did just that. We were quite stunned as were some of the Congressional wives who stood watching her.

"As we left, we still were overwhelmed by the unprecedented action of a Second Lady. I've met many a Vice President's wife at the Press Club and at the White House and I'd say only Lady Bird Johnson might have had the spontaneity and friendliness to do such a thing. We decided that such a woman, who had no pretense or stuffiness, would make a great First Lady. And what do you know, it happened."

It was amazing how quickly the press took to Barbara Bush, her white hair, her matronly figure and her tough talk. Whereas Nancy Reagan had been extremely dignified and repressed in voicing her opinions, Barbara Bush, whose husband calls her Bar, said whatever came to mind—but with warmth and good humor.

Once, when reporter Sarah McClendon—famous for needling Presidents, including Bush—was coming down the receiving line, First Lady Barbara Bush called out, "Here she comes—the troublemaker."

"I didn't mind at all," Sarah said later. "What she was saying was true, and besides, she was laughing. You have to like that woman. She always speaks her mind. You don't have to guess." Another time, Mrs. Bush warned a *People* magazine reporter with pretended gruffness, "Don't argue with me. I can throw you right over my shoulder." No First Lady ever talked like that before.

March 27—Easter Egg Roll

Anyone who has been to or seen an egg roll on the South Lawn of the White House would understand why Social Aides were never used for this function. As many as thirty thousand or more people normally attend during the four hour event and control measures range from the iron fence around the South Grounds to rope barriers and roving White House Police details.

Basic etiquette involves not throwing eggs directly at people and restraining threatening parents whose children run off at full tilt to disappear in the vast crowd. For all these reasons, the most skillful Social Aides would be of no use here. I had never been to this annual affair before, but now that Linda and I had children, it was a must-see-once event.

Many people get up way before the chickens just to come downtown and stand in line for hours to be among the first ones let in at 10:00 A.M. The parental urge to make sure children participate in this unique ritual at the President's home may be at least partially driven by their own desire to see the White House grounds.

Therefore, they are willing to endure long cold waits in line and security barriers which involve not only the metal detectors but also physical searches of purses, baby bags and Easter baskets, just to get in. Then they get the privilege of standing in line again to participate in the various events. It's a tough way to enjoy a day in the city, but a souvenir egg signed by someone famous could make it all worthwhile.

This annual ritual has been going on for over a hundred years at the White House, ever since the Congress banished the event from the Capitol grounds in 1878. Run by volunteers from various women's clubs and party loyalists in the Washington area, the event has become an institution. Anticipation and enthusiasm are not dampened in the least by the fact that several dozen children get temporarily lost in the crowds each year.

As a staff member, I was permitted to have my family join me at the Old Executive Office Building entrance on West Executive Avenue to participate in a special version of the Egg Roll starting at 9:15—well ahead of the general public.

The invitation seemed like an easy way to enjoy a charming event with a presumably much smaller crowd of people. Actually, by the time we got in, there were thousands of grown-ups and children lined up through the north entrance into the West Garden Room and then further out onto the South Lawn. The weather was absolutely beautiful after several days of rain and cold, and every person who even thought about going showed up.

We shuffled slowly to the top of the lawn and then made a dignified dash to the event of choice for our children. There were two separate locations for the egg roll and the egg hunt events as well as an egg exhibit, a celebrity autographing center, storytelling areas, comfort stations, children's animal farm, entertainment stage and the lost children and first aid station.

Already, long lines formed at every event and they never seemed to get any shorter, but they did not begin to compare with those one hour after the public was let in.

Success was measured by having each of our children find prized colored wooden eggs—one signed by the President and the other by the First Lady. It is anyone's guess how many of the 23,000 wooden eggs bore their actual autographs (remember the Auto Pen?) but several children walked out with the cherished signature eggs.

My boys would have preferred Mr. Belvedere's signature. They had heard he was there, somewhere, autographing eggs. Only their Mom and Dad know that some day they will be glad the President and Mrs. Bush won out over the testy TV butler whom they adore.

Celebrity eggs were not the only prize finds. There were also five thousand real eggs, hard-boiled and colored for the actual egg roll contest. Since half the thirty thousand-plus guests were adults who would not be permitted to take a souvenir, this total of twenty-eight thousand eggs should have been enough for the day, but some experienced parents brought their own along just in case the supply ran out before their kids got one and they needed to help out.

Thousands of helium balloons were passed out to the children who dispatched them quickly. The balloons were never expected to last very long and most were sent by air mail to the Maryland countryside long before the owners left the south grounds.

And yes, Virginia, there also is an Easter bunny.

In the past, the part of the Easter bunny was often given to someone well known on the staff or—in Reagan's time—to a spouse such as Ed Meese's wife. This year it was played by Marine Colonel Charlie Krulak, Deputy Director of the White House Military Office. Actually there were two bunnies, with Charlie's wife playing the part of the other one. Presumably, she was the figure with the apron. It didn't matter to the children.

They loved both as did the laughing and exuberant Barbara Bush. Charlie's promotion to brigadier a few days later had nothing to do with his great Easter bunny performance and his ability to hippety-hop, and everything to do with his willingness to get any job done, no matter how difficult.

The Bush White House developed a distinctive style very quickly. Rather than have a number of flashy formal parties, the First Couple preferred to invite no more than forty for an informal dinner. What really surprised everyone was that these dinners were held in the private residence, one level above the State Floor normally used for social functions and the public tours.

Dress was more casual and the delighted guests were privileged to see something that very few people who visited the White House ever saw—the President and the First Lady's private living quarters. It may seem odd that some of the guests were clearly from the political opposition but there is probably no better way in the world for differing views to come together than to have the individuals socialize. And no First Couple in recent memory has been better suited to warmly welcome significant numbers of guests into the private residence.

As a consequence of these routine informal gatherings, the services of the Social Aides were not required as much as under any of the recent four Presidents.

Some larger and more formal dinners were held downstairs, although changes were made there as well. The aide usually designated to announce the arrival of guests at the East Portico was assigned to some other duty. It was an excess that everyone (except perhaps the reporters) could do without.

There was no dancing at the smaller, private residence parties, and at some of the larger ones downstairs, dancing was also left off the schedule without explanation. However, dancing continued as a traditional feature of State Dinners.

Guests lists were also going through an evolution, taking on a different format. One of the first such lists was printed in alphabetical order with all the foreign dignitaries listed first and then the U.S. guests. Unlike previous ones under the past four administrations, the names of the Vice President and Secretary of State were buried in the middle. Later versions listed them in protocol order but then put everyone else in alphabetical order.

June 6, 1989—Arrival Ceremony for Prime Minister Bhutto

In one of those odd twists of history, the honored guest returned to the White House for a State visit, but this time she came in her father's place as Prime Minister rather than as the daughter of the head of Pakistan's government. Benazir Bhutto first appeared here in September of 1973 at a similar State visit while a guest of the Nixons.

Her father was subsequently deposed, imprisoned and later hanged. She too spent time in jail but her previous education at Radcliffe and Oxford taught her enough to lead her father's political party back to power. She seemed to be enjoying the return to Washington immensely, relishing every moment and reflecting on every detail.

George Bush was not timid in this, his first official State welcome. As if to say, "This show ain't peanuts!" the new administration rolled out the traditional trappings of the presidency to salute an old friend.

Bush obviously enjoyed participating and seeing the splendor of the whole traditional welcoming procedure. There was not a thing that was left out. The full complement of ceremonial troops, flags, cordons and musical organizations was included in the first such arrival ceremony since the new President's inauguration. The Herald Trumpets signaled the Prime Minister's appearance from the second floor balcony of the South Portico while the Navy Band played marching music for the troops. The Old Guard Fife and Drum Corps performed the final salute of the ceremony in their Revolutionary War musicians' uniforms.

It was impossible not to think back on how terribly drab and dull these ceremonies were under the Carter philosophy of greatly reduced pomp and circumstance.

Apparently the Prime Minister was also impressed. As Bush and the Commander of Troops led her through the inspection of the Honor Guard she took the occasion quite literally, walking very slowly while looking closely at each one. The group stopped in front of the colors to render proper honors and stayed much longer than necessary.

The President at one point obviously thought they had waited a respectful period of time and, dropping his hand from his heart, started to turn as if they would finally move on. He had to reverse himself when the Prime Minister failed to budge from her position of paying honor to Old Glory. They finally began to move again at a snail's pace and I wondered if the band would run out of music and have to start playing the same number over again, and in a cloudburst, which was imminent.

One of the officers supervising the conduct of this ceremony later talked with me about the particularly slow pace of the Prime Minister this morning. He agreed that she lingered much longer than necessary but that the foreign dignitaries always seemed to move at a sluggish pace. He suggested the proper music should be a waltz rather than a military march. Fortunately, he was smiling when he said it.

Just before the ceremony started, Lee Atwater walked up and stood next to me, looked around at the crowd and went back over near the President. A tourist from Louisiana (who got in with the help of a senator's office) had been standing next to me and asking lots of questions about the music, the participants and the sequence of events. This gave me a chance to turn the tables and ask him if he knew who the gentleman was who had just stopped and then abruptly left. He said with great self-assurance, "Secret Service!"

When I gently explained that the man was the head of the Republican National Committee, he said, "You mean that country and western singer?" Realizing how little some tourists know about the workings of politics, I just gave up.

Returning to my office, I discovered an award was waiting for me. One of the most elusive benefits of White House service was to receive the Presidential Service Badge and Certificate. The White House stopped awarding them to Social Aides in the 1960s, so none of us had received one despite our efforts to make hundreds of social functions run smoothly. It is a permanent and tangible form of recognition of the fact that a member of the armed forces served in a direct support role to the Commander in Chief.

One of the most dramatic impressions of the White House during my last tour was the color. It isn't true white. Also to the point, it isn't *all* white. The Executive Mansion has been repainted at least thirty-two times by official count since it was first occupied in 1800 by our second President, and there has never been any paint removed before the next coat was added. Unless of course one counts the time the British burned it in 1814 and much of the original whitewash was scorched off.

A contractor applied an acid compound to take the old layers of paint off and in the process may have identified five additional but undocumented layers of paint. Stone experts repair the outer face of the walls where damage or deterioration has been uncovered. The most serious destruction has been uncovered on the northwest corner, apparently a result of the 1814 fire.

Stones that cannot be repaired are replaced with sandstone blocks provided by the Capitol. These are some of the same pieces taken from the identical quarry during the same period that the original White House rock was cut. When each section of the job is finished, a new softer white paint is applied—an off white.

The project should be completed in time to celebrate the 200th anniversary of the laying of the cornerstone in 1992. The end result should be a much more attractive structure, particularly when lighted at night.

What happens when Washington temperatures soar to ninety degrees or more in a humid summer? I was about to find out the day that Prime Minister Robert Hawke of Australia arrived on June 27. I can truthfully say this was a particularly warm reception in every sense of the word.

One of the advantages of electing a career public servant such as George Bush is that he already knows so many heads of state and senior members of foreign governments that they do not need to waste valuable time getting to know one another. He's already an insider. President Bush received the Prime Minister like a cousin he had not seen for some time. Although this arrival ceremony was on Tuesday, the honored guest had actually come to town several days earlier. He and the President had even already had time for a round of golf.

When the Prime Minister said it was a warm welcome, he wasn't joking. It was the hottest day of the year with the mid-morning temperature approaching ninety degrees. Washington's typical summer humidity added to everyone's discomfort. We all stood in the hot sun, but at least we could move around. The honor guard of troops, which marched into place about twenty-five minutes before the ceremony started, had to stand at parade rest without moving anything but their eyelids.

They were highly disciplined troops and never flinched, regardless of the weather, but today they paid an extra price. Only a person trained in military ceremonial drill could tell how much some of them were hurting by the time the formalities actually began at 10:00 A.M.

These professionals were taught to not lock their knees because blood circulation to the legs would be cut off, but there is little that can be done to combat the combination of military parade uniforms and humidity and heat. The troops still had to endure the rapid dehydration that comes from long-sleeved dress uniforms, hats that fit tight enough to guarantee absolute stability, and close-fitting waist belts that insure no air circulates under their summer weight blouses.

Despite the constant physical training they undergo year round, the heat began to take its toll just after the principals had reviewed the troops. As several individuals collapsed one at a time, another in the proper uniform was rushed in from behind to fill the spot.

Some of the otherwise motionless troops gave warning signs by teetering on their feet. That usually indicated to the support troops that they only had seconds to get there before the soldier fell and possibly hurt himself or herself on the chrome-plated bayonet fixed to their M-14 rifles. We were fortunate that none of the officers out front or the color bearers went down. Replacing one of *them* would have been infinitely more awkward and disruptive.

Someone asked why there was only a nineteen-gun salute this day and not a twenty-one-gun salute, which is the greatest honor. Actually a prime minister is not a head of state but a head of government. For this reason, the cannon salute that is fired on the Mall near the Washington monument as he arrives is only nineteen guns. The Queen of England would receive twenty-one guns as would all those designated as a true head of state. Margaret Thatcher always received nineteen.

George Bush would receive twenty-one because he is the head of state with all that implies—all the glory when he is right and all the brick-bats when he makes a wrong decision.

I was leaving the White House too early in the administration to know which of these George Herbert Walker Bush would receive— brickbats or glory. There was so much opportunity for both. The handling of the Iraqi crisis. The handling of the savings and loan scandal. The handling of the annual budget and national debt.

Again, as I packed up, part of me was reluctant to go. But as Gilbert and Sullivan had put it so well in one of their ditties, "Duty, duty must be done—the rule applies to everyone," and I knew I would be keeping in touch with the Washington scene from my new military post in Cleveland, Ohio.

23

It's the Little Things You Most Remember...

*M*emories, memories.

I remember what the late Pearl Bailey once said—"What the world really needs is more love and less paperwork." She clowned with Richard Nixon while he played the piano. And I recall that more than one President listened to her and that she was made a member of the U.S. Mission to the United Nations.

As I finish this book, I lean back in my chair and am surrounded by the ghosts of people I have known at the White House. People gone who made a difference in the world.

Was that really me standing by and watching the parade of people involved in social and political history? Was that really me trodding the same stairs and boards where Jefferson and Lincoln and Dolly Madison walked?

And I think of things—little things—that people said. It's the little things one remembers longest. It's the little things that one has seen—sidelights of history—that most often flash through the mind.

I remember Pearl Bailey—never again will she flounce around the White House. And Freddie Prinze—a suicide. And Anwar Sadat—assassinated. And Golda Meir—heart failure. On and on—Hubert

H. Humphrey, with his infectious laugh; the Shah of Iran, with his elegant ways and ramrod posture, as if trying to look taller; Soviet Premier Leonid Brezhnev, with his eye for the ladies; Vice President Nelson Rockefeller, who was here, there and everywhere, except where he was supposed to be in the receiving line.

And I recall the living. Sometimes it's the little thing that someone says that stays in your mind the longest. Alexander Haig commenting on the fact that Washington had become the new murder capital of the nation—"What bothers me is that I can travel ten miles in this town and still haven't left the scene of the crime."

I remember Queen Elizabeth II and the fuss we made over her and what I learned about her way of silently signaling her aide. I was told that if Elizabeth is engaged in a conversation at a party and switches her handbag from her right to her left arm, it indicates she is bored and wants her staffer to rescue her with some excuse that she is wanted elsewhere.

And I often think of Henry Kissinger. Much has been said about women vying with each other to date Henry Kissinger because they were attracted to his power. Kissinger was not handsome nor did he have a reputation as a great lover. But then, Washington did not have a great reputation for romance. As someone said, "If you're looking for romance, you've got the wrong Washington—try Seattle or Spokane."

I remember the guest who most piqued my curiosity—I almost held my breath waiting for him to open his mouth and say something. *Anything.* Marcel Marceau! I didn't have to wait long.

He had come with a lovely female companion to an evening function and apparently neither had ever been to the White House before. They started asking questions the instant they got out of the receiving line. Although French was their first language, both spoke passable English and didn't hesitate to use it. For me it was almost surreal to hear the great mime speak—I had been his fan for years. Countless times, the world had seen him perform on television and never once did it hear him utter a word in any language.

His offstage personality could not possibly have been more unlike his professional act. Unrestrained and uninhibited. He talked more that night to everyone than any other guest in recent memory—he was a veritable talking machine.

Since his and his companion's interest would not be satisfied by a simple answer or two, I took them on an informal walking tour of all the rooms on the State Floor. They were a lot like excited, chatterbox tourists and simply marveled at every item of furniture, every antique clock and every painting. Many first-time visitors were like that but it was very unusual to see such an international star react so enthusiastically and to be so openly and sincerely impressed.

There frequently are amusing things going on in the lives of the First Families. There was the time Barbara Bush discovered that she had a buddy swimming along with her in the White House pool—a big rat. And there was the time Jimmy Carter was in a boat—not at the White House—and claimed he had had to fight off a "killer rabbit."

And there is all the joking about President Bush's golf game. His golfing partners come away shaking their heads over the way he plays "speed golf," or what Bush himself calls "cart polo." Whatever its name, the amusing point is that the President does not even wait to see where the ball rolls before he jumps back in the cart and speeds after it.

The score is not the point but the speed—whereas normal golfers take four hours for eighteen holes, Bush takes two and one half or less. His record is one hour, forty-two minutes for a foursome. As the President says, "We're not good but we're fast."

Bush has his fun needling the press. One day he commented, "The reason terrorists have never taken over Air Force One is that they got a good look at the way the press corps there was dressed and figured someone had already beat them to it."

Perhaps the funniest thing that happened at the White House was the pratfall Nancy Reagan took off the stage of the East Room while her husband was speaking after Vladimir Horowitz had performed at the piano. Unharmed, she stood up, brushed herself off and delivered her line—"I thought I'd liven things up."

She got her laugh but then President Reagan topped her, saying, "I told you not to do that unless I needed applause."

Those are the lighter moments. But there are the dark days.

How does a First Lady handle it when there is a scandal brewing about her husband? I remember what Pat Nixon did during the Watergate days. She confided to someone and the word got out that, for one thing, she had stopped reading the newspapers. And for another, to keep from being a virtual prisoner at the White House, hiding away from the press, Pat would slip out of the White House every day—with the help of the Secret Service—and walk around downtown Washington, disguised in dark glasses and a scarf around her head.

And what did she do? She window shopped and dreamed of the day it would all be over. And when a group of religious ladies came to see her and give comfort, she told them, "Pray for the press." She refused to show any despair and she let them know she was optimistic about the eventual outcome of the Watergate affair.

I thought of all that recently when the Nixon Library housing all his papers was opened at Yorba Linda, California, and former Presidents came to the dedication and to pay their respect—Ford and Reagan—as well as the current President, George Bush. Pat Nixon stood proudly with eyes glistening as she heard the kind words spoken in July 1990, sixteen years after she and the thirty-seventh President had packed their possessions and sadly left Washington.

One line kept coming to my mind—*Some things take a long time.* It had taken a long time and I was happy for her—*now* it was over.

Other First Ladies have lived through similar hard times. When Andrew Johnson was undergoing impeachment proceedings for disregarding the Tenure of Office Act—declared unconstitutional by the Supreme Court in 1926—Eliza Johnson took to her room.

When her husband's bodyguard ran all the way from Capitol Hill to tell her the good news that Andrew had been acquitted by one vote, she did not act a bit excited. "I knew it," she said, calmly. "I always knew it."

Bess Truman was a little more emotional when her husband was made to look bad because she had accepted the gift of a deep freeze—value $375—from an old friend. Bess said, "In the future, if someone offers me a tray of ice cubes, I'll refuse it."

I remember the Presidents I have served and how strange it is that while they are there, it feels as if they will be at the White House *forever* but suddenly they are gone. And then there is a *new* man and the *same* feeling soon reoccurs. I have liked them all, admired them all—but naturally, some more than others. I can truthfully say I tried to give equal service to all.

In their retirement, each President showed his true interest and inclination. Richard Nixon chose a quiet, contemplative life of political study.

Jerry Ford picked the very social sportsman's life on the ski slopes and golf links.

Jimmy Carter went still further in his effort to live a humble and austere life—choosing to work with his hands to help build and repair homes for the indigent.

Ronald Reagan headed back to the ambience of California to live a movie star-type life in a movie star-type home in the heart of the movie colony.

President Reagan once told how he had a recurring dream that he was looking for a house with a huge living room and a balcony and that, at the end of the dream, he had found it and could afford it. He said that as soon as he moved into the White House, the dream stopped.

Pictures of his multimillion dollar retirement home suggest that he is free of that dream forever.

I recall how most recent Presidents have had family trouble. When the Carters left Washington, some White House watchers breathed a sigh of relief that First Brother Billy Carter was gone and predicted that now we would see a perfect family life in the Reagan White House.

Billy Carter had been aptly nicknamed "the Clown Prince," and he had not hesitated to be funny at brother Jimmy's expense, even saying, during Jimmy's first presidential campaign, "I got a Mama who joined the Peace Corps when she was sixty-eight. I got one sister who's a Holy Roller preacher. Another wears a helmet and rides a motorcycle. And my brother thinks he's going to be President. So that makes me the only sane one in the family."

But the Reagans had not portrayed the perfect family life. The elder son, Michael, complained about having been shut out of his father's life by stepmother Nancy Reagan and said he was not welcome at the White House. And Patti Davis was so at odds with her real mother, Nancy Reagan, that she, too, did not visit at the White House for long stretches.

After her father, Ronald Reagan, left office, Patti went public to proclaim in an article that his policies during his eight-year administration were the direct cause of the huge wave of homelessness across the land. Economy instead of humaneness, she said, had motivated her father.

I was impressed with how Barbara Bush and her husband—the

President—stood by their son Neil, right or wrong, when he was accused of a conflict of interest in possibly benefitting from bank loans made by the Silverado Savings and Loan of which he was a director.

I was also impressed with how the Bush family, children and grandchildren always seemed to be around the Mansion.

I am not trying to pass judgment. I merely want to show that being in the White House does not automatically insure a perfect family life—or even a close one.

The Nixons, with their two daughters, were a close, happy family but I remember that Dick Nixon had the problem of one brother seeming to take advantage of the other's position.

The Fords and their children were an exceptionally close knit gang—having fun together and all ganging up to tease poor Susan, the youngest of four and the only daughter.

It was my gut feeling that a major factor in Jerry Ford's loss of the presidency after serving out the rest of Nixon's term was his refusal to help bail New York City out of bankruptcy only days before the election. It made him look rather heartless, especially in the newspapers—one headline read: FORD TO NEW YORK: DROP DEAD.

He could have played it cute and postponed the announcement of his decision, but he was a straight shooter and wanted everyone to know where he stood.

Not everyone was as reluctant to leave the White House as were Jerry Ford and Jimmy Carter. John Quincy Adams could hardly wait to get out, calling his four years there the "most miserable" of his life. Andrew Jackson, who could get no peace from job seekers, said, "What is there in this place that a man should ever want to get in?"

Harry Truman labeled the White House "a great white prison" and even Thomas Jefferson referred to the presidency as "a splendid misery."

It could also be "a splendid misery" for First Ladies.

I remember all the handshaking I saw at the White House. The receiving line can be an excruciating ordeal, and I would sometimes feel sorry for Pat Nixon and Rosalynn Carter for the handshaking marathons they suffered through—Pat Nixon, I recall, once shaking two thousand hands.

At least they didn't have it as bad as some past First Ladies who endured the ordeal of shaking thousands of hands every year at the traditional New Year's Day reception—come one, come all. It was First Lady Lou Hoover who finally decided enough was enough after her sore arm marked the beginning of 1932.

The next New Year's Day, the Hoovers conveniently arranged to be out of Washington, thus tactfully breaking with tradition. The Franklin D. Roosevelts chose not to revive the custom and the tradition was permanently gone.

Not all First Ladies went in for the democratic handshake. Ida McKinley—wife of President William McKinley—held a little bouquet of flowers at receptions to stave off guests wishing to shake her hand after they had shaken the hand of the President in the receiving line.

In the early days of the Republic, there were no handshakes at the White House. Everyone bowed, curtsied, or doffed a hat in those times.

Actually, it was President Jefferson who threw out stiff formality and began shaking hands with the guests. Even Presidents Washington and Adams had merely bowed to guests, while their wives nodded, from a seated position.

Jefferson carried informality so far that he once invited his butcher to a White House dinner. The butcher complicated the seating arrangement by bringing along his son—naturally without first getting permission to bring an additional guest. But as the story goes, Jefferson took it all with good humor.

There are many things that are hard to believe about the White House. One was that there were ever slaves.

I mention it because, as a Social Aide, I was asked many questions about the White House and its various rooms, and there were so many things I just did not mention. For example, when I was escorting one female guest to the East Room, she commented on how sad it was that Abigail Adams had to work so hard, standing in the East Room hanging up her washing. I let it go.

From the moment I arrived to be a Social Aide in the Nixon administration, I started questioning the experts and studying everything I could on White House history.

I doubt that Abigail was the one to hang the clothes. In fact, there is a painting depicting the scene which shows a black woman in Aunt Jemima headgear doing the actual hanging of sheets while Abigail stands by directing.

It's not clear if the black woman was a slave but there were indeed slaves working in the White House in the pre-Civil War years. President Jefferson, for one, brought some from his plantation. Some of the Presidents deplored slavery but there *were* slaves slaving away at the White House.

As the first First Lady to occupy the White House, Abigail Adams brought only nine helpers with her from her home in Massachusetts. They must have been really busy. In recent years the number has escalated to some eighty maids, laundresses, cooks, butlers and every other kind of helper including a Chief Usher who is in charge of just about everything *except* ushering people through the one hundred thirty-two rooms on four floors.

How things have changed since Abigail's time. She suffered more than enough. The glass hadn't been installed in all the windows yet. It was really cold at the President's House.

Even worse, the "water closets" still hadn't been installed and Abigail had to run out to a three-seater outdoor toilet. Too bad she couldn't live to see eighteen bathrooms and powder rooms installed.

Abigail had to bring her own furniture when she came to the damp, unfinished Executive Mansion in the dead of winter, 1800. She found plenty of fireplaces but no wood. And what is more, workmen were not so impressed with the Mansion and the presidency that they were anxious to help.

In a letter, she wrote of shivering and suffering rheumatism because of the cold. "Can you believe," she said, "that wood is not to be had, because people cannot be found to cut and cart it!" Perhaps fortunately, John Adams did not get reelected so Abigail did not have to endure more than four months of this difficult life-style. She moved out in March 1801.

Thomas Jefferson was next man in. No wonder he drank so much wine. The water that came from an outdoor creek was polluted. His first White House improvement was to have a well dug.

By day or night, the White House seems to be inhabited by ghosts of the past. Inside, some nights, I could almost see Jefferson going up to bed with his pet mockingbird hopping along behind him. They were quite a team and the little bird even learned to take bits of food from the President's lips.

And outside, I could almost see Calvin Coolidge talking to his pet racoon, Rebecca. He might not have had much to say to people but he was reported to be quite loquacious with Rebecca and had a little outdoor house built for her. Pretty soon Rebecca took charge—spending the daylight hours in the White House with the President and only going to her own house at night.

And for years there were huge glass greenhouses for the White House to raise its own flowers and some vegetables. A few of the Presidents actually took the time to do a little gardening on their own—John Quincy Adams gathered seeds wherever he went to make the White House grounds more beautiful and he planted many fruit and nut trees.

I would look around the White House grounds and think of how each President had enjoyed the outdoors in his own way. I could visualize them. President Herbert Hoover throwing a medicine ball in a daily pre-breakfast exercise session with his Cabinet friends—they were facetiously called "Hoover's Medicine Ball Cabinet"—and President Truman pitching horseshoes with various aides and friends. Years later, President Bush would set up his horseshoe stakes on the lawn and hold tournaments with staffers.

I could almost see President Eisenhower practicing on his White House putting green as little David Eisenhower, his grandson, ran to retrieve the golf balls. President Warren Harding had not needed the help of a child. He had trained his dog, an Airedale named Laddie Boy, to fetch the balls.

President Nixon, an ardent golfer who once made a hole in one and enjoyed talking about it, interfered with another White House sport—swimming. He shocked a lot of people when he ordered the indoor White House swimming pool, where John Kennedy had swum almost every day, covered to accommodate new press rooms. Nixon's successor, Jerry Ford, countered by ordering the construction of an outside swimming pool within easy reach of the Oval Office.

The Carters were most grateful to Ford because they all used the pool as much as possible. They also used the tennis courts and the bowling alley which Pat Nixon had enjoyed for exercise with her daughters and women friends.

As I looked around the grounds before leaving Washington, I could not help but reflect on President Reagan and how he could not use the White House grounds, though they were large enough, to indulge in his favorite sport—horseback riding. It had always made the papers when Caroline Kennedy had ridden a pony named Macaroni around the south grounds but evidently Reagan did not want to be that conspicuous. So he would go to where the horses were—Camp David, Rock Creek Park, and the Marine Corps Base at Quantico, Virginia.

There is a wonderful sidelight to his inauguration plans. Reagan had wanted to top Carter's now-famous walk down Pennsylvania Avenue by riding his favorite horse to the White House—appropriately garbed in Western dress, of course. He had to be talked out of it for reasons of security. A lone man up high on a horse was just too easy a target.

Of course history proved that even a man getting into a limousine and surrounded by bodyguards was also too good a target, resulting in Reagan almost losing his life to an assassin.

The horse that Ronnie Reagan wanted to ride, it was a white steed named El-Alamein, a gift from President Lopez Portillo of Mexico right after Reagan won the election.

The plans for the horseback ride down the Avenue to the White House had proceeded to Secret Service planning of what he would have to wear—a steel lined cowboy hat and bulletproof long johns. The plan was that the new President would be helped into this armored outfit after the traditional swearing-in luncheon on Capitol Hill.

I look back and realize that I did make many good friends because of my White House experiences—not just glamorous or famous women but men as well. I remember one friendship that led to Hollywood.

The country and western singer, Roger Miller, best known for his song, "King of the Road," was a guest one evening and brought along his very personable manager, Dann Moss. Formerly the husband to and manager of the beautiful Vikki Carr, Dann was like most guests, interested in the surroundings and history. He eventually asked me about myself and in turn talked about his life. As he left, he invited me to a party at Roger's private suite in the Key Bridge Marriott.

Expecting a small quiet social gathering, I was surprised at the number of people there. Miller's entire band and support staff showed up, and no one left until the early morning hours. Partying was something these Hollywood people were exceptionally good at.

I mentioned that I was going to be on a business trip to the Los Angeles area and Dann surprised me by inviting me to spend the weekend at his Bel Air home. It was interesting to drive through the prestigious area past many stars' mansions.

It turned out that Dann Moss lived at the top of a hill in a U-shaped house with a pool in the center of it. His home was next door to that of the son of Groucho Marx. From the front terrace, there was a breathtaking panoramic view of Hollywood that at night looked like the backdrop for the Johnny Carson Show. As we stood on the patio next to the hot tub, Dann pointed out the homes of Cher and Jim Nabors who were farther down the hill.

But Dann was no stay-at-home. We got into his car and spent the evening going from one private discotheque club to another where Dann met and brought home the girl who lost out to Susan Anton as the new White Owl Cigar commercial spokesperson. The would-be star proceeded to give us her audition routine in his living room sometime well after midnight and it was apparent that the cigar maker made the correct choice.

The next day, several people dropped by the house, including an NBC executive and a Marriott Hotel vice president. One young lady who also appeared was Sondra Theodore from Bakersfield, California. At the time she had been in Hollywood only four weeks, and her biggest claim to fame was that her father owned one of the largest strawberry farms in the nation. Sondra related to all of us how she only the day before had persuaded legendary agent Swifty Lazar to represent her.

Realizing the vulnerabilities of starlets, I asked her privately about the moral pressures some people might have put on her in exchange for helping her get ahead. She was surprisingly calm in relating that it happened all too often but she had simply refused to do business with them. Now Swifty's professionalism would start her career in the right direction without forcing her to make immoral sacrifices. She struck me as a sweet, smart, and apparently innocent girl who knew exactly where she wanted to go.

Six months later, Sondra was a *Playboy* centerfold and had become the constant companion of Hugh Hefner. She was at his side for a number of years, until she was replaced by someone younger, but not prettier.

To be at the White House was to hear all kinds of quaint things about the guests. One tidbit that showed that if you are wealthy enough, you can get away with little quirks of behavior, is that Nelson Rockefeller—Ford's Vice President—would casually stir his coffee with the stem of his eyeglasses and then simply put them back on without even wiping the earpiece dry.

Everything Nelson Rockefeller did was of great interest to the social set and Washington ears really perked up to hear that he also had a quaint economy that would make him quite at home with the lower middle classes—he had the worn collar of his shirt turned around and resewn to extend the shirt's life.

But at least he believed in tipping. The word was that "Cousin Cheap," who was so adept at saving money at the White House for his cousin, Jimmy Carter, saved money himself by not tipping waiters. No wonder that when he married a stewardess, insiders chuckled that he had found a way to save money on transportation.

It always interested me to see what First Ladies collected since it showed their humanness—from Pat Nixon's humble sea shells to Nancy Reagan's regal blue porcelains. Barbara Bush struck a middle ground by collecting tiny silver pill boxes.

Sometimes it was presidents who surprised me by the things they collected—Dwight Eisenhower with his cookbooks, which he used as bedside reading (I'm told he made a mean vegetable soup) along with his Wild West books, and FDR with his small wood carved animals which almost covered his desk in the Oval Office.

John F. Kennedy collected something that certainly would be frowned on today—scrimshaw—ivory carvings from such things as elephant tusks.

Richard Nixon's hobby was wines. He collected lore about them. From the debunking of the belief that you must allow time for wine to breathe before you taste a new bottle to anecdotes about which wine was preferred by famous figures of history.

His personal wine favorite was a Bordeaux which had been the choice of the statesman Benjamin Disraeli—Château Margaux. And it's ironic that Nixon's least favorite wine was champagne, the one drink that protocol frequently forced him to drink. As he explained it, after sixty-nine days of being served champagne at both lunch and dinner during a trip abroad as Vice President, he and Pat Nixon "couldn't stand the taste of it" any more.

I remember the procession of White House Military Social Aides I have known and even one who didn't quite make it, having offended the powers that be during the entrance process. She was a very attractive lieutenant whom I had met only once while she was making the interview rounds. Reports of the favorable results from her interviews and our brief meeting in the hall suggested that she would be an ideal addition to the staff.

Even the Social Secretary had said she was accepted into the program just as soon as her routine background investigation was completed. After a considerable period of time, I casually asked the senior Social Aide when the lieutenant would come on board. He informed me that she had been disapproved because of the findings of the investigation.

Astonished, I immediately wondered aloud what could possibly keep her out. He advised me that one of her neighbors had apparently told an investigator that a man was seen coming out of her apartment early one morning. Since she had no brothers, it was assumed that a boyfriend had spent the night and she was considered a risk, on the basis of morality.

Another Social Aide did get into the program in spite of a serious social flaw—bad breath. Eventually, his superior discussed the chronic problem and suggested a remedy. At the next White House party, he seemed to have taken the advice and everything was fine. We were all relieved.

However, the following function indicated he had relapsed. The aide was never invited back to work at a White House reception again though he remained officially on the Social Aide roster until his departure from the area more than a year later.

And I remember one aide who tried to use his White House position to further his career. During the final weeks of his Washington tour of duty, he volunteered for almost every function and always arrived early. Whether at an afternoon tea or evening dinner, he could be seen working the crowd, finding the most influential people and letting them know he was moving on and would be available if a good job came along. He literally threw himself at people or stood in their way as they were headed out the door, offering his services at every turn.

Others on the social staff were particularly critical of him and accused him of offering a copy of his résumé to anyone who appeared the slightest bit interested. If his fellow aides were put off by this activity, it is fair to assume that the guests were even more annoyed.

There was no action taken against him, and he kept it up until the day he left for a routine overseas posting assigned by the Air Force and not some plum of a job arranged by one of his quarry of the past few weeks.

The guests had probably found him to be a trifle intimidating, just as we found one group to be. The Daughters of the American Revolution made an annual visit which some of us began to refer to as the DAR Spring Offensive. When these ladies arrived, it was clear that they belonged at the Executive Mansion, and they knew just about everything and could have served as expert tour guides. We felt like excess baggage at their annual tea. Directions from us aides were seldom required as the ladies knew exactly where they wanted to go next and what they wanted to do. Often, their plans were even quite similar to those the Social Secretary had passed out. Individually, the ladies were very nice but as a group, they generally turned the event into one similar to the Children's Christmas Party where some of us found an excuse to be absent.

I have gained great respect for our First Ladies.

Few people know how many important programs in the field of social welfare were started by or promoted into resounding success by dedicated First Ladies—Lady Bird Johnson and her Headstart Program for preschoolers; Rosalynn Carter and her Halfway Houses for the mentally ill; and Nancy Reagan with her Foster Grandparent Program in which senior citizens bring joy into the lives of children with special needs, and her "Just Say No" Program to teach children how to avoid drugs.

All modern First Ladies have tried to do something for humanity and not just sit around the White House having tea. Eleanor Roosevelt was cruelly ridiculed when she sponsored a housing project for the poor and traveled the country to study working conditions— even descending into a coal mine.

Betty Ford was sharply criticized, even by some members of her husband's political party, when she worked actively to get the Equal Rights Amendment passed into law. Choosing less controversial projects, Lady Bird Johnson started a National Beautification Program to place wild flowers instead of billboards along the highway, and Pat Nixon and Jacqueline Kennedy concentrated on acquiring historic furnishings and art objects for the White House.

I was proud of Rosalynn Carter for devoting herself to a project that many found distasteful—the problems of the mentally ill and the elderly. Because of her, mental patients who needed only minimal help were enabled to live in group houses away from institutions.

Though we take these programs for granted and quickly forget how they came about, history records the great service that the wives of presidents have rendered to all Americans.

To be a Social Aide is to be privy to innumerable tense moments, some of which have happy endings and some of which don't. You never know where trouble will pop up next around the White House, in spite of endless planning. Take the arrivals of presidents and foreign monarchs which occur below the Truman balcony on the south lawn of the White House.

Usually, everything goes in apple pie order. The American President and the foreign chief of state make their welcoming remarks as they read from their notes on index cards and then, if necessary, an interpreter repeats their words.

But just once there was an impending disaster when the unflappable Ronald Reagan reached into his overcoat pocket and realized he had the wrong welcoming words when he almost said, "Your Highness."

He recalled in a flash that these were the notes he had used to welcome the Grand Duke of Luxembourg. The guest standing in front of him today was no aristocratic figure but a freedom fighter, up from poverty—a patriot who endured torture before becoming the president of Venezuela—Jaime Lusinchi. Reagan was in deep trouble but he did what he had to do—he started to ad lib when he suddenly remembered he had put his speech in his jacket pocket and not his overcoat.

Such things were always happening to Reagan. I consider him the luckiest President I have known because, whatever happened, he always came through unscathed.

Nixon was just not as lucky a man as Reagan. Neither was Pat a lucky woman.

Embarrassing little things would happen to her, and we would hear about them.

On the amusing side was what occurred one day when a representative arrived from the bowling industry on a serious mission. He was there to measure Pat Nixon and daughter Tricia for new bowling balls so they would have the proper equipment when they wanted to use the alley in the White House.

The occasion would be good publicity for the bowling industry, of course, and a White House photographer took a picture that would be made available to the press.

Unfortunately, the caption under the picture showing Pat and Tricia being fitted for bowling balls had been slightly abbreviated, leaving out the type of balls, which is undoubtedly the reason the picture was not distributed. It could have been a great collector's item.

I was surprised, in researching this book, to discover that the Nixons and I had something in common—our interest in the government's procurement process. Long before running for political office, Richard Nixon was terminating government contracts for Martin Corporation in Maryland and Pat was a contract price analyst in San Francisco while Nixon was serving overseas. Both of these functions are integral parts of the acquisition system which I am part of even today.

I consider Jimmy Carter the most unlucky President I have known. Unfortunate things just kept happening to him—like the time at a welcoming ceremony when there was a mix-up and the wrong national anthem was played for President Nicolae Ceausescu of Romania. Unlike in the case of a similar situation with Reagan, it was too late to make a neat recovery and ad-lib.

Starting at the inaugural festivities, things happened that were almost guaranteed to reflect on the new president—and embarrass him. First Brother Billy Carter arrived at the Washington Hilton carrying his own half-gallon "jug" of Jim Beam bourbon and poured himself a double.

Then he complained loudly that John Wayne had been invited to be part of the Inaugural Gala, saying, "Anybody getting John Wayne to come to a Jimmy Carter thing has got to be nuts...after he campaigned for President Ford and Ronald Reagan. I believe Amy and I could have written a better show."

And the fates still seemed determined to needle Jimmy Carter even after he was out of the White House.

Even Amy Carter, as a college student, managed to keep stirring things up in the world with her campus activities. When asked a couple of years ago about her twenty-one-year-old daughter's political statements and subsequent encounters with the law, Rosalynn Carter said, "Amy is basically a shy person. Her activism is a surprise to us. We are proud of her. She has only been arrested four times."

As I remember Amy Carter skittering around the rooms at party time and reading a book at formal dinners, I realize she was a saint compared with Alice Roosevelt who played many pranks around the White House and jumped fully dressed into a ship's pool when she was seventeen. President Teddy Roosevelt's comment was, "I can do one of two things. I can be President of the United States or I can control Alice."

Amy and her cat—how can I forget them?

In fact, one amusing memory of the Carters is the scene in which they are descending the Grand Staircase with the Portillos for the State Dinner in honor of the Mexican president and his wife, when suddenly an interloper appeared.

It was Misty Malarky, Amy's Siamese cat, who had decided to come to the dinner too, and was marching down the stairs most regally and surefooted, leading all the rest. It was an effort for Amy's father to pretend not to see the cat and to keep from stepping on her—but he managed.

You could tell Jimmy Carter would prefer that this undignified procession remain unnoticed and unmentioned. But the press was there and the photographers. As I've said many times—you can't keep a secret at the White House.

And the latest secret to pop out is that President George Bush has transferred his affections from the famous First Dog Millie to a second dog—a previously unknown and unsung spaniel named Ranger.

It wasn't totally Millie's fault. Millie just could not handle fan adulation, TV appearances with coauthor Barbara Bush—sometimes referred to as "The Silver Fox" for her mane of white hair—and still have time to cater to the President.

George Bush admitted that his nose was out of joint and accused Millie of having switched her loyalties to Barbara. But he was not the kind of man to sit around as second fiddle. Instead, he took action, getting himself another dog, Millie's son, from granddaughter Marshall, to whom Ranger had been given.

Of course, the President maintained that Ranger was only on sort of an extended loan—and one has to believe a President.

One bright sunny afternoon while strolling across Jackson Place to Lafayette Park, I heard the unmistakable wail of distant sirens. So many people had been murdered in Washington, D.C., in the past year that hearing the sounds of emergency was not unusual, until the sound came unmistakably nearer. The noise from several of these alarms was suddenly painful, even before the first police motorcycle came into view.

The huge white Harley-Davidson machines leapfrogged each other as they moved down the street, blocking each side entry to the main road. No one would be permitted to create a crisis by inserting himself into this motorcade.

They swept around the corner and headed straight for me, lights flashing and sirens howling. At the top of Jackson Place (the northwest corner of President's Park), the motorcade turned west to go down Seventeenth Street to Pennsylvania Avenue and Blair House to discharge the VIP passengers.

Next to appear amongst the phalanx were two city patrol cars with several occupants, bigger lights and louder sirens. Close behind them were two black Secret Service war wagons loaded with live bodies that appeared to be wrapped in clothing too heavy for summer. The image of cloth dissolved into flak jackets as the lead vehicles turned into the sun.

More motorcycles flanked three or four limousines, and all had to slow somewhat to get around the corner. This was definitely a weak point in the operation, and the Secret Service knew it. By now I had stopped to observe this display of Chief Executive commuting style, impressed that they never had to stop for a red light. In an instant the agents turned to check me out as they slowed for the corner. Even wearing a coat and tie and carrying a briefcase, I was and should have been suspect.

The moment the main limousine had passed, another war wagon full of well-dressed soldiers sped by, followed by three city police cruisers, more motorcycles and, of all things, an ambulance. Every siren on every vehicle was screaming. It must have been quieter on the runway at National Airport.

The deafening noise reverberating among the tall buildings, the swirling red lights, and the roar of the multiple supercharged engines racing through the city made this simple act of moving a visiting head-of-state down the street one of the most memorable sights in Washington.

Looking back at the presidency and those who have filled the post, my favorite story is still the little incident involving Jerry Ford and his dog. It happened on one of Ford's skiing vacations in Vail, Colorado, when the Ford dog made a mess on the floor.

A White House steward rushed over with a cloth to wipe it up. Gerald Ford, President of the United States, took the cloth from him, saying, "No man should have to clean up after another man's dog." And he did it himself.

For me, it sums up the quality all the presidents should bring to the Oval Office.

Bibliography

Boller, Paul F., Jr. *Presidential Anecdotes*. New York: Oxford University Press, 1981.

Bryant, Traphes, with Frances Spatz Leighton. *Dog Days at the White House*. New York, Macmillan, 1975

Carter, Hugh, with Frances Spatz Leighton. *Cousin Beedie and Cousin Hot: My Life with the Carter Family of Plains, Georgia*. Englewood Cliffs, NJ: Prentice-Hall, Inc., 1978.

Carter, Jimmy. *Keeping Faith*. New York: Bantam Books, 1982.

Carter, Rosalynn. *First Lady from Plains*. Boston: Houghton Mifflin, 1984.

Eisenhower, Julie Nixon. *Pat Nixon: The Untold Story*. New York: Simon & Schuster, 1986.

Ford, Betty. *The Times of My Life*. New York: Harper & Row, 1978.

Gallagher, Mary Barelli, with Frances Spatz Leighton. *My Life with Jacqueline Kennedy*. New York: McKay, 1969.

Gulley, Bill. *Breaking Cover*. New York: Simon & Schuster, 1980.

Haldeman, H.R. *The Ends of Power*. New York: Times Books, 1978.

Jeffries, Ona Griffen. *In and Out of the White House*. New York: Wilfred Funk, 1960.

Johnson, Haynes. *The Working White House*. New York: Praeger, 1975.

Kissinger, Henry. *White House Years*. Boston: Little, Brown and Company, 1979.

Leighton, Frances Spatz. *The Search for the Real Nancy Reagan*. New York: Macmillan, 1987.

Leighton, Frances Spatz. *They Call Her Lady Bird*. New York: Macfadden-Bartell, 1964.

McLellan, Diana. *Ear on Washington*. New York: Arbor House, 1982.

Nessen, Ron. *It Sure Looks Different from the Inside*. New York: Playboy Press, 1978.

Packard, Jerrold. *American Monarchy: A Social Guide to the Presidency.* New York: Delacourt, 1983.

Parks, Lillian Rogers, with Frances Spatz Leighton. *My Thirty Years Backstairs at the White House.* New York: Fleet, 1961.

Parks, Lillian Rogers, with Frances Spatz Leighton. *The Roosevelts: A Family in Turmoil.* Englewood Cliffs, NJ: Prentice-Hall, Inc., 1981.

Regan, Donald T. *For the Record: From Wall Street to Washington.* San Diego, CA: Harcourt Brace Jovanovitch, 1988.

Roosevelt, Selwa "Lucky." *Keeper of the Gate.* New York: Simon & Schuster, 1990.

Smith, Hedrick. *The Power Game: How Washington Really Works.* New York: Random House, 1987.

Weidenfeld, Sheila Rabb. *First Lady's Lady.* New York: G.P. Putnam's Sons, 1979.

NEWSPAPERS, MAGAZINES AND BROCHURES

The Washington Post
The New York Times
USA Today
Time
Washingtonian
People
The New Yorker
The First Ladies. Published by the White House Historical Association, with the cooperation of the National Geographic Society.
The Living White House, an Historic Guide. Published by the White House Historical Association, with the cooperation of the National Geographic Society.

Index